Theology after

Freud

An interpretive
inquiry

Theology after Freud

An interpretive inquiry

BY PETER HOMANS

The Bobbs-Merrill Company, Inc.

Indianapolis   New York

For permission to reprint excerpts in this book, acknowledgment is made to the following publishers:

Abingdon Press—for excerpts from Roland Bainton, *Here I Stand: A Life of Martin Luther,* New American Library, 1955. Copyright 1950 by Pierce and Smith. Reprinted by permission of Abingdon Press.

Beacon Press—for excerpts from Herbert Marcuse, *Eros and Civilization: A Philosophical Inquiry into Freud,* Vintage Books, 1962.

Harper & Row, Publishers—for excerpts from Martin Buber, *The Knowledge of Man,* translated by Maurice Friedman and Ronald Gregor Smith, edited by Maurice Friedman, 1965; and from Philip Rieff, *The Triumph of the Therapeutic: Uses of Faith after Freud,* 1966.

International Universities Press—for excerpts from David Shakow and David Rapaport, *The Influence of Freud on American Psychology,* Psychological Issues, No. 13, 1964.

The Macmillan Company—for excerpts from Gibson Winter, *Elements for a Social Ethic: Scientific and Ethical Perspectives on Social Process,* 1966.

W. W. Norton & Company—for excerpts from Allen Wheelis, *The Quest for Identity,* 1958. Copyright © 1958 by W. W. Norton & Company, Inc. Reprinted by permission of W. W. Norton & Company, Inc.

Rand McNally & Company—for excerpts from David Bakan, *The Duality of Human Existence,* 1966. Reprinted by permission of the author and publisher.

Random House—for excerpts from Norman O. Brown, *Love's Body,* 1966.

The University of Chicago Press—for permission to adapt my articles: "Transference and Transcendence: Freud and Tillich on the Nature of Personal Relatedness," *Journal of Religion,* Vol. XLVI, No. 1, Part II (January 1966); "Toward a Psychology of Religion: By Way of Freud and Tillich," *Zygon: Journal of Religion and Science,* Vol. II, No. 1 (March 1967), reprinted in *The Dialogue Between Theology and Psychology,* ed. Peter Homans, copyright © 1968 The University of Chicago; "Transcendence, Distance, Fantasy: The Protestant Era in Psychological Perspective," Journal of Religion, Vol. XLIX, No. 3 (July 1969).

Van Nostrand Reinhold Company—for excerpts from David Bakan, *Sigmund Freud and the Jewish Mystical Tradition,* 1958. Copyright © 1958 by Litton Educational Publishing, Inc.

Wesleyan University Press—for excerpts from Norman O. Brown, *Life Against Death: The Psychoanalytical Meaning of History,* Random House, 1959. Copyright © 1959 by Wesleyan University. Reprinted by permission of Wesleyan University Press.

Yale University Press—for excerpts from Paul Tillich, *The Courage to Be,* 1962.

Acknowledgments

I WOULD like to thank in particular two colleagues, Charles Long and Perry LeFevre, for having taken the time to read the manuscript in earlier draft form and for their valuable comments, criticisms, and suggestions. My thanks also go to Donald Capps and Doris Dempsey for their considerable help in editing and in general preparation of the final draft. And I am especially indebted to Richard A. Underwood, who first read the manuscript at the request of the Bobbs-Merrill Company, and whose interest and suggestions were particularly useful and encouraging. For their patience during the writing of this book, thanks also to my wife and children.

Contents

Preface

AN investigation of the relation between theology and psychology has never been of special interest to either theologians or psychologists. Theological studies express only modest concern for the forms of personal and social life and, in so doing, give occasional attention to psychology. But, when the theologians' more considered methodological discussions move to materials outside classic kerygmatic and doctrinal sources for assistance and a fresh perspective, they usually turn to philosophy and historiography, even to literature, rather than to, say, psychology or sociology. And when psychologists from time to time reflect on matters beyond the limits of their own imperatives to scientific rigor, they, too, turn to philosophy, history, and occasionally to literature, but never to theology.

While the grounds for such mutual indifference are complex and varied, it is true to say that both theology and psychology actively prefer it. But the wisdom of their conviction is not at issue in this book, which *is* about theology and psychology. The significance of such indifference lies in one of its formidable although unanticipated consequences: the obscuring of an extremely important set of connections between declining theological images of person and society, on the one hand, and their displacement by predominantly psychological images, on the other hand. Has theology's preoccupation with philosophy in effect obscured its capacity to engage those contemporary modes of thought and experience that are predominantly psychological in character? Has psychology's indifference to theological views of the self cut it off from the deepest, most obscure roots of its own past, thus permitting an excessive sense of its own novelty and distinctiveness?

At this point, sometimes referred to as the problem of secularization, a study of theology and psychology does become important. What such a study requires, however, is an approach that not only discloses lines of similarity between the two very separate views of the human person but also one that accounts for the differences and the cultural consequences of these differences. The approach must be both descriptive and interpretive.

Much of the apparent indifference between theology and psychology lies, I think, in the unattractiveness of the several approaches or styles already available in discussions of theology and the human sciences. These can be characterized, at least from the perspective of theology, as either reductive, integrative, or dialogical. In this study, as well, there is an attempt to create a sustained interplay between theology and one of the human sciences, psychoanalysis. But, unlike previous discussions, there is also an attempt to explore the consequences of such interplay when the rules for interplay that theology and psychology have made are suspended, examined, and even interpreted.

Reductive approaches to the relation between theology and psychology—attempts to explain one in terms of the other—are important and even valuable, especially once the true intent is clear. Equally clear, however, is the pattern that has established itself in such attempts: generous initial discussion with a mood of openness and reciprocity, followed by an emphasis on inevitable differences and points of final and absolute disagreement. The crossing of boundaries is itself reduced to a kind of tourism, and the inevitability of disparities remains unchallenged. As such, reductionism has vexed theological studies of psychology and many psychological studies of religion and religious beliefs as well. On the other hand, attempts to integrate into theology the "new insights" of the human sciences do call attention to similarities but tend to overlook the very formidable differences. A variation on these two styles, that of "dialogue," takes as its primary assignment the more modest task of locating and describing the boundaries and of establishing respective areas of specialty and expertness. The limitations of this third style are inherent in its modesty.

Whether the approach is reductive, integrative, or dialogical, and especially in the case of the last, each has in its own way for the most part worked within the two sets of rules that the disciplines in question have set up, or else there is a quite deliberate attempt to challenge one set of rules on the basis of the other, criticizing and finally removing the former in the light of the latter. In this study, I shall neither simply accept the rules set by theology and psychology nor simply abrogate them. Instead, I will first explore the ways in which theology and psychology, on their own terms, view each other, and then expand and complicate the discussion, introducing new considerations, questions, and problems, especially as these bear on the meaning of secularization. Therefore, although this study does from time to time engage in reductive, integrative, and dialogical approaches, it also attempts, in a more inclusive manner, to suspend their conclusions in the interests of "something more," which tends to remain hidden by the very insular self-definitions of the two disciplines themselves.

Theology, psychology, and secularization, then, are three interrelated problems that together make up the subject matter of this book. There is, first of all, contemporary Protestant theology, and, secondly, there is Freud's psychological thought. These two groups of material are my point of entry into the wider, general question of theology and its relation to the human sciences and into the still wider problem of secularization. The argument begins, therefore, in a very specific and rather narrow manner, with an inquiry into the way in which contemporary theologians have regarded psychology, in particular, Freud's psychology. There are two parts to this question: How does theology conceive its own work and its own view of the human self? And how does it view and judge, on the basis of its own understanding, the psychological analysis of the nature of the self? I call this the problem of "theological response to Freud" and ask, How does theology view Freud's psychological thought, and what are the grounds, intrinsic to theological work itself, that require this view?

This question generates a second problem quite naturally and inevitably: How are we to understand aright Freud's thought? So this book is unavoidably about Freud's psychology every bit as much as it is about theology. His thought is rich, complex, and daring, and there are different ways to understand the force of his psychology, each highly plausible. Is it, for example, a scientific theory of personality? Is it a clinical theory, at a low level of generalization, of personality change? Or is it a theory of cultural interpretation, of myth and symbol? The problem of analyzing theological responses to Freud cannot be separated from the problem of reading Freud. On the other hand, the problem of how to read Freud is itself more sharply focused by introducing the perspective of another discipline than it is by strictly limiting discussion to the Freudian materials themselves.

If there are different readings of Freud, does theology read Freud correctly? Or does theology reduce Freud's thought and in so doing omit its "higher," more implicitly theological possibilities? In asking these questions, this book enters into a debate with theology, an argument in behalf of what I call the implicit psychological form of Protestant thought. I propose to disclose those psychological aspects of theological self-understanding that remain for the most part unacknowledged by those working too strictly within the "theological circle." I propose to seek the latent dimensions of childhood that underlie theological images of man, the psychological meanings that underlie doctrinal statement—what I also call from time to time the psychological infrastructure of Protestant thought and spirituality. Whereas the *odium theologicum* is well known within the psychological sciences, this study is more concerned with the *odium psychologicum* in theological circles. By criticizing theology's inadequate view of Freud, we move to a psychological criticism of theology based on a more generous view of Freud.

The inquiry, therefore, begins descriptively and then becomes interpretive, moving toward a psychological perspective on Protestant thought. Thus, it can be characterized fairly as an attempt to place the "Protestant era" in psychological perspective. In this sense, it resembles, in an external way, the reductive approaches that psychoanalysis has often taken in relation to religion. Yet, the meaning of reductionism depends on the view of psychology to which theology is allegedly reduced. I will press toward a higher view of psychology, one absent from both theology's view of psychology and from psychology's view of itself, at least in the more official moments of each. This higher psychology, because it differs so from both, might even be called theological in form. The lines of relation between theology and psychology are more complex than either imagines and, I will argue, more rich and open to innovation. Distinctions must be made that are not made by either.

But the perhaps rather esoteric questions of theological response to Freud and of readings of Freud are only special instances of a wider problem in morals and meaning, that of secularization. The comparative approach to theology and psychology of necessity opens out into the question of secularization. However, that question cannot be posed apart from careful comparative analysis of a theological and a psychological system.

Christian thought, for the most part, has been a theology without a psychology, and Christian man has regularly decided to understand his psychology, when he wanted it at all, under the control of his theology. What Christian thought today calls modern, secular man is also called psychological man. In this case, psychological man in effect means nontheological man. Modern, secular, psychological man, it seems, has decided to reverse the argument of his Christian forebears, has turned the tables on his past, to see if a psychology without a theology works any better; or, at best, he has decided to get his theology from his psychology. To study theology and theological images of man is to study what modern man used to be; and to study psychology, especially psychoanalysis, is to study what Christian man has become.

Is psychoanalysis a psychology of secularization? If so, we need to know in exactly what sense psychoanalysis really does differ from theology. Is psychoanalysis more theological than its proponents are capable of acknowledging? Are theological images of man more psychological than their custodians believe? In any case, the question of secularization is intimately related to the way that theology differentiates itself from psychology and to the readings one gives to Freud's psychology.

The purpose of this book, then, is to explicate the issues and lines of relation between these three foci: the way that theology, in defining itself, distinguishes itself from psychoanalysis; the possibility of different understandings of psychoanalysis that such a distinction raises; and the part psychoanalysis has to play in what theologians and others call the process of secularization.

I must note here that theology, and not religion, is the object of psychological criticism and interpretation. This book is not a study in the psychology of religion, in the conventional sense of that phrase, but rather in the psychology of theological constructs, of theological thought—especially the theological doctrine of transcendence. Nor is this a study of psychological aspects of ecclesiastical leadership; it is not a study in pastoral psychology. Although most psychoanalytic studies in fact have addressed themselves to religion rather than theology, I am concerned with the implications of psychoanalysis for theology because I believe that theology contains and presents the deepest core of meaning in which institutional experience and leadership are embedded. Hence, a psychological approach to such experience and leadership, if it is to be fundamental, must be first of all an approach to theology. Theology, too, has understood psychoanalysis to be primarily a psychological theory of religion rather than a theory of the origins of theological doctrine. As a result, each in its own way has been able to avoid discussing a higher psychoanalytic psychology of doctrine. Yet, what Freud called "religious ideas" have as much in common with doctrine as they do with institutional experience and pastoral leadership.

In using the term "psychoanalysis," I refer only to Freud's psychological thought. Freud remains central to most of modern psychology, and in this regard I am concerned with clarifying the deepest strands of his thought, those root ideas and assumptions that have been put to use in so many different ways in different systems within the broad spectrum of contemporary psychology. Therefore, although attention is given to psychoanalysis as metapsychology and as clinical technique, the force of this discussion is always to disclose the still deeper strands of Freud's thought.

The style of the argument of this book bears an important relation to its content. The assumption that one particular problem can be made to open out into another, that exploring the second problem is a way of further exploring the first, albeit indirectly, is a procedural as well as a material feature. This procedure, best characterized as "linking together and working through," consists in starting with a particular problem, theological doctrine, then making distinctions by asking psychological questions, and then demonstrating connections between the new problems and the initial formulation.

Consequently, the meanings of specific constructs undergo change as the argument itself progresses. This is not, however, to introduce periodically capricious or arbitrary assertions but is, rather, simply the consequence of opening theological and psychological constructs and processes to one another in a way not permitted by the rules built into each discipline. My procedure is an attempt to press mere dialogue and comparative analysis to the point where something new emerges or, at least, to the point where it is possible for something new to emerge. I assume that there are levels of meaning in any discussion and that such levels become more visible as the discussion progresses, even though the particular discussion can of course be conducted at only one level at any one moment.

In Chapter 3, for example, I explicate the psychoanalytic notion of transference, beginning with its most obvious and acceptable meaning as a clinical phenomenon. However, I also argue that this construct and the processes to which it refers can also be used to characterize Freud's thinking about religion, although he does not use it in precisely this manner, and I suggest the term "transference-God" to suggest the link between clinical process and Freud's thought about religion. At this point, the term is psychoanalytically psychological. However, I also draw it into dialogue with Tillich's critical rejection of what he calls the "God of theological theism," arguing for the close similarity between the two. At this second point in the analysis, the psychological construct has acquired implicit theological meaning as well. Still later in the argument, I carry this discussion further and propose that transference can also be viewed from a religious perspective—that it is a form of nostalgia. Establishing this connection permits interplay between theology, psychoanalysis, and the phenomenology of religious structures. Other constructs are employed in other contexts, less extensively, but following the same procedure of linking together and working through.

For some, the possibility of a psychic basis for theology is always reductive by definition—they feel no need to listen or to inquire further. For others, that theological thinking is "defensive," "sublimation," "regressive," and the like is equally self-evident. Within psychoanalytic circles Freud is considered primarily as scientific psychologist or as intuitive psychotherapist —and only then as one who developed, *en passant,* a general theory of fantasy, myth, and symbol. That his work might be considered to be first of all and fundamentally religious may seem perverse to both psychoanalytic theorists and theologians. Again, that depends on how you look at it. The most imaginative discussions of Freud's thought have come from without the field of psychoanalysis and, if within psychoanalysis, from those clinicians with nonclinical backgrounds or nonclinical interests. Least of all have they come from scientifically trained psychologists or theologians.

The practical purpose of this book is to provide a stimulus for thought to persons concerned with the fate of theology in an age given over to predominantly psychological thinking—those who, although they cannot but affirm the psychological, still sense that genuine meaning resides in the theological. Perhaps this book will be of value in helping such persons create new paradigms of religious and psychological understanding rather than simply repeating those of either theology or psychology.

A remark once made by Freud to Oskar Pfister, the Swiss pastor who practiced psychoanalysis and who was personally acquainted with Freud, illustrates well the fundamental intent of this study. Pfister had written for comment on one of his cases, and Freud became impatient: "Your analysis suffers from the hereditary weakness of virtue . . . one has to become a bad fellow . . . to transcend the rules . . . sacrifice oneself . . . without some such criminality there is no real achievement." Pfister was a theological liberal. I have selected the neo-Reformation theologians for many reasons, but the simplest lies in the conviction that their work, like Freud's, implicitly contains "some such criminality," an impulse to transcend the rules, very much in the spirit referred to by Freud in this letter. This book attempts by interpretation to free that impulse, to render it explicit, in both theology and psychoanalysis, and in doing so moves on to a third orientation, one neither doctrinal nor psychoanalytic, one best described as hermeneutical. Perhaps this approach to such theology and such psychology, in proposing to move beyond reductionism, integration, and dialogue, can eventuate in some "real achievement."

Part One

---

*Theological response
to Freud*

One: The problem

---

*The hazards
of reading Freud*

TODAY, Freud's thought is everywhere—not just in the psychological and social sciences, but also in the humanities, the professions, and in the "culture." To take a term dear to psychology itself, Freud has been "integrated" into the fabric of many disciplines, and fundamental decisions regarding the final worth and limits of psychoanalysis now seem possible. Even the theologian, the last to make use of something new, has, it seems, recognized the challenge, considered and weighed the evidence, made his decision, and moved on to fresh problems. The Freudian revolution has largely run its course.

Still, in another and not necessarily contradictory sense, one might also argue that Freud's thought is not everywhere, but nowhere. Instead of consolidation of psychoanalytic understanding there seems to be simply more proliferation and variation in the "uses" of Freud. This ambiguous situation calls for second thoughts. Paul Ricoeur has asked, "How is one to read Freud?"[1]

---

[1] Paul Ricoeur, *De l'Interpretation: Essai sur Freud* (Paris: Editions du Seuil, 1965), pp. 67–72.

His question suggests that one's response to Freud is intimately related to the use one makes of his psychology in rethinking the nature of hermeneutics. His question also suggests, by implication, that the problem of response to Freud lies as much in the very act of reading as it does in the more detached drawing of hopefully correct conclusions about what is being said. Presumably, the act of reading is a properly distantiating one in which thought precludes the more immediate features and some of the better-known dynamics of personal relations. Reading seems to be more "objective" than talking. Yet, it would seem that the act of reading presumes a relation to an object or person that in some ways is no different from speaking. Some books, we find, are more "interesting" to us than others; some require more effort, and sometimes that effort cannot be explained entirely in terms of conceptual complexity.

Much of the discussion of Freud's work—in psychology as well as in theology—assumes that the problem of understanding Freud is largely one of sifting, collating, rejecting, amending, and the like, without much regard for whether or not there are special hazards or pitfalls that present themselves in the very wish simply to understand. We are faced today with a plurality of very different readings or interpretations. Is this kind of disagreement inevitable? Does one's particular academic discipline, professional training, sociology, and the like necessarily create a different reading? Or are we simply to conclude that some readings are right and some are wrong? Although just about everything a critic may say Freud said is true, nevertheless it is also clear that not all interpretations of Freud are correct.

Theological responses to Freud, in particular, are at the same time theological responses to the discipline of psychology as a whole, responses to the responses to Freud within psychology, and also responses to the very critical prior responses of Freud to religion and theology. It is not entirely possible to isolate theological readings of Freud from these contexts and factors. To provide a context for our theological discussion of Freud, let us glance at the way psychology has responded to Freud.

By and large psychology has given us two clearly recognizable and just as clearly conflicting responses to Freud; and the general style of these responses is reflected in theology as well, although both theology and psychology have tended to work independently of each other. In American psychology at least, these readings are structured by the methodological dichotomies (and, of course, by the wider sociological and historical forces that inevitably play upon the formation of a new discipline) that resulted from attempting to ground a scientific psychology in the method of introspection and the problem of consciousness. Behaviorism took as its defining characteristic a rejection of both the problem of consciousness and the method of introspection, creating what Watson himself called an "objective" psychology. Criticisms of behaviorism perforce attempt to develop a subjective psychology. Following Gordon Allport's familiar allusion to this development, his distinction between the Lockean and Leibnitzian traditions in psychology,[2] we may note a mechanistic as opposed to a dynamic reading of Freud.

The Lockean approach appears in behaviorism and learning theory in their characteristic emphasis on such methodological criteria as experimental replication, prediction, causality, clearly discernible mechanisms of response, and the behavioral field, as well as in their preference for work with animals under controlled conditions.

Of the Lockean point of view Allport says: "Its representatives are found in associationism of all types, including environmentalism, behaviorism, stimulus-response (familiarly abbreviated as S-R) psychology, and all other stimulus-oriented psychologies, in animal and genetic psychology, in positivism and operationism, in mathematical models—in short, in most of what today is cherished in our laboratories as truly 'scientific' psychology."[3] Allport summarizes this point of view by means of four fundamental presuppositions that he believes these different

[2] Gordon W. Allport, *Becoming: Basic Considerations for a Psychology of Personality* (New Haven: Yale University Press, 1955), pp. 7–16.

[3] *Ibid.*, p. 8.

movements share: Each assumes that what is external and visible is more fundamental than what is not; each assumes that what is small and molecular is more fundamental than what is large and molar; they assume a "strong belief in equivalence of species," that is, that every basic feature of human nature can be studied without essential loss among lower species; and they assume with regard to development that what is earlier is more fundamental than what is later and more contemporary.

Such an approach, committed to a particular model of scientific inquiry, either attempts to extract from Freud's work whatever it can find there that resembles its own approach,[4] or asserts that what little truly scientific work Freud did was hopelessly lost in a morass of unscientific speculation. This unscientific speculation has received a variety of designations—vitalistic, pansexual, teleological, mystical, metaphysical, religious, or simply subjective rather than objective.[5] As Boring remarks, "Behavioristics does not readily assimilate psychoanalysis, which is so subjective as to be suspect of harboring *homunculi ex machina* . . . in its superego, ego and id."[6] Let us simply refer to the Lockean reading of Freud as a scientific-mechanistic or objective reading, thus noting its inherent disapproval of concern with the internal, socially private aspects of the person, depth of inner conflict, and psychic participation on the part of the observer in research situations.

The Leibnitzian or dynamic reading of Freud has been taken up especially by the group now recognized as neo-Freudian and also by certain figures within ego psychology, personality theory, and existential psychology. The Leibnitzian point of view forms

[4] For a relatively early example of this sort of reading, see E. B. Holt, *The Freudian Wish and Its Place in Ethics* (New York: Henry Holt, 1915). The most well known later discussion is John Dollard and Neal E. Miller, *Personality and Psychotherapy: An Analysis in Terms of Learning, Thinking, and Culture* (New York: McGraw-Hill, 1950).

[5] For an example, see Knight Dunlap, *Mysticism, Freudianism and Scientific Psychology* (St. Louis: Mosby, 1920).

[6] Edwin G. Boring, *A History of Experimental Psychology* (New York: Appleton-Century-Crofts, 1950), p. 714.

a polar opposite to the Lockean emphasis. It is the tradition of the active intellect, maintaining that the person rather than the environment is the source of acts, that these acts are purposive rather than mechanical, and that they refer to the future as well as to the past. Allport's own style of doing psychology follows that of his introductory discussion in *Becoming:* first to describe the Lockean, positivistic, or objective approach in psychology; then to allude to dynamic alternatives; and then to develop his own approach in critical contrast to these. In calling attention to Allport's polar opposites, we are not attempting to define two methodological procedures in the field of psychology, but only to note two extreme methodological styles, styles that can also be taken as guides to the approach of American psychology to Freud's psychology. Indeed, much of the thrust of personality theory may be seen as an attempt to reconcile these two epistemological traditions in psychology.

One might expect to find this a more tolerant reading of Freud. That is so, but only up to a point. Eventually, there is the same combination of tentative qualified acceptance and final rejection. In this case, however, Freud's work is thought to be helpful in understanding the functionally lower and developmentally earlier processes but is rejected as an explanation of higher and distinctly personal psychological processes such as decision, formation of self-concept, thinking, and the like. In this response to Freud we have a dynamic reading, one that seeks to cull out nonreductionistic findings, hypotheses or data from what is believed to be the more generally reductive intent and context of his writings.

In sum, the mechanistic or Lockean motif in psychology finds Freud insufficiently reductive, whereas the dynamic or Leibnitzian motif finds Freud to be ultimately too reductive. Each wishes in effect to hand him over to the other.

This characteristic ambiguity of response is well illustrated by Shakow and Rapaport's comprehensive discussion which places the response of American psychology in both its method-

ological and broader sociological context.[7] They discuss three
major surveys of experiments testing psychoanalytic theories.
Of the work of Dollard and Miller, they write: "The attempt
made by Hull and the Yale group to reconcile psychoanalysis
with conditioned-reflex theory generally resulted in an invasion
of the literature by Freudian terms, but at the price of turning
Freud's concepts into conceptions only barely related and sometimes contradictory to the original concepts."[8] Of the experiments of Robert Sears, Rapaport and Shakow say that:

> . . . perhaps the major limitations of Sears' study involves its
> basic philosophical orientation. His strongly behaviorist-en-
> vironmentalist point of view seems to have prevented him from
> recognizing the nativistic-genetic quality of psychoanalytic
> theory. In keeping with the then prevailing behaviorist frame of
> reference, his discussions appeared to be directed at translating
> psychoanalysis into learning-theory terms. . . . It is, of course,
> too much to expect Sears to have transcended the limitations of
> the *Zeitgeist* of his particular environment. Nevertheless, if he
> had been able to do so, as an experimental psychologist who *was*
> interested in psychoanalytic theory, he might have been more
> creative about experimental approaches *combining* the nativis-
> tic with the learning-theory orientation.[9]

The theology to be examined in detail below has defined
itself methodologically as against a mechanistic (scientific) understanding of the world, arguing that the reality that Christian
faith seeks and the methods it employs transcend those of science.
This affirmation has structured theology's response to Freud's
psychology, conceiving it to be an instance of the science of psychology. Whenever theologians have asked themselves whether
Freud's psychology was "really" science or whether it was something quite different, they have generally preferred the first con-

---

[7] David Shakow and David Rapaport, *The Influence of Freud on American
Psychology* ("Psychological Issues," No. 13; New York: International Universities Press, 1964).

[8] *Ibid.,* p. 159.

[9] *Ibid.,* p. 169.

clusion. Like the Lockeans in psychology, theologians have been concerned with Freud's scientific credentials, and this is an important feature of their methodological style with regard to psychology.

Theology has taken advantage of—or, perhaps, has simply been influenced by—the rather uncritical willingness of psychology to work on the basis of such dichotomies as Lockean versus Leibnitzian, mechanism versus dynamics. Theologians have found in this polarity a lock-and-key parallel to their own epistemological preoccupations with the subject-object relation and the theological transcendence of that relation. Thus, theology has placed Freud on the mechanism side of the debate, although there have been moments when deeper affinities between psychoanalysis and theology have been sensed. In other words, the theologians' reading of Freud has been mechanistic, but there has been some recognition of those portions of Freud's work that cannot be reduced to mechanism.

Three extremely influential books, all written from a Protestant point of view, illustrate this polarity of theological response to psychoanalysis and in so doing implicitly link psychological and theological styles of response to Freud. Albert Outler, in *Psychotherapy and the Christian Message,* seeks to separate the techniques of psychotherapy from what he believes to be its deeper anthropological presuppositions, and he does so because he wishes to avoid the mechanistic world view often implicit in the presuppositions of scientific psychology. In so doing, he effects at important points a mechanistic reading of Freud. However, in *Psychotherapy and a Christian View of Man,* David Roberts employs a different strategy. He finds, in some of the assumptions of psychotherapy that Outler rejects, a close parallel to the dynamics of Christian theology's understanding of sin and salvation. It is the dynamic features of psychotherapy that interest him rather than its mechanistic limitations. The work of Seward Hiltner also illustrates this polarity in theological approaches to psychology. He distinguishes several approaches to counseling: a social-adjustment view and an inner-release view which, taken together, make possible a broader approach that he calls an objective-ethical view. In so doing, he attempts to integrate the emphases given by both Outler and Roberts.[10] For the most part, however, the mechanistic reading of Freud and of psychology generally has prevailed in theology.

Why are there different readings of Freud? Are we obliged to choose between them? And if we do, must our choice be the most "objective" one? The logic of these questions insists that we accept the bias of one particular reading. But that is hazardous not only because it cuts us off from the possible resources of the others, but also because it excludes further discussion of the context out of which a particular reading takes shape. Let us, then, suspend these questions for a moment and instead further extend or complicate the problem. To do this, let us examine not only intellectual and conceptual considerations, but also the more personal aspects of response. We can, in this case, consider who Freud was alongside of what he said. This in turn could be extended one step further to include the technical side of psychoanalysis, that is, what Freud did.

Erik Erikson has written psychoanalytically about the origins of psychoanalysis as these are to be found both in Freud's person and in his work. He speaks of three major and interrelated issues that together form the necessary dimensions of discovery in psychology: first, a crisis in therapeutic technique; second, a crisis in the conceptualization of clinical experience; and third, a personal crisis.[11] He has also written at length concerning the interlocking of ideology, identity, and the sense of professional role created by what he calls various historically given work techniques. Together we may think of these, albeit in a somewhat more general fashion, as thought, person, and work—Freud's conceptual system, Freud as a person, and the craft or technique of assisting in the psychological difficulties of another person.

[10] See Albert C. Outler, *Psychotherapy and the Christian Message* (New York: Harper, 1954); David E. Roberts, *Psychotherapy and a Christian View of Man* (New York: Scribner's, 1953); and Seward Hiltner, *Pastoral Counseling* (New York: Abingdon-Cokesbury Press, 1949), pp. 26–33.

[11] Erik H. Erikson, "The First Psychoanalyst," *Freud and the Twentieth Century,* ed. Benjamin Nelson (New York: Meridian Books, 1957), p. 87.

If, as Erikson argues, all three are necessary aspects of psychological discovery, it follows that, in formulating one's response to Freud, one responds to the ideas, but not only to these. One responds also to the person. And one responds not only to the person and his ideas, but also to the technical or practical side of psychoanalysis as well.

The reciprocal of this more inclusive and wholistic understanding of response to Freud must be included as well, again however with the same appropriate qualifications. As an individual's own intellectual point of view—his questions and problems —is endowed with personal significance, features of his own developmental, psychic career are from time to time brought into play. And so as well with his vocation or work, his "professional" orientation. Insofar as interplay between such considerations is necessary and, if necessary, is then permitted, then at least an approach to what might eventually become an "objective" reading of Freud becomes possible.

By and large theologians—and academic psychologists, too —have tended to focus on the thought of Freud and in so doing have excluded considerations of his person and work. It has been pastoral psychology and clinical psychology that have extended the responses of their respective disciplines in a wholistic direction. Does this suggest that considerations of craft or technique— in theological language, considerations of care and casuistry—are perhaps irreconcilable to more purely conceptual theological problems? Or, does it suggest that Freud was less successful in drawing these together than Erikson has indicated?

What we have been considering might be expected to eliminate certain possible hazards in reading Freud. Once different views are available, we are in a position to select. But, in fact, they only exacerbate the problem further, for they simply provide more and different points of view. This additional hazard appears in the efforts of certain psychotherapists to examine the person of Freud. The exemplary pattern of patienthood that lies behind a particular psychotherapist's own theoretical constructions (his thought) and his own techniques of transformation (his work) become the basis of his image of Freud as a person.

Erikson's own work is a case in point. Just as "identity" is the keystone for the more important Eriksonian reconstructions of libido theory, theory of identification, of the superego, and so forth,[12] so it appears that Freud's person is to be understood through his identity crisis.[13] Which comes first in the Eriksonian reconstruction: his theoretical discussions *qua* ego-psychologist, his clinical discernments, or the sense in which these intersect with his own understanding of the meaning of personal crisis? Erikson's point, which we have adopted here, is that these cannot be understood in simple, sequential manner.

Just as the distinction between productive and nonproductive orientations remains central to Erich Fromm's analysis of the self, so is he inclined to see in the life of Freud a man suffering from the failure to break out of nonproductive cycles of behavior and their inner dynamics.[14] Carl Rogers sees in Freud a man enduringly "incongruent," one who was never able to undergo that sense of self-expressive release so important for the client-centered client.[15] Rogers speaks of the relation between Freud's theory of therapy and his failure to feel accepted during his self-analysis. Yet, Ernest Jones quotes with approval Freud's allusions to the kind of self-confidence that came from having been his mother's favorite. According to Jones, it was this privileged relation that gave Freud the inner security and self-confidence to achieve success.[16]

Philip Rieff has given us a distinctly Puritan Freud.[17] Although Rieff is primarily concerned with Freud's thought, his

---

[12] See Erik H. Erikson, *Identity and the Life Cycle* ("Psychological Issues," No. 1; New York: International Universities Press, 1959).

[13] This point is the substance of Erikson's "The First Psychoanalyst."

[14] See Erich Fromm, *Sigmund Freud's Mission: An Analysis of His Personality and Influence* (New York: Harper, 1959), pp. 10–18.

[15] Carl Rogers, "The Nature of Man," *Pastoral Psychology*, XI, No. 104 (May 1960), 23–26.

[16] Ernest Jones quotes Freud's remark as follows: "A man who has been the indisputable favorite of his mother keeps for life the feeling of a conqueror, that confidence of success that often induces real success" (*The Life and Work of Sigmund Freud* [3 vols.; New York: Basic Books, 1953], I, 5; see also I, 14).

[17] Philip Rieff, *Freud: The Mind of the Moralist* (New York: Viking Press, 1959).

allusions to Freud's person clearly indicate that he finds Freud to be a stern moralist concerned with voluntaristic mastery and discipline of the instincts. David Bakan has argued that the clue to Freud's person, and to his thought and work as well, lies in certain historical strands of Jewish mystical thought.[18] Bakan's Jewish mystical Freud stands in intriguing contrast to Hobart Mowrer's theological discussions of Freud, which find something demonic in the moral implications of psychoanalytic therapy. Mowrer has spoken of Freud as the Devil.[19] Psychologists, it would seem, are unlikely consultants when it comes to understanding a man many consider to be the greatest psychologist of all.

We may see such attempts on the one hand as insufficiently informed, as confused, or even as biased. Furthermore, we notice a disturbing circularity between what Erikson calls the dimension of psychological discovery and the typology of readings just proposed. A mechanistic reading of Freud's thought creates an image of Freud's person as Newtonian scientist—abstracted, detached, relating to his patients and colleagues externally rather than internally and participatively. This in turn is linked to an understanding of psychotherapy as didactic reeducation or as drive extinction. The more dynamic reading leads to romantic interpretations of Freud's person as a healer, a conqueror (a reference Freud himself once used),[20] or as a great man; psychotherapy becomes the cure, self-fulfillment, self-realization, perhaps even a process of mystical descent into one's own inner life. In the hands of the theologians, Freud is a secularist or atheist, and his therapeutic work is an idolatrous substitute for the kind of self-understanding that comes only through revelation.

On the other hand, this fragmenting of views may be understood as a series of necessary projections exemplifying both the

[18] David Bakan, *Sigmund Freud and the Jewish Mystical Tradition* (Princeton, N. J.: D. Van Nostrand, 1958).

[19] See O. Hobart Mowrer, *The Crisis in Psychiatry and Religion* (Princeton, N. J.: D. Van Nostrand, 1961), chap. ix.

[20] See Jones, *Freud*, I, 5.

advantages and vicissitudes of a particular perspective and its particular set of questions and interests. So understood, the presence and circularity of such a variety of readings testifies to the hazards of ignoring the particular interests and questions that form the perspective from which a particular reading emerges.

Such considerations raise the apparently crucial question: Is it possible to read Freud without projecting? This, however, is a pseudo-question. A more preferable and surely more manageable problem is whether or not it is possible to read Freud in conjunction with other readings and in consideration of different questions. I therefore want to project what will in time come to be a "higher" reading of Freud, one that is theological in form and that I refer to as a "third reading"—indicating its place in relation to the mechanistic and dynamic understandings. I will argue (in Chapter 5) that a third reading is not only possible, but also that it is the one most consistent with the deepest strands of Freud's thought. That is, both the mechanistic and dynamic motifs in Freud's thought can be viewed as more abstract derivatives of another motif, which I call the iconic motif. Freud's psychology is fundamentally about images, symbol and myth, about interpretations that presuppose levels of meaning, and about culture rather than therapy. But this reading, which at this point has only the status of a question, lies embedded in the theological materials themselves, especially in the latent intricacies of theological response to Freud.

Theological existentialism and the
thought of Freud

THERE has been a good deal of theological literature responding to Freud, but only certain portions retain consistency in depth from one statement to the next. What is required first of all is a theology that has responded with something more than sheer polemical-apologetic violence. Secondly, such a theology should register its response positively, preferably even using Freud in a constructive sense. Thirdly, it should possess a particular style, should evince the characteristics of a genre—that is, one should be able to move from one particular theological figure to another with some sense of continuity, even though emphasis and vocabulary undergo change.

Although it is banal to note that Protestant thought has found Freud congenial whereas Roman Catholic thought has preferred Jung, it is also true and important. For extremely interesting reasons, which I hope to be able to clarify, Protestant thought has distinctly preferred Freud's psychology, whereas it has remained offensive to the Catholic theological imagination. In particular, there is a branch of Protestant thought characterized by emphasis on God's extreme otherness that has its roots in St. Paul and St. Augustine and then in Luther, Pascal, and Kierkegaard. Those theologians who derive from this tradition I call theological existentialists, and it is they who have been drawn to Freud.[21] There are, of course, many exceptions to this generalization, but they do not provide even the moderately sustained interest and the consistency of response that can be found in this type of theology.

Beyond the more obviously popular and ideologically toned theological responses, the first theological attempt to deal with psychoanalysis was made by pastoral psychology. Several such efforts appeared during the 1930s, to become an established part of Protestant theological education during the 1940s and 1950s. However, this response largely to the work of Freud has not even now created a synthesis of sufficient intellectual depth for sustained examination. While psychology was undergoing its transformations from structural psychology to functional psychology and to behaviorism, and at the same time beginning to

[21] I use this term to refer primarily to the work of Barth, Brunner, Bultmann, Tillich, Reinhold Niebuhr, and to the later writings of H. N. Wieman.

read Freud, theology was also undergoing a revolution of its own. Besides their efforts to rethink the nature of theology, Tillich, Niebuhr, Brunner, and Barth all had time to become acquainted in varying degrees with Freud during the 1930s and, in the case of the first two, continued to discuss him periodically throughout their work.

In contrast to pastoral psychology, theological existentialism displays a recognizable style with regard to the human sciences, and this is the context in which discussions of psychology and Freud's psychology can be found. This genre has until recently dominated the Protestant theological scene, and the writings of Paul Tillich and Reinhold Niebuhr at least have been influential in intellectual and professional circles beyond the immediate theological community. Perhaps most important, theological existentialism displays an intriguing readiness first to articulate with psychoanalysis at certain predictable points and then to correct it apologetically. What are the more obvious features of this response?

Its salient features are inseparable from its style, and the insistence with which methodological self-definition is regularly attempted is an outstanding feature of that style. The problem of method—or, more precisely, what I would call the problem of methodological identity—remains formidable in this particular type of Protestant theology. Consider the ever-present prolegomena or methodological prefaces. These theologians cannot resist defining themselves. If not clearly visible in the first part of a systematic work, its equivalent is to be found within the context of other considerations. The distinctiveness of theological method is defined primarily in relation to philosophy and science, and, if a single term brings together these otherwise diverse efforts, surely it is that of "transcendence": In what sense does and does not theological method transcend the methods of science? In what sense does the object of theological statement transcend scientific knowledge?

This simplistic and highly general observation no doubt will seem for the most part self-evident. Its meaning can be illustrated diagrammatically, to show a particular pattern in the way in which methodology is conceived within this group of thinkers. If we construct a horizontal line, we can locate Karl Barth's theology at the extreme left on the line, Tillich's theology in the middle, and the work of H. N. Wieman at the extreme right. We could then place Brunner between Barth and Tillich and Bultmann and Niebuhr between Tillich and Wieman. By means of this "gradient" we may note a progressive movement with regard to the meaning of theological method, of theological anthropology, and of the place of psychology in theology.

With regard to methodology, we note that as we move from left to right, the requirements for a highly systematic prolegomenon decline. Barth, Brunner, and Tillich give us well-formed prolegomena. For the remaining figures to the right of Tillich, methodology is tangled up with other considerations. It is, of course, formidably present nonetheless, but it is also more difficult to locate and one must hunt for it. Wieman's methodological considerations appear, for example, in his concern with scientific method, Niebuhr's in his grappling with the presuppositions of social and political theorists, and Bultmann's in the particulars of his biblical-historical analyses and in his discussions of the relation between ontology and faith. As we move from left to right, we see an increasingly immanental style of theological method. As we move in the other direction, theological method increasingly requires that a dissociation of high integrity be effected between theological and scientific matters. The problem of methodology in theological existentialism is reducible finally to a debate regarding the subject-object relation and its theological transcendence. (This epistemological problem in theology and the questions that psychoanalysis brings to it are discussed in detail with reference to Tillich's thought in Chapter 3.)

The methodological problem bears a circular relation to a second problem that has preoccupied the contemporary Protestant imagination, that of theological anthropology. The doctrine of man, the problem of theological self-understanding, is the reverse side of the methodological problem. Whereas the key category in theological method is that of the transcendence of God, the key category in theological anthropology is that of the self and self-transcendence. "Spirit," "self," "the I," "the centered self"—these anthropological categories refer back to the structure and dynamics of man as sinner, to his "boasting," his "pride," his "hubris and concupiscence," his "I-certainty," his "emancipation."[22] How is theology to understand this crucial mark of the human condition? How is it to speak truthfully of its transformation?

Again making use of our diagrammatic approach, this time with regard to theological anthropology, we note a similar kind of progressive shift of emphasis as one moves from Barth's position to Tillich's and from there to Wieman's position. In this case we find increasingly direct concern for theological anthropology, and a great deal of effort is given to theological legitimation of this concern. There is an increasing sense of the rightness of using nondoctrinal sources in theological anthropology and a sense of permittedness regarding the use of verification criteria from other than doctrinal sources. Thus, Brunner's secondary critical principle, Tillich's correlation, Bultmann's demythologizing, Niebuhr's historical empiricism, and Wieman's natural-empirical theology all achieve much of their force from their capacity to validate their sources in critical relation to the "high" approach of Barth. (The question of anthropology and the kind of questions psychoanalysis can bring to it are taken up in detail in relation to Niebuhr's thought in Chapter 2.)

These two very central issues are the framework in which psychology is considered by this type of theology. The methodological question becomes: At what point is the way to theological understanding coordinate with the means of psychological understanding and at what point must it be said to transcend psy-

---

[22] These designations are the more familiar dynamic and anthropological categories employed, respectively, by Bultmann, Niebuhr, Tillich, Barth, and Brunner. In the case of Wieman it is not so easy to find a single outstanding term, especially one that gives exceptional emphasis to a hubris of self-seeking and domination.

chological knowledge? The anthropological question becomes: What is the meaning of psychological processes in the normative development, formation, and functioning of the person? Does theological self-understanding occur within developmental matrices, as these have been delineated by the psychological sciences? Is there a psychodynamic of faith?

Our diagrammatic approach can shed some light on this general question of the status of psychology in this genre of theology. Again, moving from left to right, from the "high" theologies of the left that emphasize transcendence to the "lower" theologies of the right that emphasize immanence, we find psychology to have increasing value for theology. Not only is the task of theology thought to be enriched by the methods and knowledge of psychology, but also the task of theology itself is considered to be more clearly psychological in nature. Conversely, movement in the other direction requires an increasing sense of dissociation between theology and psychology.

However, a paradox appears when we consider another question, that of the proper kind of self-involvement required of the theologian. Because psychological processes are more likely to be considered legitimate sources for theology as one moves to the right, it might seem that the psychological features of the theologian's own life situation—what we might call the relation between his person and his thought—would become increasingly important determinants. Yet, the apparently opposite point can be made as well. For, on the right, theology is limited by its relation to other disciplines. Theology, it is in this case maintained, must be responsible to these disciplines in some way or other, and, therefore, theology is limited by them. But as one moves to the left, theology is less and less limited by other disciplines. Rather, it is more likely to be limited only and entirely by the theologian's sense of his tradition, his participation in his community of faith, and his sense of the otherness of the object of his inquiry. One might therefore argue that *more* self-involvement is required in this case than in the more psychologically concerned theological position. Perhaps the use of psychological materials has some compensatory relation to the absence of these in the community of faith.

In any case, further inquiry is required regarding the intricacies of this theological style, which prizes the skill with which it debates the magnitude of the gap between theology and other disciplines. (This question is posed directly toward the end of Chapters 2 and 3, and an attempt is made to clarify it in the first two sections of Chapter 5.)

The consensus of response that I wish to explore, although articulated by different theologians in complex and often different vocabularies, remains in one respect rather simple. In its most distinctive moments, Protestant theological existentialism is deeply concerned to protect what it conceives to be the theological dimension of human life from reduction to psychological processes and psychological understanding; and the thrust of its remarks with regard to psychology has remained under the control of this concern. Although avowedly sensitive to the constructive implications of psychodynamics for theological self-understanding, it defines what is distinctively theological in the life of the person in opposition to the psychological such that psychological processes are always considered part-processes. The theological dimension that characterizes the existence of the person transcends psychological processes. Psychological studies can clarify distortions in the life of the self, they can document the processes and mechanisms of development, and they can delineate the various modes of adjustment and socialization. But in this very doing they necessarily come upon only part of the total meaning of the person and his existence. The anthropological reality of which such Christian theology speaks transcends developmental and socialization processes—as these are delineated by the psychological sciences—just as, methodologically, theological method transcends the methods of inquiry employed by the psychological sciences. One encounters God as one moves away from—or beyond—the effects of development and socializa-

tion. In such fashion is theological meaning protected from reduction to psychological interpretation.

Such a stance, with its characteristic concern for reductionism, is from time to time extended to include Freud's psychology.
Freud, it is said, proposed an exhaustive account of human life,
and in so doing reduced higher processes of life to the lower. In
pointing out the irrational roots of religion, social organization,
art, and culture, he collapsed the fundamental significance of
these phenomena into the developmental modalities of childhood.
He resolved the essential, the ontological, and the normative into the existential, the psychological, and the descriptive. Transcendence, which can be understood only in terms of its own inner
meaning, has been submitted to the objectifying modes of empirical science or to the subjective, internal irrationalities of the
unconscious and infantile life. The root dynamics of man's problematic—his pride, his propensity for self-elevation, and his corresponding capacity for freedom and self-transcendence—have
been brought under control of the rationalizing processes by
which therapy and development are understood. The theologian
cries, "The cure becomes the disease."

In order to explore this stance in depth and with some
systematic precision, I shall examine the work of two highly representative figures. Within the Protestant theological group,
Reinhold Niebuhr and Paul Tillich have thought and written
about Freud a good deal more than have the others. Further,
their work closely matches the two issues central to this consensus. Niebuhr's work is almost entirely anthropological rather
than methodological in intent (perhaps this is the meaning of
his cryptic and often quoted remark, "I am not a theologian");
and Tillich's thought, although it clearly encompasses both considerations, has addressed itself to the methodological problem
as much as or more than any other.

Through a discussion of the work of these men it is possible
to explore the roots of tentative theological approval and final
theological objection to psychoanalytic psychology. And,

through a critical interpretation of this theological objection, it is possible to bring into view both a higher reading of Freud and the implicit psychological form of theological anthropology and methodology. There is a connection between theology's reductive reading of Freud and its failure to recognize how deeply psychological are its own formulations.[23]

[23] In discussing only two theologians we have employed a single case approach. The "single case" approach permits exploration in depth, allowing features of both psychology and theology to appear that might otherwise be obscured by the broader, survey approach. No doubt there is in each case both gain and loss. But the very style of this type of theology, so ambiguous with regard to its assessment of psychology, requires discussion in some depth; and because a recognizable consistency of style is shared by this theological movement, the single case can in a number of ways be expected to speak for the movement as a whole. This approach is, therefore, the more rewarding.

Two: Anthropological response
to Freud: Reinhold Niebuhr

The conceptual styles
of Niebuhr and Freud

REINHOLD NIEBUHR'S work is generally considered to be a representative restatement of classic Protestant theological views of the nature of the person and his relation to God. His writings have provided an American counterpart to European theological existentialism, the genre of theology which we wish to examine. Further, Niebuhr has made the problem of the nature of man central to his many and otherwise extremely diverse interests and concerns. In the course of his efforts to write a Christian anthropology he has commented on Freud's thought on a number of different occasions. The views of Niebuhr provide us with representative and fitting definitions of theological concepts. These concepts in turn provide the basis for a comparative discussion with psychology, and for assessing the extent to which theological meanings do or do not in fact undergo secularization at the hands of psychology. Most important of all, Niebuhr's views will serve as an ideal type for determining the validity of a higher psychological criticism of theology.

In this chapter I begin with a brief review of Niebuhr's concept of the self. Since I will subsequently develop a rather thoroughgoing criticism of Niebuhr, I have tried to make the present discussion as inclusive as possible, allowing Niebuhr to speak for himself, in order to avoid the charge of misrepresenting his thought to fit my own arguments. The way one reads Niebuhr is as important as the way one reads Freud.

It is possible to provide a framework for comparing Niebuhr and Freud in terms of several categories of the self that emerge directly from the theological and psychological materials—that is, directly from what I call the conceptual styles of Niebuhr and Freud. These categories will in turn serve as a general conceptual framework for subsequent discussion of theological and psychological materials. Niebuhr himself notes that Freud's psychoanalytic psychology presents a definite theory of the self and is therefore consistant with the general aims and intent of his own work.[1] If the theologian is to reject Freud, he will have to do so on grounds other than the simple fact that Freud is a psychologist. A direct debate with psychoanalysis is possible. At what specific points is the debate to be conducted?

There is a high degree of similarity in the conceptual styles of both systems of thought as these apply to the concept of the self, and this formal likeness is the most advantageous point at which to begin. I understand these systems as attempts to define the nature of the self, and find that they break down into four fundamental emphases: structure, dynamics, socialization, and methodology. These emphases provide the framework for analyzing theological and psychological approaches to the nature of the self, and I begin by reviewing their meaning and place in the writings of Niebuhr and Freud.

Structure refers to enduring elements in the life of the self, whereas the dynamics of the self denotes the modes or processes by which and through which the elements of the self are said to interact. Niebuhr's analysis of the self begins with three such elements: body, mind, and spirit. Man is a self, or, as Niebuhr likes to put it, man lives at the juncture of nature and spirit; he is a

---

[1] See Reinhold Niebuhr, "Human Creativity and Self-Concern in Freud's Thought," in Nelson, ed., *Freud*, p. 259.

unity of body, mind, and spirit, and he knows that his nature requires that he unite these elements.

Structural and dynamic considerations together constitute what is essentially human in the life of the self, the full range of both its possibilities and limitations. The self knows it is an essential unity of its elements, and consciousness of this unity includes some awareness of possible disunity. Niebuhr describes such awareness objectively as temptation; subjectively the awareness of temptation is experienced as anxiety. Man is always tempted to overemphasize his spiritual possibilities at the expense of his bodily limitations, or else he is tempted to deny his spiritual possibilities and to overemphasize the bodily aspects of his life. While the self is ideally a synthesizing of body and spirit, human life consists in a perpetual denial and overemphasis of one at the expense of the other.

Structure and dynamics refer to the internal life of the self. But this includes the fact that the self exists in and through a multiple series of social relations—groups, institutions, and historical movements. The self, which is the fundamental unit of analysis in Niebuhr's system, seeks to complete itself in social and historical life. Therefore social life is characterized by the same dimensions as individual life: it has a bodily, organic, and unconscious aspect; a rational, contractual, and voluntaristic aspect; and a spiritual, dramatic, and existential aspect. Niebuhr refers to these three dimensions of sociality as organism, artifact, and drama, and he uses these categories to analyze the structure and dynamics of social and historical life.

These three emphases or dimensions in the life of the self are complemented by a fourth, the methodological, which refers to the ways the self knows itself and knows its world. The natural and rational dimensions of the self provide the ground for those processes whereby the self knows itself and its world through its own efforts. They refer to approaches taken by science and philosophy, to empirical and rational ways of knowing. However, Niebuhr insists that, with regard to the most fundamental recesses of the self, it is finally known from "beyond" itself. The self can, in and of itself, know its world and to some extent its own internality; but its knowledge of its essential nature is grounded in a fundamental or special experience which it cannot of itself create. Niebuhr refers to the experience of being comprehended by a principle of comprehension beyond comprehension. We will attempt to clarify in more detail below this difficult, perhaps cryptic and esoteric statement, for in it lies the meaning of self-transcendence and revelation—that is, the distinctively theological components of Niebuhr's anthropology—and the grounds of his rejection of Freud's image of man. There are, therefore, two ways of knowing: the objective modes of self-knowledge employed by science and philosophy; and the intuitive and dramatic encounter with a principle of comprehension or meaning the source of which lies "beyond" all those meanings constituted through human achievement.

The thought of Freud, when analyzed in terms of the image of man resident in it, yields a pattern identical in all respects to Niebuhr's but this holds only at the formal level of analysis. Taking our cue from the rather central notion of metapsychology, we must say that, structurally, the Freudian self is "an awareness beset by instinct and culture," Freudian man lives at the "juncture" of instinct and culture. When fully developed, the Freudian self is a unity of instincts and psychic apparatus, each divided further into ego, id, and superego, on the one hand, and into the life and death instincts on the other hand. Niebuhr's characterization of the body of the self as the natural impulses to procreation and self-preservation is reminiscent of the component or partial instincts in Freud.

Dynamic considerations, however, take precedence over structural ones in Freud's thought. As theologians have pointed out, Freud, too, projected an original situation all his own—a psychoanalytic Garden of Eden—phylogenetically, in his vision of a primal societal unity preceding the oedipal crime, and ontogenetically, in the sense of the unity and closeness enjoyed by child and parent prior to oedipal disenchantment. In both the developmental and the mythological transition to the "actual" situation of life, the Freudian self becomes anxious, only to experience guilt and loss of freedom in its fall into repression and neurosis, into self-deception and its behavioral consequences. The remainder of the work of development, enhanced as it is by the formation of defenses, especially sublimation, and by the work of psychoanalytic therapy as well, is given over to mitigating this state of affairs through insight and recollection. Freud, too, had his doctrine of grace as well as of sin.

Freud turned to the societal context of selfhood as to a new and fascinating patient, only to see there on a wider scale what he had all along guessed to be the case regarding the individual. The structure and dynamics of the self, internally conceived, remain the interpretive perspective in Freud's understanding of culture—developmentally in terms of group psychology, and historically in terms of the primal crime. The Oedipus myth articulates for all men the innermost problematic depths of selfhood and, as such, is the psychoanalytic counterpart of Biblical myth. The energies of a culture, like those of the individual, are circumscribed by Eros (cultural process) and by Thanatos (return of the repressed).

Like Niebuhr, Freud affirms a necessary circularity between his psychological anthropology and his conception of method. The way the self knows itself is intimately associated with what it conceives itself to be. The scientific attitude is a function of development—that is, a function of the extent to which the ego is reality-oriented. Science is "normal thinking." Psychoanalysis is in this sense therapy for the world of science, and therefore for the world. Although the self knows itself and the world in the same manner, the repressed self is faced with the task of apprehending what in effect lies beyond itself. What lies beyond the ego is the truth about itself, truth that for dynamic reasons it cannot always take into itself. The unconscious is, in this sense, "beyond comprehension."

Freud simultaneously accentuated two different stances for psychological inquiry into the repressed dimensions of selfhood. While claiming the objectivity of science as a fundamental goal, he also found it necessary to encourage free association—he sought a disciplined form of subjectivity. This insistence upon objective formulation and dynamic intuition is reminiscent of Niebuhr's distinction between the empirical and dramatic modes of self-understanding.

At this extremely formal level of analysis there seems to be an identical pattern of thought, an identical conceptual style, in our theologian and psychoanalyst. Minimally this suggests that the Freudian image of man may bear some sort of internal and necessary relation to that particular type of Christian theology of which Niebuhr is so representative. If that is the case—and this is in great part our argument—we are now under obligation to pursue further the possible interconnections between these two images of man. We now turn to a more detailed but still descriptive application of Niebuhr's view of the self, in terms of structure, dynamics, socialization, and method. What, more precisely, is the theological nature of selfhood, and what features of psychoanalytic psychology require correction?

Niebuhr's phenomenology
of selfhood

NIEBUHR's three constructs of body, mind, and spirit refer specifically to the nature of the self. Their meaning, however, is derived from three general categories, those of nature, reason, and spirit, which provide the framework for all his discussions. Nature and spirit are polar dimensions in the analysis of human situations. Nature is the generic term for that which limits man and his world, despite his intentions and efforts; whereas spirit refers to that dimension of selfhood and to those moments in human experience in which the self must limit itself. Nature defines the extent of human limitation, and spirit the forms of human possibility. The general meaning of nature is, therefore, suggested by experiences of derivation, dependency, and in-sufficiency, subjectively; and of the physical and biological world, objectively. In each case the self comes upon situations of limita-tion which it did not produce and to which it must conform.[2]

The most outstanding general characteristic of the world of nature is the fixed and highly patterned way in which it combines vitality and form, energy and order. On the one hand, Niebuhr speaks of the vital impulses of nature, referring to the natural im-pulses that men share with the whole world of nature and which, in his words, "carry life beyond itself," driving each organism to seek completion and harmony in the life of another. This energy and exuberance takes the form of two impulses, the vital force of the sex impulse or the impulse to procreation, and the will to survive or the impulse to self-preservation. Nature is dynamic and organic. It is the energetic basis for self-extension, through which the self relates itself to its world.

But the vitalities of nature have form and order built into them. The outstanding specific feature of nature is its causality and ordered sequence. Nature is repetitive, cyclical, and mecha-nistic—it "knows no history but only endless repetition within the limits of each given form."[3] In contradistinction to spirit, nature contains repeatable processes and recurrences, and these create the necessary conditions for scientific experimentation. The forms of nature make possible empirical knowledge in which "the mind is compelled to draw one, rather than another, conclusion."[4]

On the one hand, then, the vitalities of nature are ex-perienced as ineluctable and unavoidable forms of limitation; on the other hand, vitality is a highly patterned urging with forms

[2] This review of Niebuhr's conception of nature is drawn primarily from *Nature and Destiny of Man* (2 vols.; New York: Scribner's, 1953), I, 26, 27, 40, 54–55, 69, 166–189; *Faith and History: A Comparison of Christian and Modern Views of History* (New York: Scribner's, 1949), pp. 77–79; *Moral Man and Immoral Society: A Study in Ethics and Politics* (New York: Scribner's, 1932), pp. 25–29; "The Truth in Myths," *The Nature of Religious Experience, Essays in Honor of D. C. Macintosh*, ed. Julius S. Bixler, R. L. Calhoun, H. R. Niebuhr (New York: Harper, 1937).

[3] Niebuhr, *Nature and Destiny of Man*, I, 26.

[4] Niebuhr, "The Tyranny of Science," *Theology Today*, X (January 1954), 466.

of its own. Each physical impulse has its own restraints that hedge it about in nature. But natural vitality limits the self from beyond the reach of its rational and volitional functions. The self must come to terms with its vital impulses. The nature that science observes and interprets lacks such features as consciousness, subjectivity, uniqueness, and identity. Therefore, the natural dimensions of the self need to be complemented by rational and spiritual functions.

Reason and spirit designate those aspects of selfhood in which consciousness and self-limitation are increasingly significant. Reason denotes separateness between self and world, whereas spirit denotes the capacity for still further discrimination, for self-consciousness.[5] Reason permits an orderly world, the fact that events in experience are somehow amenable to representation, organization, and expression by the self. From this follow reason's three functions. First, it is the capacity to form ideas, rational principles of coherence and patterns of thought, and to relate these to events in the external world. Secondly, reason constitutes "the extent to which we become conscious of the real character of our own motives and impulses."[6] And, thirdly, reason functions to restrain and channel the energies of nature. But because reason cannot reform or transform these energies, it exercises only a limited spiritual function. For Niebuhr spirit is clearly the clue to the essential nature of the self.

Spirit refers to those aspects of human experience in which self-limitation is required of the self, rather than given to it. Its most characteristic marks are therefore those of independence, self-derivation or aseity, self-determination, and self-sufficiency. Spirit is the active, self-initiating, and self-generating core of selfhood.[7]

[5] Niebuhr's most precise discussions of mind and reason can be found in *Nature and Destiny of Man,* I, 4–18, 26–30, 54–56, 123–125, and *Moral Man and Immoral Society,* pp. 25–29.

[6] Niebuhr, *Moral Man and Immoral Society,* pp. 27–28.

[7] This review of Niebuhr's discussion of spirit is drawn from *Nature and Destiny of Man,* I, 13–14, 17, 26–27, 55–56, 70–75, 123, 150; *Faith and History,* pp. 91–101; and *Self and the Dramas of History* (New York: Scribner's, 1955), pp. 26–29.

In Niebuhr's thought spirit is synonymous with self-consciousness and self-transcendence, although the latter is the more significant term. And here we find a theological definition of transcendence in which to anchor later psychological discussions of secularization, so often referred to as the loss or absence of transcendence. Self-transcendence is a phenomenologically real activity of the self. Niebuhr means by it an imaginative sensing and grasping of the world and especially of oneself as the seat of this activity. He writes: "The human spirit has the special capacity of standing continually outside itself in terms of indefinite regression. Consciousness is a capacity for surveying the world and determining action from a governing center. Self-consciousness represents a further degree of transcendence. . . ."[8]

By indefinite regression Niebuhr means that the self has the capacity to discern and construct many possible meanings in any situation, even when all apparent meaning seems to have been exhaustively grasped at any particular moment. The self's capacity for viewing alternatives is one of ever-increasing ranges of reflection and self-reflection. At no point is the capacity to reflect upon reflection potentially limited; at no point does satiety intervene, except insofar as the self itself creates and chooses its own moments of limitation or closure. In the realm of spirit, limitation comes from within the self, not from nature, society, or history, except insofar as the self so chooses.

Therefore, spirit is the basis of ethics, in particular of freedom and individuality. Transcending both natural process and its own reason, the self is able to inspect different environments and situations and to choose one rather than another. Both self-transcendence and freedom presuppose a sharp and discrete sense of individuality, a sensing by the self of its apartness and distinctness from the events and entities of the world.

Structurally, of course, the self is neither nature nor spirit but a concretion of these. Self-transcendence is neither simply a yearning upward into ranges of unlimited potentiality, nor simply a gravitating downward into natural limitation. What lies

[8] Niebuhr, *Nature and Destiny of Man,* I, 13–14.

at the core of the self is the essential possibility of establishing a proper sense of rhythmic alteration between these modes. Therefore Niebuhr speaks of depth, organic relatedness, and wholeness in the self, to suggest internal relations between elements of the self.

Niebuhr calls this view of the self as a unity of nature and spirit an essential or ideal, rather than an actual or historical, unity. Under actual, historical conditions the self is a tension between nature and spirit in which one is constantly being overemphasized at the expense of the other. Niebuhr insists that his delineation of an essential unity is grounded in the Biblical doctrine of creation. The self's essential unity is his term for the original righteousness and for the innocence from sin presented in the first chapter of Genesis.

Therefore, any rupture or breaking of the synthesizing and unifying function of the self is in effect a "fall," in the Biblical sense, away from unity and into disunity or sin. Niebuhr defines the loss of unity or fall as the dynamics of the self.[9] The self is anxious because it knows itself to be both limited and limitless, and because this knowledge tempts it to actualize its unlimited possibilities by denying or overcoming the dependent and contingent character of its existence. Man thereby refuses the project which God has set for him—he rebels and "falls," breaking his own inner unity, becoming at once more and less spiritual, more and less natural and bodily, than he essentially is.

The dynamics of the self consist of two phases or movements.

[9] For Niebuhr's discussions of anxiety, see *ibid.*, I, 178–207, 233–240, 269–280; II, 107–126; "Human Creativity and Self-Concern"; *Self and the Dramas of History*, pp. 158, 232; *The Structure of Nations and Empires* (New York: Scribner's, 1959), p. 31. Niebuhr's thought has become progressively more dynamic. His theological ethics have given way to a moral psychology of self and society. See his most recent *Man's Nature and His Communities: Essays on the Dynamics and Enigmas of Man's Personal and Social Existence* (New York: Scribner's, 1965), where the terms "self-seeking" and "self-giving" occur, also suggesting a more phenomenological approach. Note also the appropriation of the work of Erik Erikson. This later work also gives theological attention to female sexuality. Niebuhr's thought has become more patently psychological, suggesting that these emphases may have been latent in his earlier thought.

There is first the fall and the dynamics of what is called self-deception, and then there is the reverse of this, the movement of transformation whereby the self recovers some sense of its original righteousness, unity, and balance. In Biblical language these are the movements, respectively, of sin and grace in the life of the self.

Under the condition of anxiety the freedom to perceive and know alternatives leads to an overemphasis of spirit, which Niebuhr calls pride, and to an overemphasis of natural vitality, which he calls sensuality. These dynamics are so forceful in the life of the self that it must continually deceive itself about the deepest roots of its motives and acts. Niebuhr speaks of the mechanism of self-deception to refer to the self's refusal to recognize its finite, contingent aspects, and to its overestimation of its spiritual capacities. Pride or self-concern is the ethical consequence of such overvaluation.

However, anxiety is double-edged. It leads not only to pride or self-concern; it also leads to creativity and transformation, to reversal and renewal. Niebuhr refers to this second dynamic of the self as the shattering of the self. It is a process of reorganization of the inner life. The self surrenders its anxious grasp and claims upon its own prerogative of final limitation, and brings into proper limitation the inordinate emphasis upon excessive transcendence and limitation. This is a process which requires a recentering of loyalties around a transcendent reality that lies beyond the self's own powers to limit and be limited: "The self is shattered whenever it is confronted by the power and holiness of God and becomes genuinely conscious of the real source and center of all life."[10] Such a process is in effect a glimpse into the essential structure and dynamics of the self, a genuine confrontation with its striving both to deny its contingency and to flee its possibilities.

But such recentering is never an accomplished reality. Niebuhr's estimate of human achievement, so characteristic both of

[10] Niebuhr, *Nature and Destiny of Man,* II, 109.

his thought as a whole and of the theological tradition he so arduously represents, is unabashedly grim: "The final exercise of freedom in the transcendent human spirit is its recognition of the false use of that freedom in action. Man is most free in the discovery that he is not free."[11]

The social discussions of selfhood are little more than an application of the structural and dynamic considerations already mentioned. The human community is the necessary locus of the self's activities, so that self-transcendence is inherently social. The three categories of nature, reason, and spirit, when used to interpret social life, are redefined as organism, artifact, and drama. They indicate three different levels of motivation in social and historical life.[12]

Organic factors in social life refer to patterns or styles of social relation that develop and function unconsciously, either apart from or in spite of conscious, rational, individual effort. Because organic factors are least subject to self-conscious scrutiny, they are least accessible to intentional change. They constitute the unrecognized assumptions, values, and interests of a particular group or epoch. Artifact designates the consciously contrived, voluntaristic dimensions of collective life. At this level, community is contractually integrated by means of rational discourse and voluntary consent. The dramas of history refer to social events, actions, and decisions motivated by factors which transcend organic and rational considerations. The term drama, then, specifies yearning for limitless possibility, insofar as such yearning characterizes a group or nation. The dramatic dimension of history transcends both the organic, unconscious forces and the contractual, consciously contrived arrangements of social life.

---

[11] *Ibid.,* I, 260.
[12] This discussion of the sociality of the self is drawn from *Christian Realism and Political Problems* (New York: Scribner's, 1953), p. 25; *Self and the Dramas of History,* chaps. x and xx; and *Nature and Destiny of Man,* II, 15–34.

Niebuhr does carry his analysis of the individual self over into social life, but he establishes one important quantitative difference. Tension between spirit and nature, he insists, increases with increased social involvement. The more men seek to complete themselves in the wider ranges of social life, especially institutional life, the more vulnerable they become to pride and self-deception. It is the essential paradox of social life that collective involvement permits more freedom and therefore the possibility of more self-concern. Collectivities have no specifiable structure of self-transcendence. One of Niebuhr's earliest and best-known books carries this emphasis in its title: *Moral Man and Immoral Society*.

We complete this brief review of theological anthropology by summarizing Niebuhr's thought on methodology, his analysis of the fundamental sources of self-understanding. At this point the doctrine of revelation is central for any Christian theologian, although here again the polarity of nature and spirit, the key to Niebuhr's theology, makes itself felt, requiring as it does a distinction between general and special revelation.[13]

General revelation is a common experience potentially accessible to all men. Like nature and reason, it refers to experiences of divinity which all men can, from time to time, construct and project on the basis of their own capacities and intentions. Niebuhr believes, in a fashion reminiscent of the early psychologists of religion, that there is accessible to all men a universal religious experience with certain common features—awareness of the awe-inspiring and majestic aspects of life, recognition that one's life touches a reality beyond itself, and the experience of being commanded and judged, also referred to as a general experience of conscience. Such experiences, which are individual and personal rather than historical, create a longing for completion

---

[13] For Niebuhr's discussions of revelation, see *Nature and Destiny of Man,* I, 123–149; II, 25; *Self and the Dramas of History,* chaps. xii and xiii; *Faith and History,* pp. 26–31, 102–105, 141–150.

and forgiveness, and thus make both necessary and possible the experience of special revelation.

Special revelation, however, is not a common experience, because it only occurs at a special time and place in history. It clarifies and completes the experiences of general revelation, just as spirit completes nature and reason, and is therefore the ultimate and transcendent source and ground of the self's capacity for self-transcendence. Like natural and rational forms of understanding, the contents of general revelation are within the grasp of human intention and understanding; general revelation is in fact an extension and projection of human forms of meaning. Special revelation, however, transcends general, natural, and human forms of meaning; it is a source of meaning which is said to lie beyond comprehension. In special revelation divine mystery completes human meaning. How would Niebuhr have us understand such completion?

The content of special revelation is an historical event, the life, death, and resurrection of Jesus Christ. This event cannot be experienced directly, but is mediated through the form of Biblical narrative. Biblical narrative expresses in mythological form the same heights and depths of human possibility which the categories of nature and spirit attempt to suggest. The paradox of the Cross and Resurrection—which is never resolved historically but which is resolved in the life of God—constitutes a dramatic paradigm for the tension between nature and spirit, between immanence and transcendence. The capacity for self-transcendence, the most distinctive feature of human nature, is therefore ultimately grounded in God's revelation to man, in his relatedness to and transcendence of the world. Biblical narrative embodies the paradox of human self-understanding. That paradox, as we have repeatedly noted, consists of the tension between the self's capacities and its needs: between its natural and rational capacity to comprehend itself and its world, to construct its own meanings, and the need, generated by these very activities, to be comprehended by a source of meaning beyond its own systems of understanding. The mystery of God's transcendence clarifies and completes human meaning. Special revelation clarifies and completes general revelation. That is the theological view.[14]

---

*The Freudian view of the self
and its Niebuhrian critique*

TRANSITION from such a theological anthropology to the world of Freud must at first seem abrupt and jarring, even for so skilled an apologist as Reinhold Niebuhr. For here we find Freud approaching only indirectly, circuitously, and, for the most part, implicitly those considerations that Niebuhr has chosen to assault frontally. Selfhood in its allegedly mature or developed state is broached largely through the study of childhood; the present is understood through the study of the past; the scientific effort which insists upon objectifying psychic processes creates the need for an alternative, indirect access to the subjectivity of wish, fantasy, and dream; the study of the forces of life are illuminated by inquiry into the forces of death; the desire to understand growth leads to the study of regression; and so forth. The Freudian analysis places in the foreground of consideration the actual, the on-going, the immediate—immanence rather than transcendence.

Niebuhr's criticism in its most general sense turns on this very question of the reduction of self-transcendence to the ra-

[14] Niebuhr's distinction between special and general revelation is the basis for another distinction which takes on importance in relation to subsequent discussions of Freud's psychology of Biblical myth. Niebuhr distinguishes between primitive and permanent myth. Primitive myth can and must be interpreted by the human sciences, and aspects of Biblical myth can be so interpreted. But there are features of Biblical narrative that are permanently inaccessible to naturalistic and rationalistic approaches. See "The Truth in Myths."

tional and natural, to the more immanental modes of self-understanding.[15] And his most specific criticism centers on the limits of "mechanism," understood as both a style of thinking and as a series of conclusions about the human self. According to our theologian, the psychological processes delineated by Freud fall within the realms of nature and to some extent reason, but not spirit. The validity of this view can be challenged on the grounds that Freud's thought is addressed precisely to that mid-point, that juncture between nature and spirit that Niebuhr believes can only be discussed by means of theological statement. (See the following section.)

To expand the critique: the anxiety of temptation is reduced to the developmental process of repression; the shattering of the self that can lead to self-understanding in the form of creativity and self-transcendence is reduced to insight; the dramas of history and their concomitant possibilities of social achievement in democracy and justice are collapsed into the organic dynamics of the family, which are largely those of a preformed self; the ultimately efficacious sense of mystery that always awaits recognition at the fringes of self-understanding is replaced by a rationalized and self-conscious psychological meaning, that of scientific thinking. In short, the Freudian self is capable neither of reaching so high nor of plunging so deep as the Niebuhrian self. Freud stops short of both the heights and the depths of self-understanding. He has domesticated man's capacity for both misery and greatness.[16] We must review the outstanding points

[15] This summary of Niebuhr's views on Freud is drawn from *Nature and Destiny of Man* I, 42–44, 52–53, 121; "Human Creativity and Self-Concern"; *Self and the Dramas of History,* pp. 8–11, chap. xviii; and *Moral Man and Immoral Society,* chap. ii. In these discussions, Niebuhr relies primarily on two of Freud's works, *New Introductory Lectures on Psychoanalysis,* trans. W. J. H. Sprott (New York: W. W. Norton, 1933), and *Civilization and Its Discontents,* trans. Joan Riviere (Garden City, N.Y.: Doubleday, 1958). *Totem and Taboo,* trans. James Strachey (New York: W. W. Norton, 1952), and *Beyond the Pleasure Principle,* trans. James Strachey (New York: Bantam Books, 1959) are mentioned.

[16] See Albert C. Outler, "Freud and the Domestication of Tragedy," *The Tragic Vision and the Christian Faith,* ed. Nathan A. Scott, Jr. (New York: Association Press, 1957).

in Freud's psychological anthropology in order to grasp fully the basis of Niebuhr's objections. What is the Freudian self to which Niebuhr takes such exception?

In the most simplistic sense possible, the Freudian self may be rendered structurally as an awareness beset by instinct and culture. It is a structure of instinct and mind, each of which has a substructure; there are two basic instincts, those of life and of death, and there are three elements in the structure of mind, the id, ego, and superego. The Niebuhrian criticism makes a great deal of Freud's mechanistic modes of thought, and the evidence for it is familiar and plentiful. With regard to the structure of the self, this criticism asserts that a mechanistic reading of instinct will be followed by an excessively rational understanding of mind and that a sociologically relativistic or merely situational view of self-transcendence will be advanced through the concept of the superego.[17]

Freud clearly spoke of the instincts in neurophysiological and mechanistic terms.[18] His remarks often convey the impression of a detached observer inspecting a spatially and temporally circumscribed apparatus and seem to be simply a continuation of his own prepsychoanalytic physiological work. The instincts are internal stimuli or needs, continually flowing sources of somatic stimulation. They create a sense of demand—that is, they press ineluctably upon the ego for representation and discharge. Their energies are directed toward objects, and their purpose is the reduction of tension, returning the organism to homeostatic

[17] The most obvious example of the mechanistic point of view in Freud's work is "Project for a Scientific Psychology," *The Origins of Psycho-Analysis: Letters to Wilhelm Fliess, Drafts and Notes: 1887–1902,* ed. Marie Bonaparte, Anna Freud, and Ernst Kris; trans. Eric Mosbacher and James Strachey (New York: Basic Books, 1954). This criticism is a familiar one and is found in religious and philosophical existentialism and existential psychology, as well as much personality theory.

[18] See, for example, Sigmund Freud, "Instincts and Their Vicissitudes," *Collected Papers* (5 vols.; "The International Psycho-Analytic Library," ed. Ernest Jones; New York: Basic Books, 1959), IV; "Anxiety and Instinctual Life," *New Introductory Lectures;* "Three Contributions to the Theory of Sex," *The Basic Writings of Sigmund Freud,* trans. and ed. A. A. Brill (New York: The Modern Library, 1938).

quiescence. The analogies which Freud used to discuss the flow of libido in this context are equally mechanistic—motor forces, electric charges, columns of water. The theory of the instincts itself suggests further and more subtle fragmentation—duality in terms of conceptual specification (Eros and Thanatos) accompanied by fusion and unity in terms of actual dynamics. Clearly, it seems that Freud renders human motivation in mechanistic terms. Note that Niebuhr's own analysis of natural vitality into the two major impulses of procreation and self-preservation matches what is usually referred to as Freud's first instinct theory.

The mind fares little better with regard to the unity of selfhood that Niebuhr is constrained to defend.[19] Although Freud protested that his geographical, "place-thing" habit of conceptualization was only a convention and that the id is not a region in the mind anymore than the mind itself is a mental place, he nevertheless seems to have proposed, even in his later thinking, no alternative, less reductive terminology.[20] The id is without a form of its own—it is without logic or intention, entirely lacking in constructing and synthesizing capacity. On the other hand, the ego is without dynamic energies of its own. It is, in effect, pure form, without what Niebuhr would call vitality, either natural, rational, or spiritual. Its function is that of giving form to the inner life and to the representation of external reality. The ego-id relation, therefore, is normatively characterized by a splitting between what Niebuhr calls vitality and form. The activity of giving form consists in imaginatively construing causal sequences, relations, networks of determination. The ego constructs the external world and the internal world in the same way. Thus, the ego is really a framework (Freud spoke of the perceptual apparatus) of conscious self-awareness that gradually expands

---

[19] For an early discussion of the ego, see "Formulations Regarding the Two Principles of Mental Functioning," *Collected Papers,* IV.

[20] See, for example, *An Outline of Psychoanalysis,* trans. James Strachey (New York: W. W. Norton, 1949), p. 14, and *New Introductory Lectures,* pp. 102–103.

under conditions of growth to include objects and the causal relations between them, as these are found in the external world or as they are found through reflective objectification of the internal world. The psychoanalytic therapy becomes the (scientific) rationalization of the mind, and by implication, of the self as well, a facilitation of the mind's own attempt to objectify its origins and emergence.

This criticism, which is a specific instance of the general criticism of mechanism, has quite far-reaching implications. It suggests that Freud's mechanistic thinking, epitomized in "Project for a Scientific Psychology," is more applicable to lower forms of psychological organization in a structural but also in a developmental sense. To transcend the categories of causality in an epistemological sense, therefore, perhaps bears some relation to the process of developmental integration itself.[21] The superego, like self-transcendence, pertains to what Niebuhr calls self-limitation, those aspects of experience which expose the self to possibilities and alternatives for thought and action, wherein it cannot defer to natural processes for self-limitation. Its three functions—self-observation, conscience, and the holding up of ideals—all serve the freedom side of the self, permitting a plurality of alternatives to confront the self. However, the superego is formed through identification; although these identifications are subsequently worked through during puberty, the superego retains its fundamental oedipal structure. The superego is heir to the Oedipus complex. Therefore, the realm of possibility—the capacity of the self to stand outside itself in indefinite regression—receives final sociological constriction. Since the superego is "simply" the internalization of cultural norms by way of the individual's father, it simply legitimates as normative what is "essentially"

---

[21] See Maurice Merleau-Ponty, *The Structure of Behavior,* trans. Alden L. Fisher (Boston: Beacon Press, 1963), pp. 176–180. Merleau-Ponty's discussion does not, however, refer to what we have called the "work" of Freud. This second aspect of psychoanalytic psychology is discussed below (chap. 3) through the notion of transference, which, it is there suggested, itself contains this kind of criticism and which is therefore a corrective from within Freud's psychology.

not the case. According to Niebuhr, the self retains its essential unity even under the conditions of actuality, and the possibility of transcending all familial, interpersonal, sociological, and historical conditions remains.

Niebuhr objects that Freud's view of the self is a "one-sided" dialectic, that is, Freud's system regularly collapses the possibility of transcendence into immanence. Structurally, the Freudian self lacks that synthetic capacity that permits creativity in both thought and action, in imagination and will. According to Niebuhr, the self "knows" that it is more than its id, ego, and superego at any particular time. He writes:

> Since Freud's system is a consistently naturalistic one, it cannot, despite the subtleties of its analyses of the intricacies of human selfhood, do full justice to the transcendent freedom of spirit of which the self is capable. . . . For the capacity of transcending every social situation and its own self bears within it all the possibilities of creativity.
>
> The self in its self-transcendence can always use its freedom both to justify and to accuse itself. . . . Retrospectively, it is always possible to establish scientifically what pressures prompted the self to certain actions. It is only prospectively that the self is free.[22]

The place assigned to anxiety by the two images of the self makes this point even more apparent.[23] For in both cases anxiety is the experience through which the possibilities and limitations of the self are mediated. Freud labored long and hard over the crucial problem of the origin of neurosis, and it is significant that one of his more careful and thorough discussions of this problem should have taken place alongside an equally careful and thorough attempt to think through the meaning of anxiety. He seems to have had little doubt as to the theoretical and clinical capacities of psychoanalytic psychology and its workers eventually to

---

[22] Niebuhr, "Human Creativity and Self-Concern," pp. 269–270.

[23] Most of this review is drawn from Freud, *The Problem of Anxiety,* trans. Henry Alden Bunker (New York: The Psychoanalytic Quarterly Press and W. W. Norton, 1936), esp. chaps. viii, ix and pp. 101–117.

arrive at more and more sophisticated and discriminating *descriptions* of anxiety and the formation of neurosis. He was, however, far less sanguine about his own and others' ability to, in Niebuhr's words, penetrate the mystery of human behavior that lay behind the phenomena of neurosis and anxiety.

Anxiety, Freud said, is an ego function, a physiologically felt sense of unpleasure, an unpleasant affect, emerging in the ego as a result of the pressure of a dangerous situation. The danger could be described in several ways: as either internal or external, as instinctual or realistic, or as either neurotic or objective. Anxiety is further described as a prototypical experience that retains its form while undergoing developmentally appropriate transformations throughout the individual's life. The prototypical experience by means of which all later forms of anxiety are to be understood is that of the infant's separation from his mother at birth. This trauma produces what Freud called mental helplessness, a flooding of the psychic apparatus with affect that could not be "bound" by sufficient intentional and imaginative organization. In childhood, separation anxiety is experienced as loss of love and as object loss; in the oedipal period, castration anxiety concerns the fear of separation of the desired member from the body; in latency, there is the fear of the superego; in puberty, there is fear of society; and, finally, throughout the remainder of life, there is a fear that one will become separated from the powers of destiny. The last three stages all express the fear of the superego in different forms.

Two points are worth noting. First, however cumbersome and simplistic, Freud was attempting, through homology and analogy, to develop a theory of anxiety that would draw together the varieties of developmental experience in such a way as to permit a unitary theory of the self. Freud writes:

> It decidedly seems as if this anxiety were an expression of helplessness, as if the still very undeveloped creature did not know what else to do with his longing. Anxiety thus seems to be a reaction to the perception of the absence of the object, and there at once spring to mind the analogies that castration anxiety has also

separation from a highly valued object as its content and that the most basic anxiety of all, the "primal anxiety" of birth, arises in connection with separation from the mother.[24]

Secondly, Freud asserted that the meaning of anxiety lay less in the objective fact of separation and more in the undeveloped ego's failure to cope with and master its own inwardness or, in Niebuhr's terms, its inability to give form to its own vitality. Its desire and longing for the lost object might also be spoken of as a nostalgia. Anxiety is an expression of helpless longing, "as if the still very undeveloped creature did not know what else to do with his longing." Separation creates desire for union, and this longing creates helplessness, which is in turn accompanied by anxiety.

Yet, this formulation did not satisfy Freud. His desire to pursue the origins of neurosis and anxiety led to a series of further distinctions—internal and external, instinct and objective reality, inner and outer—distinctions that he finally tried to clarify by distinguishing between neurotic and objective anxiety. Internal, instinctual danger is neurotic, for it can be resolved only by defense formation. External danger is objective because the organism can reduce its anxiety by removing itself physically from the situation. Freud debated the point and then decided that whether a situation is really dangerous or not is not the point, for eventually "neurotic anxiety has, under our hands, turned into objective anxiety, into anxiety felt towards certain external danger-situations."[25]

This conclusion apparently did not help much either, and Freud remained throughout his discussion unpersuaded about a possibly deeper understanding of why the still very undeveloped creature does not know what else to do with his longing. He concluded: "What is the source of neurosis, what is the ultimate, its specific, underlying principle? After decades of analytic effort this problem rises up before us, as untouched as at the be-

24 *Ibid.,* p. 76.
25 Freud, *New Introductory Lectures,* p. 129.

ginning."[26] He resigned himself to a series of descriptions—the biological factor of mental helplessness, a phylogenetic factor of latency, and the psychological factor: "By reason of the dangers which reality offers, the ego is compelled to adopt an attitude of defense. . . ."[27] It is a theory of psychic fault, of structural flaw. Freud summarized:

> We have understood that the seemingly extremely intimate relation between anxiety and neurosis derives from the fact that the ego protects itself against an instinctual danger . . . but that in consequence of an imperfection of the psychic apparatus this defensive activity eventuates in neurosis. . . . An instinctive recognition of dangers threatening from without does not seem to have been among Nature's gifts to man, save to a very moderate degree.[28]

The Niebuhrian critique both is and is not to the point here. On the one hand, the repression that follows separation anxiety can be construed (although he does not do this) from the Niebuhrian vantage point as perhaps a first, developmental instance of the dynamics of temptation. In desiring the lost love object that developmental (or historical, it makes no difference) necessity has removed as a relational possibility, the self inordinately attempts to transcend the limits that have been placed on it by the fact of its own creation and creaturely condition. It then deceives itself as to the true source of its anxiety (repression) by means of symptom formation (neurosis). In this sense, the oedipal situation is a "drama of history," and the Oedipus complex is conceived in order to deceive the self regarding its contingent, finite origins. According to this line of reasoning psychopathology has theological meaning.

But this is not Niebuhr's view. Instead, he contends that psychoanalytic theory is not applicable to the historically completed self, the self free from such idiosyncratic developmental

---

[26] Freud, *The Problem of Anxiety*, p. 92.
[27] *Ibid.*, p. 101.
[28] *Ibid.*, pp. 115–116.

failures as an Oedipus complex. In this case the notion of a psychic fault, a significant feature in the Freudian image of the self, is viewed simply as a denial of the possibility of the self's essential unity. This is the point Niebuhr prefers to make.[29]

Whether it strikes the reader as plausible or perverse, his point is not, however, a moralistic one. It does not suggest that the self "ought to be able" developmentally to integrate all separations; that is precisely the moralistic stance that creates repression. Repression occurs when anxious longing is no longer psychically possible. Rather, Niebuhr's point is addressed to the fully formed self's therapeutic rediscovery of its oedipal situation. The self, Niebuhr insists, will never really extricate itself from self-concern except insofar as it recognizes that even the deceit of repression arises from a wider historical (dramatic) and existential (spiritual) context. A notion like "oedipal fall" obscures those capacities for self-deception that characterize the self in its innermost depths. The self is not merely driven by internal instincts and external obligations, nor does it "decide" perversely in full awareness. It is of the essence of the internal maneuvering of the self that it should choose to speak of drives and obligations, of its being driven internally and externally, in order not to escape the claim that ultimately it drives its driveness. Repression is tragic, but the guile of self-deception, that is irony. But is repression perhaps more akin to irony than Niebuhr admits? Does the process of repression pertain to nature, to reason, or to spirit?

The virtues of psychoanalytic therapy are no more commendable than those of the theory, Niebuhr contends. Indeed, regarding the transformation of the self, his theological critique asserts itself with even greater impatience and conviction. Freud had a "way," a process, a hermeneutic for the life of alienation, by which repression could be alleviated. Through it, the bifurcations of instinct and mind, self and society, objective and subjective

---

[29] There are infrequent moments when Niebuhr shifts his discussions of Freud slightly. He says, for example: "The whole of Freudian psychology, not in what it declares but in what it implies, is really a striking proof of how remarkably spirit and nature, animal impulse and spiritual freedom, are compounded in human existence" *(Nature and Destiny of Man,* I, 43).

could be rendered at least less marked. The readiness of Protestant theology to register methodological horror at the very mention of techniques and procedures is well represented in Niebuhr's work.

Notions of technique, so powerfully reminiscent of the grasping quality of pride and self-concern, are themselves reductionisms, for they place into the hands of a sinful self the possibility of conducting its own self-authentication, its own unification, without reference to that fundamentally necessary principle of proper limitation that underlies the essential unity of the self. Free association, regression, transference, and repetition; integration, recollection, and working through; in short, psychoanalytic insight, all reduce the "problematic" that arises from the fact of a juncture between spirit and nature to a "problem" in therapeutic management.

But, more important, the object of truly therapeutic recall is, for the theologian, not the lost image of the mother or of the ambivalent father behind memory traces, hallucinations, and fantasies of an anxious ego; rather it is the lost image of essentiality in its transcendent, nondevelopmental reality. This image cannot be constructed in fantasy or objectified in thought; it can only be surrendered to in its only accessible form, that of Biblical narrative, of permanent myth. Thus, the dynamics of psychoanalytic recollection, it is argued, cannot encompass the more powerful and majestic trends toward both unity and disunity within the self.

There are two remaining considerations in this brief review, the self in relation to its collectivities, and the question of methodology. Freud sees the social side of psychoanalytic psychology as a viewing "upon a wider stage" of what has been demonstrated in the analysis of the individual personality.[30] The individual personality is, in its most constitutive and problematic moments, an oedipal personality, which is to say that Freudian psychology is a family psychology. The developmental thrust of the Freudian

[30] See Freud, *An Autobiographical Study,* trans. James Strachey (New York: W. W. Norton, 1952), p. 138.

self is to become itself in relation to parents and then to endeavor to remain what it has become without their support. Just so do the parental images of the family mediate between self and society. The theory of the primal horde, the psychology of the group, and the structure and dynamics of civilization are all patterned after the ego's progressive synthesizing of itself on the basis of, and final detachment from, parental images. Just as Eros and Thanatos, polarized into female and male in the oepidal situation, drive the individual self, so do they drive the cultural process, undergirding both science and social solidarity as well as the return of the repressed. However, with each increase in the range of social relatedness, the ego loses some of its capacity for insight and integration. Consequently, it is here that the ego is most vulnerable, for it finds itself confronted with wider ranges of social relatedness. Standing at the beginning and at the end of history, respectively, the primal father and the great man serve to remind the ego of those needs and their fulfillment that collective life has created for it. So it is that the oedipal myth organizes into dramatic form the phylogeny as well as the ontogeny of the self.

By now the Niebuhrian critique should be self-evident and even somewhat tiresome. The structure and dynamics of the self are in both cases the unit of historical analysis. Freud has, in effect, projected familial dynamics into the wider and wholistic context of the self and its world, and in doing so he has attempted to construct history along natural and rational, rather than spiritual, lines. Just as he insisted that psychic defect lies at the root of the ego's failure to bind in self-transcending activity the sense of object loss, so he finds that the institutional life of man aggravates even more grievously this psychic fault.

That the Freudian self is dialectically conceived only in a one-sided sense is nowhere more clearly betrayed than in the progressive ego dysfunction experienced by the self in its efforts to cathect institutions in an integrative way. According to Niebuhr, however, although there is no institutional embodiment of self-transcendence, the anxiety of temptation moves the self in *both* destructive *and* creative directions, making sociality both potentially and actually creative. Democracy does not have, as Freud once described it, an "injurious" effect.[31] The creativity and destructiveness of historical life issue from a single tension— not from a duality of drives—within the self, making itself felt in a confusion between drama and organism, egoistic self-assertion and unavoidable organic determinants.

Niebuhr's distinction between primitive and permanent myth, one of his more important methodological points, rounds out his response. For Freud, science is not an activity of the mind abstracted from psychological functioning; it is "normal thinking," by which he meant that it is subject to all the developmental vicissitudes that characteristically beset the ego. Science is a bright spot in an otherwise grim picture, a comfort to discontented humanity, for through scientific understanding internal drives and external obligations can be sufficiently mitigated to permit the ego an occasionally uncontaminated apprehension of its world. Freud's methodological remarks—for example, the distinction between conventions and phenomena, interpretations and constructions, genetic and dogmatic modes of teaching, the critique of religion and metaphysics in the interest of metapsychology—all reflect the model of psychoanalytic psychology as a method or mode of ego-expanding inquiry into the hidden, latent, or depth factors within and behind the apparently superficial and arbitrary "surfaces" of the perceptual world.[32]

Consistent with this view is Freud's not infrequent use of the word "riddle"—the riddle of sex, of life, of the universe—and he

---

[31] Freud, *Civilization and Its Discontents,* pp. 66–67.

[32] But the reverse is also true. With the exception of "Project for a Scientific Psychology," written at the very beginning of Freud's psychoanalytic career and rejected by him shortly thereafter, there are few extended discussions by Freud of scientific method, especially when those that do exist are placed alongside the remainder of his writings. Although there are frequent allusions to being scientific, it seems clear that Freud was not interested in what might today be called formulating research designs and methodologies. The sparsity of such discussions makes any insistent criticism of mechanistic reductionism seem somewhat out of place, and, for that reason, calls for investigation.

offered psychoanalytic psychology as the interpretive key to these riddles.[33] In doing so he implied that all mystery, the very possibility of a mystery that transcends meaning, is really a riddle that is in principle capable of being exhausted through psychoanalytic psychological method. Mystery and meaning do not support each other dialectically, as they do in Niebuhr's constructions, such that mystery, *qua* mystery, may be understood as the companion of meaning. In Freud's world, mystery is the enemy of meaning. For this reason, there can be no permanent myth encountered within or beyond primitive myth. Permanent myth, as Niebuhr speaks of it, objectifies the deepest possibilities and yearnings within the self, possibilities that, although they can never be brought under rational ego control and perception, nevertheless can be apprehended and designated as efficacious to the ultimate intentions of the self.

The Niebuhrian critique is therefore the same at this point as it has been at all others. The tension between spirit and nature, between transcendence and immanence, is such that its existential reality can be known only through revelation, that is, through the dramatic-narrative structure of Biblical myth. To come to know that one's image of God is a projection or extension of one's ideals, hopes, and wishes is the beginning of the sense of mystery of which Niebuhr speaks; at such moments, the self is rendered existentially "safe" to discover these projections and to trust the wider context in which they occur. On the other hand, for Freud the discovery of projection is a signal to return to the ego's self-understanding, for mystery, *qua* mystery, can never enrich meaning. Mystery can enrich meaning only by giving way to it. For Niebuhr the discovery of projection *creates* the dialectic of meaning and mystery; for Freud this discovery *collapses* it in favor of meaning. In behalf of meaning, Freud tears mystery out of the heavens, thereby rendering it manageable.

The issues in this discussion are finally reducible to a debate

[33] Freud, *Beyond the Pleasure Principle*, p. 106; *An Autobiographical Study*, p. 68; *New Introductory Lectures*, p. 236; *The Problem of Anxiety*, p. 23; and *Collected Papers*, V, 357.

about the meaning of personal freedom. This problem lies at the root of both systems of thought, and it underlies the structural, dynamic, and sociohistorical dimensions of the self. According to our theologian, the self is free insofar as it is capable of synthesizing in and for itself the radically dialectical manner in which meaning and mystery permeate the self's existence. This principle underwrites the central features that characterize the human self; the tension between the essential unity and actual disunity of the self; the tension between the destructive *and* creative possibilities of anxiety; and the tension between love and justice, between family and society, between organism and drama. Freedom, as the right relation between meaning and mystery, lies at the center of Niebuhr's interpretation of the self.

In like fashion, the Freudian construction of meaning and mystery also indicates the extent to which the self is free. The self is free insofar as it can reduce tension between the instinctual life and cultural obligation through the development of the ego. It is free insofar as it can draw meaning from the many and various forms of psychic irrationality that beset it, knowing further that the very pressure of such irrationality can only block the self's pursuit of self-understanding. The self is free insofar as it can eschew cultural entanglements, knowing that the deeper such involvement becomes, the more vulnerable is the self's integration. Freedom lies in the progressive collapsing of the "over against" in human life—be that the unconscious, the superego (individual and collective), or the world-historical projections of religion. Psychoanalytic psychology is a method whereby meaning is extracted from mystery rather than reconciled to it.

This is the Niebuhrian reading of Freud's thought. It shows the intimate connections between Niebuhr's view of selfhood and the manner in which he has chosen to conceptualize Freud's view. We have given free rein to this perspectival tendency in order to illustrate the scientific-mechanistic reading of Freud. It is extremely common, perhaps the dominant reading, both within and without psychology. Our argument is that this reading is neither simply correct nor simply incorrect, that the issue at hand is not one of choosing one reading instead of another. The issue is whether there remains a more fundamental aspect of Freud's thought that puts this reading, without abrogating it, in a different context.

In the following section, I begin to explore the question of a more fundamental aspect of Freud's thought, insofar as the materials themselves allow. I argue that there is a circular relation between Niebuhr's view of Freud and his inability to become as phenomenologically definite about the interfaces or juncture between nature and spirit as he is about the distinctiveness of these two dimensions themselves. This raises the question of the origins of actual disunity in the self, and, paradoxically, this question drives us back to the question of the origins of psychoanalysis.

The implicit psychological form of the Niebuhrian anthropology

CONSIDER these two images of the self from the point of view of methodological style, disregarding for a moment considerations of content. Niebuhr's style, and that of the theological genre that he has been so influential in creating and of which he is also representative, is a style of "discontinuity" or what I would prefer to call, in a more colloquial way, a "style of the gaps." His anthropological vision is really a celebration of the gaps, and, as such, it is more concerned with self-limitation than with self-completion. Again and again his perceptions recur to the fundamental reality of the self's impulses to idolatry, its tendency to transmute each and every thing it touches into an occasion of its own self-concern, its own self-aggrandizement. A deep and pervasive suspicion of the ubiquity and tenacity of this impulse creates the necessity for a methodological style of the gaps: the gaps between family and society (moral man and immoral society), between essential unity and historical disunity, between empirical and dramatic modes of self-understanding, between meaning and mystery, between man and God.

This style necessitates remaining execeptionally alert to any and all statements about the nature of selfhood that appear to disregard the depth and ubiquity of this impulse. Hence the insistent and sometimes strident quality of Niebuhr's criticism of psychoanalysis; for Freud's methodological style and, for that matter, the style of the school of psychology that he created and of which he remains clearly the single, outstanding instance is clearly a style of continuity, of closing the gaps.

It is the essence of psychoanalytic method that all inquiries begin with the recognition of the apparent—one might almost say phenomenological—discontinuity that appears to characterize any particular phase or aspect of psychic life. It is, in effect, a hermeneutic of continuity, proposing that continuity obtains between the imaginative, relational, and meaning-constructing functions of the self—or, as we have chosen to put it here, between the structural, dynamic, sociohistorical, and methodological dimensions of the self.

In this sense, psychoanalytic psychology is really the mirror image of Protestant theology—its *doppelgänger*—both as regards method and as regards the significant features of the self. For psychoanalytic method seeks "meaning," understood as imaginative, associational interplay amidst apparently diverse functions and constructions of the self. It is mistaken to point out, as this genre of theology so often does, that the final status of these integrations and connections may be and often are in doubt. For the moment the point is one of style rather than final conclusions.

The theological criticism of mechanistic reductionism, therefore, can serve—and it is our point that in this case it does so serve—to obscure or to mask a critical objection of a different kind, a more subtle objection to the very notion of continuity itself. Here, the premise or principle of discontinuity becomes a barrier to the very processes and understandings that it is intended to serve. Rather than protecting the unity of the self in its functions and relations from premature closure in the direction of either idealism or naturalism, the criticism of mechanistic reduction can exacerbate the self's propensities for disunity. In such a case, an objection to mechanism is, at a deeper level, an objection to relation. What reason can there be to insist that the higher dimensions of the self—its spiritual and social formations —are "reduced" simply by virtue of an attempted clarification of their relation to the lower dimensions? Under what conditions does relation come to be understood as reduction?

The problem goes back, I think, to a root methodological polarity so characteristic of this theological genre, that of mechanism and transcendence. It is the manner of posing the question of selfhood rather than the manner of resolving it that creates the necessity for a style of discontinuity. The polarity is perhaps more recognizable, both in Niebuhr's thought and in Protestant theology generally, as that of the subject-object relation and its transcendence. (This more familiar phrase will be discussed in detail in Chapter 3 below.) First, however, the polarity of mechanism and transcendence must be examined. According to this polarity, nature—in this case, the psychological or the mental— is rendered as mechanism and spirit or self-transcendence is rendered as "getting beyond" mechanism. Thus, at times, transcendence is thought of as a denial of mechanism, and this can eventuate in an understanding of transcendence (whether it be so recognized or not) that continues to embody those very features of mechanism that are so critically rejected.

It is our thesis that Freud's view of the self is not primarily a mechanistic one at all and that it therefore does not fit this reductionist criticism. In fact, we argue that Freud shares with the theological stance we have been discussing a similar criticism of mechanism, although this aspect of his psychology is not so easily recognized. If the deeper strands of Freud's thought are not caught by the metaphor of mechanism, then we must ask: In what sense does Freud's psychology, like theology, strive to go beyond mechanism, that is, to transcend mechanism? If it does, then his *psychological* criticism of mechanism provides a dynamic link between the *theological* polarity of mechanism and transcendence. Let us now begin to include in these considerations of Freud's thought considerations of his work and let us keep in mind as well considerations of his person. In so doing, we expand and complicate our problem, on the basis of materials already given, in order to explore that problem further.

Students of the origins of psychoanalysis have often commented on the changing conceptions of science and scientific method to which Freud ascribed and which served as a basis for his theoretical work. Of special interest has been the early transitional period beginning with his medical work at the University of Vienna, so much informed as it was by anatomical, physiological, and neurological problems, and ending with the first truly psychoanalytic formulations. That period, extending roughly from 1882 to 1902, spans the contacts with Breuer (1882–1887) and then with Fliess (1887–1902). The bearing of Freud's relation with Fliess upon his methodological thinking has been pursued with special interest.[34]

In the spring of 1881 Freud passed his medical examinations at the University of Vienna and proceeded directly to pursue further his interest in physiology, which he hoped would lead in time to a permanent position in the Brücke laboratory. Both dur-

[34] There are two points of view regarding the period during which Freud's understanding of science, his self-analysis, and his relation to Fliess all assumed importance. One argues that the relation with Fliess was primarily a means of carrying out intellectual-scientific discussion. The other argues that the relation was far more emotional.

Of Freud's debt to the Helmholtzian, mechanistic view of science, Shakow and Rapaport say, ". . . we have perhaps made Freud's identification with the program appear too explicit and deliberate. In point of fact it may not even have been *implicit* except in the earliest days" *(The Influence of Freud,* p. 45, n. 21). They continue: "It is our impression that Fliess played primarily the role of a sympathetic listener, particularly suited to Freud's needs at that time." And they conclude, "Freud's strength was that, insofar as it was possible, he applied an acceptable Helmholtzian method—observation—to the Romantic (but also Enlightenment) content" *(ibid.,* pp. 46–47, n. 22). Because Shakow and Rapaport attempt to take into account other discussions, we follow their overview of this period and then rely on Erikson's analysis for special interpretation.

ing his medical studies and for the brief period after this and before entering clinical work, Freud became strongly identified, through the influence of Brücke, with the physical physiology point of view of the Helmholtz School of Medicine. Shakow and Rapaport find this point of view summarized in portions of a letter from du Bois-Reymond, a physiologist who succeeded Johannes Müller at the University of Berlin and who was also a friend and colleague of Helmholtz:

> Brücke and I pledged a solemn oath to put into power this truth, no other forces than the common physical-chemical ones are active within the organism; that, in those cases which cannot at the time be explained by these forces one has either to find the specific way or form of their action by means of the physical-mathematical method, or to assume new forces equal in dignity to the chemical-physical forces inherent in matter, reducible to the force of attraction and repulsion.[35]

This statement became a guiding position for the Helmholtz point of view and, as such, we may assume also for Freud's work under Brücke at Vienna.

A year later Freud resigned in order to take up clinical medical practice, and we need not pursue the complex reasons for this. The period 1882–1887 included his marriage, his work in the various clinical departments of the General Hospital, the work with Breuer and especially the case of Anna O., and the fellowship with Charcot. During this period, Freud, still equipped with a characteristically Helmholtzian point of view and interests, found himself struggling to understand clinical situations that did not fit the methodological premises and styles of that training.

The locus of clinical inquiry during the Breuer period was external to the worker, either as researcher or as clinician. Freud at this time was carrying out his work on the basis of a composite professional self-image, that of good scientist (that is, properly objective) and good clinician (that is, detached but helpful). The years immediately following, however, produced a contrasting

[35] Quoted in *ibid.*, p. 34.

shift in the locus of inquiry to the inner life of the investigator himself, and here the relation with Fliess assumed importance. This was the period of self-analysis, and during it Freud moved methodologically away from a mechanistic and physiological point of view and began to endow the psychological forces with that dignity that had heretofore been reserved for the physiological.[36]

What, precisely, took place during this time? Different students, we have noted, comment in different ways. With regard to the first and central point, the abandonment of the Helmholtzian mechanistic and physiological understanding of the manner of scientific investigation, Fliess was a peculiarly well-suited ally. He was, like Freud, in private practice. His qualifications as a scientist were sufficiently convincing so that Freud could regard him as a representative of the Helmholtzian philosophy. On the other hand, Fliess was also given to having thoughts of his own that departed quite radically from the official views of the day. He held "heterodox opinions of his own in the sexual sphere"[37] and was open to nonmechanistic ways of thinking concerning the motivations of his patients. Thus, his person and work became a likely context for the evocation of whatever incipient heterodox clinical or scientific notions were emerging in Freud's thinking. As a result, Freud was able to make the problem of the "motivational-psychological" his primary sphere of concern and to face directly the question of a different method appropriate to the new clinical problems confronting him.

---

[36] Shakow and Rapaport say: "This was the phase in which Freud was emancipating himself from the narrower Helmholtz view which involved at least the use of chemical and physical methods, if not a reduction to physical and chemical concepts. Emancipation was not accomplished, of course, without considerable conflict about giving up the physiological, as is revealed in the recently discovered 'Project for a Scientific Psychology.' In the 'Project,' Freud made a valiant attempt to develop a neurological theory of psychopathology and psychology, but when he 'failed' in this, he turned to what amounted to a search for forces 'equal in dignity' in the psychological sphere. This was not, however, the sphere of academic psychology, for the problems Freud settled on—those of affectivity—were more consonant with the subject matter of moral philosophy" *(The Influence of Freud,* pp. 44–45).

[37] *Ibid.,* p. 44.

Secondly, when this relationship is viewed in a more dynamic and personal sense, it appears to have had certain features characteristic of the clinical process known as the transference relationship, "that peculiar mixture of overestimation and mistrust" that in moments of crisis one all too readily brings to important persons. Freud called Fliess his "Other one" to whom he could entrust what he was not ready to entrust to "the others."[38] According to Erikson's discussion of this phase of Freud's life and work, this underlying irrational dynamic was an essential ingredient for the new theoretical orientation that Freud was in the process of discovering. Having worked through the universal father image and its distortions, "Freud now could break through to the first prehistoric Other of them all: the loving mother. He was free to discover the whole Oedipus complex, and to recognize it as a dominant theme in world literature and in mythologies around the world."[39] That is to say, he became able to see in himself what heretofore he and Breuer had been struggling to see in their patients, and he was able to return to that clinical mode of learning and assistance, equipped with the instrumentation of what Erikson in another context has called "disciplined subjectivity."[40]

Thirdly, we note that, at least by implication but perhaps directly as well, this reorientation, which was both methodologi-

---

[38] Erikson, "The First Psychoanalyst." Erikson's description should be cited in more detail: "Freud, we now say, must have overestimated this friendship in an irrational, almost pathological way. But what, after all, do thinkers need friends for? So that they can share speculations, each alternately playing benevolent authority to the other, each be the other's co-conspirator, each be applauding audience, and cautioning chorus. Freud calls Fliess his *'Other one,'* to whom he can entrust what is not ready for 'the *others.'* Fliess, at any rate, seems to have had the stature and the wide education which permitted Freud to entrust him with 'imaginings, transpositions, and guesses.' That Freud's imaginings turned out to be elements of a true vision and a blueprint for a science, while Fliess' ended in a kind of mathematical mysticism, provides no reason to belittle the friendship. The value of a friend may sometimes be measured by the magnitude of the problem which we discard with him" (pp. 93–94).

[39] *Ibid.,* p. 95.

[40] Erik H. Erikson, "The Nature of Clinical Evidence," *Insight and Responsibility* (New York: W. W. Norton, 1964), p. 53.

cal and developmental, was accompanied by a reorientation in the understanding of human sexuality as well. The movement away from mechanism as the guiding metaphor for scientific inquiry and the regressive experience that produced a progressive, comprehensive kind of insight had consequences for the meaning of sexuality in the total life of the person. Once again, Erikson's remarks are instructive. As he points out, during the course of this friendship and as a result of the discovery of the oedipal theme, "a balance was righted: 'feminine' intuition, 'childlike' curiosity, and 'artistic' freedom of style were recognized and restored as partners of the masculine 'inner tyrant' in the process of psychological discovery."[41]

From these discussions it is clear that Freud's movement toward conceptual or methodological reformation of the mechanistic understanding of science is to be linked significantly with a highly personalized and private relationship and also with an opening out onto the oedipal dimensions of the self, exposing at the same time an erotic element in "methodological" thinking. Freud's crisis indicates that a movement away from mechanism and by implication toward transcendence is also a developmental movement toward uncovering the oedipal organization of the self. If such oedipal organization is an important link between mechanism and transcendence, one might expect oedipal sexuality to have a place in theological discussions of the self. But that is not the case. Instead, we find at this point a gap or blank. To move, as these theological discussions do, from a critique of mechanism to the assertion of transcendence without indicating intermediate process and considerations is reminiscent of the characteristic theological aversion for continuity.

Furthermore, if we inquire into the content features of this gap or blank, we find that it has certain oedipal characteristics. We therefore can now begin to take the term "oedipal" to stand somewhat metaphorically for that generalized psychoanalytic insistence on continuity, without at the same time denying its more

[41] Erikson, "The First Psychoanalyst," p. 96.

literal, developmental meaning. In what sense, if any, is there an absence of such psychological thinking or its equivalent in Niebuhr's theology? Let us explore this argument or possible criticism briefly as regards the several dimensions of the self. Since theology is so much more inclined to focus on the structural and the historical, let us consider the argument first at the point of self and society, the third of our four dimensions of the self.

Here, the evidence for the absence of psychological thinking or its equivalent in Niebuhr's thought is strongest. In characteristic fashion Niebuhr denies any continuity, in the sense already indicated above, between the formation of the self in the family, on the one hand, and the historical dramas of the self, on the other hand. "Moral man and immoral society" are epithets critically addressed to any ethic (and not simply the social gospel) that understands moral achievement at the level of institutions to be in principle no less difficult or different from moral achievement in personal relations, especially family relations. As such this principle of discontinuity between family and society is inconsistent with the psychoanalytic insistence on dynamic continuity between learned behavior expressed in the family and any transfer of learning to wider ranges of sociality. Therefore self-transcendence, as a feature of the developed self, depends on "leaping" out of the family and into society. Furthermore, according to Niebuhr, family life is innocent, as we have noted, and the leap is also a fall into the condition of self-concern and the dramatic complexities of sociohistorical life. This leap from family to society is also, we are arguing, a leap from the oedipal structure of development into a wider social context, and the possibilities of that developmental transition depend on an analysis of its dynamics.

Despite this theological disinterest in the possibly darker meanings of family life, the family is given importance in the Niebuhrian analysis. Its importance is structural but not dynamic. The family is the link between the individual and the community. It is at once the locus of individuality and the smallest of social groups. It provides the context for the exercise of the self-preservative and procreative instincts. It is, further, the referent for the language and imagery that Niebuhr uses when he speaks of the self's dramatic encounter with God. Yet, there is no sustained analysis of family dynamics, and the family remains a model of moral achievement that cannot be found—and that moralists should not expect to find—in social life. The familiar Niebuhrian incisiveness, his brilliance in exposing moral and spiritual pretension, is not exercised in discussions of the family. Clearly, something is missing.

Niebuhr's innocent family is rationalized and sentimental, a betrayal of his own Biblical realism for the moral idealism about which he has so persuasively warned us. The gap that he thereby creates between family and society is at least in part closed—but not necessarily reduced—by psychoanalytic psychology, which is, after all, a family psychology. It is also a psychology of continuity between the various ranges and different levels of socialization that confront the developing self. Niebuhr's anthropological analyses require a fully developed self, one which has overcome, it would seem, repression and early conflict.

In what manner is continuity between the early, developmental self and the later, mature self to be discovered? This is to inquire into the nature of psychoanalytic insight and the extent to which it is either a "merely rational" or a spiritual process. The cognate term for repression in the Niebuhrian anthropology is "the mechanism of self-deception." Self-concern becomes more problematic as the self seeks its completion in the social order; but self-deception is exacerbated by this yearning, for the self cannot will its mastery of its own self-concern. Psychoanalytic insight, Niebuhr argues, creates precisely this premature sense of mastery and is therefore itself a subtle instance of self-concern.

Yet, Niebuhr's analysis rests on a mechanistic reading of insight. A nonmechanistic reading of Freud generally, and of the repression-insight question specifically, establishes more than a formal connection between the theological and psychological processes. Repression and insight are the dynamic links between the polarity of mechanism and transcendence. The theological injunction to self-transcendence, therefore, must contain an implicit although unacknowledged psychological injunction, an injunction to "overcome" repression. In this case, the oedipal situation is not the early, developmental structure that is, so to speak, "left behind" as the self reaches out into wider ranges of sociality; it is that, but it also becomes the medium through which the self discovers the dramas of history and, upon reflection, the dramatic quality of its own developmental life. It is repression that creates a sense of discontinuity between different levels and sectors of personal and social life. In an expanded, nonmechanistic reading of Freud, psychoanalytic method becomes an attempt to reestablish continuity—to reestablish a sense of self-transcendence through an immanental immersion in the apparent discontinuities of imaginative and moral life. Niebuhr's fear that insight will be taken up into the circular, destructive dynamics of self-concern—a point the validity of which we are clearly *not* discussing here—prevents our considering immanental forms of self-understanding. A nonmechanistic reading of insight opens out into precisely that "juncturing" of nature and spirit that Niebuhr identifies with essential humanity—and, we should add, with theological inquiry.

Freud's remark at the end of the case of Little Hans is important:

> For analysis does not undo the *effects* of repression. The instincts which were formerly suppressed remain suppressed; but the same effect is produced in a different way. Analysis replaces the process of repression, which is an automatic and excessive one, by a temperate and purposeful control on the part of the highest mental faculties. In a word, *analysis replaces repression by condemnation.*[42]

These remarks juxtapose a mechanistic view of psychological processes with a higher, moral conception. Overcoming repression is not a leap, except insofar as it is guided by a translucency

[42] Freud, *Collected Papers,* III, 285.

in which all that was there before remains, but it remains under the conditions of a different organization.

Gaston Bachelard provides us with a truly lovely description of what we mean by an expanded understanding of insight and, by implication, an expanded understanding of Freud's thought, in a manner that is at once erotic, moral, and phenomenological, yet retaining the meaning that Freud intended to convey. He says:

> . . . the truly anagogical cure does not consist of liberating the repressed tendencies, but of substituting for the unconscious repression a constant will to self-correction. . . .
>
> Then the fire which was consuming us suddenly enlightens us. The haphazard passion becomes the deliberate passion. Love becomes family; fire becomes hearth and home. . . . The charm of novelty yields progressively to the knowledge of character.[43]

It is in the vicissitudes of that "deliberate passion" that Freud seeks to instruct us, and, in so doing, he provides us with a dynamic phenomenological glimpse into the paradoxes of vitality and form, of nature and spirit.

Of course the point can be made structurally as well as dynamically. The superego represents the demands of culture on the early, developmental life of the self. Niebuhr argues that the self's capacity for self-transcendence can never be reduced to a simple appropriation and replication of cultural norms, for the self has the essential capacity to transcend all socially given norms. Once again, the gap: finite freedom and the discovery of real guilt rests on an implied abrogation of the superego rather than upon an imaginative opening up of the self to this very important dimension of itself. The psychoanalytic attempt to comprehend the harsh superego—"We replace repression by condemnation"— is an attempt to create continuity between immanence and transcendence. Self-transcendence, as a feature of the mature self's stance toward social norms, depends on imaginative immersion

---

[43] Gaston Bachelard, *The Psychoanalysis of Fire,* trans. Alan C. M. Ross (Boston: Beacon Press, 1964), pp. 100–101.

in the cultural superego. For that matter, much of Niebuhr's brilliant and incisive historical analysis of thought and institutions can be seen from this higher Freudian perspective as an attempt to clarify the contents, and thereby to reduce the coercive power, of the cultural superego.

Niebuhr's methodological injunctions make themselves available to similar considerations, for his theological circle is a tight and highly consistent one. The style of discontinuity, its polarization of mechanism and transcendence, appears in the parallelisms of meaning and mystery, primitive and permanent myth, empirical and dramatic modes of self-understanding, and, finally, special revelation and general revelation.

Much of the burden of our argument thus far has been to extend, without reduction, the theological notions of immanence and nature to include their psychoanalytic equivalents: Oedipus complex, repression, and harsh superego. These characterize what is problematic in human selfhood and as such open up the question of transcendence. Niebuhr's attempts to describe the experience of general revelation—especially his reference to the longing for forgiveness and for the self's desire to complete itself in the life of another—resemble Freud's descriptions of the superego. As we shall see, what Niebuhr means by the experience of general revelation is closely linked to Tillich's discussions of conscience—the bad, moral conscience (which he openly identifies with the Freudian superego) and the good, transmoral conscience, the ethical counterpart of the theological doctrine of justification. Tillich, of course, refers this experience back to Luther's spiritual anxiety, his *Anfechtung*. According to Niebuhr, special revelation "clarifies" the vague longings of general revelation. This nucleus of problematic psychological processes—Oedipus complex, superego, repression, insight—bears an important relation to special revelation. Freud's psychology, therefore, is addressed to the theological question of transcendence. It bears upon the juncture between nature and spirit, so definitive of Niebuhr's anthropology. The link between Niebuhr's reading of Freud and the defects of his analysis of that juncture have been disclosed.

When Niebuhr asserts, as he often does, that the self is known through introspection and dramatic encounter and not by empirical methods, his analysis further demonstrates the dichotomy created between mechanism and transcendence. This is all the more remarkable because the thrust of his Biblical realism is clearly to eliminate this dichotomy. Freud's psychology is an introspective psychology which—at least when it is not under the control of mechanistic interpretations—is neither merely empirical nor entirely dramatic. It is therefore qualified to assist in renegotiations between the dramatic and the empirical, between the subjective and the objective. However, once the offer of assistance is accepted, the polar structures undergo modification. Here, theology articulates directly and without qualification with the deepest strands of Freud's thought and in so doing opens itself to an unexpected therapeutic. We want to know in far greater detail precisely what is at stake in such a therapeutic, and the answer to that question is the burden of Part Two. But first we need to explore and clarify our argument in relation to another theologian, Paul Tillich, who has also risked opening his system to Freud's thought.

Gaston Bachelard has described his project for a psychoanalysis of objective or scientific knowledge as "an indirect and secondary psychoanalysis which would constantly seek the unconscious under the conscious, the subjective value under the objective evidence, the reverie beneath the experiment."[44] The following discussions, especially those of Part Two, continue the search for the psychological infrastructure in Protestant thought and its methodological implications. In so doing we transpose, but only somewhat, Bachelard's approach: we seek the reverie beneath the doctrine, the doctrine of transcendence.

[44] *Ibid.*, pp. 21–22.

Three: Methodological response
to Freud: Paul Tillich

Theological method and
psychological understanding

THUS far, we have juxtaposed theological and psychological conceptions of the self and a theological response to the psychological materials. We then adduced the beginnings of an alternative reading of Freud, showing that the fundamental intent of his psychology is obscured by the criticism of mechanistic reductionism, and we linked this criticism with Niebuhr's inability to become as concrete about the interfaces or juncture between body and spirit as he was about these two dimensions taken separately. Niebuhr's misreading of Freud can be seen to obscure, at a deeper level, the critical and clarifying power of Freud's thought. Freud's psychology is one of continuity, of mediating between the gaps created by theology. This failure throws into motion a spiral of ominous consequences. Transcendence, in the style of the gaps, begins to take on the very features it is intended to correct through the criticism of mechanism. The self, freed from the deterministic effects of mechanism, comes under an even more formidable principle of determinism, that of theological determinism. The experience of self-transcendence, so defined, becomes the enemy of man, the occasion of his divisions and alienations.

In particular, we were able to insinuate a nuclear set of psychological categories alongside of the theological view of the self. Transcendence comes to be, in effect, the transcendence of the superego. This structural concept is central to Freud's psychology. Its dynamic counterpart is the double process of repression and insight, and its developmental or societal counterpart is the Oedipus complex. The superego is heir to the Oedipus complex. We will return to this link between the superego and transcendence, each nuclear constructs in psychological and theological views of the self. For the moment, we simply note that a concept of transcendence that abrogates rather than passes through the dynamics of the superego is, in effect, a higher form of repression—divine repression or, rather, the theological legitimation of a higher repression. Niebuhrian anthropology possesses psychological form; there is a psychological infrastructure. Once this infrastructure is recognized, further questions must be asked about theology.

We need to clarify, develop, and test this argument further, however, and will do so now at two points. We have noted how Protestant theological existentialism polarizes around the problems of anthropology and methodology. In this chapter, we explore the question of a psychological dimension to theological methodology. Here, the root problem of mechanism and transcendence remains but in its theological-epistemological form. "Mechanism" no longer refers to the self's experience of necessity, but to a way of knowing sequence and causality; and "transcendence" refers to a higher knowing rather than to the experience of freedom. We juxtapose this theological discussion against the clinical and dynamic notion of transference, although the bearing of each on the other may not be immediately apparent.

The dominant methodological construct in theological existentialism is the subject-object relation and its transcendence. This theology states in various ways that, in the reception of revelation, the self's knowledge of God and subsequent self-understanding transcends the subject-object structure of knowing. I take the problem of the subject-object relation in a stereotypical sense, to be representative in a general way of the methodological question that preoccupies these theologians and have selected Paul Tillich's position to serve as my single case. How can Freud's thought be drawn into this discussion?

In the preceding chapter, we discussed Freud's struggle with the way scientific method bears on psychoanalysis; Freud was forced to define what is distinctively psychoanalytic by rejecting a particular view of scientific method, and we have noted the role of transference during this period in his thought.

The wider implications of transference are sometimes obscured by the predominant clinical emphasis on technique. Transference, however, is the more dynamic and concrete psychological process on which more abstract and formal metapsychological constructs are based. As such, the phenomenon of transference is central to what we have earlier called a second reading of Freud's psychology, the clinical-dynamic one. But transference is significant in a second sense. For it is also the basis—more correctly, the object—of understanding and interpretation, so crucial to psychoanalysis. In this sense, psychoanalysis is not so much a theory of personality as a method of inquiry, and transference is the object of understanding and interpretation. Transference is a special form of subjectivity that, for this reason, requires a special kind of objectivity, the kind least found in the view of science rejected by Freud. As we shall see, the problem of objective understanding in clinical interpretation is not unrelated to the problem of objectification and authentic existence in theological epistemology.

Furthermore, the notion of transference is central to Freud's thought about culture and religion. We have yet to discuss Freud's psychology in relation to his views on religion and should note right away that, with the exception of theory and therapy, religion attracted Freud's attention more than any of the several applications of psychoanalysis. In fact, although he attempted from time to time to approach religion somewhat ironically as a social form to which the findings of psychoanalysis could simply be applied, he was forced to conclude that psychoanalysis is best defined in direct opposition to religion. Religion, for Freud, is a way of knowing that can seriously compete with and damage psychoanalytic understanding. If transference is central to psychological process, then it is also central to Freud's view of religion.

We must therefore begin with a review of Freud's psychology from the perspective of the phenomenon of transference. Then we turn to Tillich's discussion of the subject-object relation and its transcendence. The theological imperative to transcend the subject-object relation has a psychological side to it that is implicit in the theological discussion itself. Just as superego processes are implicit in Niebuhr's view of the experience of self-transcendence, theological knowledge is related to the kind of understanding that results from interpreting transference. The double focus of this chapter is, then, transference and transcendence.

The centrality of transference in Freud's thought

FREUD never wrote a definitive paper or monograph on transference, nor did he even attempt to collect his thoughts on the subject from time to time, as he did, for example, on dreams, anxiety, or primitive religion. Yet the phenomenon of transference appears throughout his writings,[1] and it will always be found in psychoanalytic discussions.

[1] Freud wrote three papers bearing directly on the meaning of transference, and in this discussion I draw heavily on them. They are "The Dynamics of the Transference"; "Further Recommendations in the Technique of Psycho-Analysis, Recollection, Repetition and Working Through"; and "Observations on Transference-Love," *Collected Papers*, II. The chapter on transference in *A General Introduction to Psychoanalysis*, trans. Joan Riviere (New York: Washington Square Press, 1952), is also helpful. The German word is *Ubertragnung*, which Strachey, like Brill, translates as "transference." Strachey suggests that the term has an internal or intrapsychic meaning as well as an interpersonal reference. See *The Standard Edition of the Complete Psychological Works of Sigmund Freud*, trans. James Strachey (London: Hogarth Press, 1953), V, 262. Important references by Freud to transference as an internal phenomenon may be found in "The Interpretation of Dreams," *Basic Writings*, sec. vii, esp. pp. 508 and 514.

Transference must be taken in several ways. It can be understood as an internal or intrapsychic phenomenon, corresponding roughly to what we have called structural and dynamic considerations. It can also be understood as an interpersonal and then as a social and cultural phenomenon, corresponding to what we have called the self-society relation. But transference is also a construct that bears closely on the nature of psychoanalytic inquiry, and it is, therefore, a methodological construct as well. For Freud insisted that psychoanalysis was a mode of inquiry or investigation even before it was a theory or a therapy.[2] In the *General Introduction to Psychoanalysis* he attempted a clear and simple but also extremely thorough definition of his psychology for an audience that was both unfamiliar with it and quite skeptical of it.

All psychoanalytic investigation, Freud said, has its inception in the self-conscious, in scrutiny of mental processes or psychological phenomena, best illustrated at least for introductory purposes by the study of the psychopathology of everyday life, especially the errors of speech. Overly simple as it may seem, the study of the psychology of errors is to be taken as a model for psychoanalytic investigation of all mental phenomena.[3]

In cases of speech error there is a momentary and abrupt interruption of a comprehensibly organized sequence of mental events; something quite different from and unrelated to the intended and the expected occurs. For conventional, everyday understanding, the error is arbitrary and meaningless. Freud's point —and, fundamentally, his only point—is that there is "something more" to this psychic situation. He described this "something more" in different ways: tendency, intention, counterwilling, and meaning. We shall use the last as representative.[4]

The assertion of meaning in the face of the apparently arbitrary expands the analysis of psychic process at several points. It suggests that psychic life occurs at different levels—a surface level, the workaday, conventional world of everyday life, and a

[2] See Freud, *General Introduction,* chap. iii; see also p. 44.
[3] *Ibid.,* chap. vi, esp. p. 106.
[4] See esp. *ibid.,* chap. iv, pp. 63–71.

depth level, which, when acknowledged, renders meaningful what is otherwise apparently meaningless. "Depth" in this case also connotes moral direction, intention and will. Medard Boss has commented on Freud's attention to hidden intending as "his tacit awareness of man's existence as an open, lucid realm into which something can unveil itself and shine forth out of the dark."[5] This fully luminous sense of reality remains constricted and opaque, however, at least under conditions of repression, which require that the meaning remain hidden. That is, depth and surface are related in a way that is never simply harmonious nor completely dissociated. A dynamic opposition or conflict obtains between surface and depth, so that Freud designated depth as "counterwilling" or a "countertendency."[6]

Dreams, symptoms, and exceptionally close and intense personal relationships (especially the doctor-patient relationship) along with the errors of speech constitute the four basic forms of psychic life that psychoanalysis claims as its special object of understanding.[7] Again, each has its conventional and apparently self-evident side that stands in contrast, given the psychoanalytic

[5] Medard Boss, *Psychoanalysis and Daseinsanalysis,* trans. Ludwig B. Lefebre (New York: Basic Books, 1963), p. 62.

[6] Boss argues that the entire psychoanalytic theory was guided by Freud's "secret" appreciation of what Martin Heidegger understands to be the meaning of *Dasein,* but that Freud's articulation of this was obscured by the mechanistic framework that he employed (e.g., *ibid.,* p. 284). Freud's understanding of "hidden intending" is well-nigh identical, too, I think, with what Reinhold Niebuhr has meant by the twin notions of the dramatic nature of selfhood and the dialogues of the self. For the dramas of history transcend the artifacts of history, and the defining feature of artifact is highly self-conscious, contractual arrangements. Freud's attempt to discern depth beneath the phenomenal, everyday world is therefore an attempt to transcend it. For that matter, once the mechanistic "barrier" is removed from discussions of Freud's work, then the "Psychopathology of Everyday Life" *(Basic Writings,* sec. i), may be seen as a protophenomenology—highly dynamic and highly erotic—of language. There is some recognition of this in Gibson Winter's attempt to develop a phenomenology of "the world of every day." Winter says, "We can say that Freud presupposed an intentional consciousness. That which was unconscious thus becomes 'motive' through becoming accessible to consciousness. When the Freudian tradition is reinterpreted in terms of the intentional self, the deterministic aspects of unconscious forces can be set in their proper perspective" *(Elements for a Social Ethic: Scientific and Ethical Perspectives on Social Process* [New York: Macmillan, 1966], p. 154).

[7] Freud, *General Introduction,* pp. 268–269, 440.

point of view, to deeper levels of intending and willing. In this sense, dream interpretation requires that a distinction be made between manifest content and latent thought, which are linked through conflict between levels of intending and willing. It is in this sense, we suggest, that the Freudian vocabulary often employs the term "wish." To wish is to intend in a latent, hidden way.

Symptoms, either as behavior (external) or as thought (internal), present a surface dimension to the investigation of speech (the "presenting problem" of clinical work) and are contrasted to a depth or counterwilling dimension. In like fashion, the transference relation represents the conventional expectations of the doctor-patient relationship and the deeper "unreasonable demands" of the patient.

It is in this context that the primary meaning of transference is to be found. Indeed, transference "means" meaning, it means the primary connection that obtains despite the apparent gap between surface and depth. Here two points of view are possible, the one reductive and the other more positive. It can be argued that the notion of transference is a reductive one, that it serves to neutralize and depotentiate in the mind of the physician an affectively charged interpersonal (or internal) situation.[8] Early in Freud's psychoanalytic career, a female patient "suddenly" embraced him during her analytic hour. Freud later concluded: "Transference."[9] Perhaps he used this term to avoid facing his own feelings, which might have been aroused by the sudden break in the conventional expectations of the doctor-patient relationship. Taking another view, one might argue that in adducing the notion of transference Freud was attempting to find her behavior whole, fundamentally sensible, and meaningful. This patient was

[8] Objections of this sort can be found, for example, in the client-centered school of psychotherapy. See Carl R. Rogers, *Client-Centered Therapy* (Boston: Houghton Mifflin, 1951), pp. 198–218, and Dieter Wyss, *Depth Psychology: A Critical History,* trans. Gerald Onn (New York: W. W. Norton, 1966), pp. 404–410.

[9] Jones, *Freud,* I, 242–243. See also Freud, *An Autobiographical Study,* pp. 47–48.

in this act momentarily constructing her life in a manner more consistent with deeper levels of feeling and willing. In this sense, all pathology comes to be understood as implicit curative gesture.

Freud was far more preoccupied with the dynamics rather than the structure of what we have called depth and surface. He was more concerned with the symbolic transformations that occur between these levels than with the ontological problems that emerge in the assumption of levels of psychic life. Transference, sometimes preceded by "a" or by "the," was the most consistently employed term for these symbolic transformations between surface and depth.

Symbolic transformation, in which depth "grasps" and re-orders surface, is a double process of statement-concealment, a shift of feelings, ideas, attitudes, energies, and wishes from one locus of psychic reality to another. Freud attempted to characterize this shift with such notions as displacement, substitution, and compromise. Dream symbols, for example, are composed of day residues (surface level) as well as attitudes displaced on them from deeper and earlier levels of experience. These processes are also substitutive, for the memories or day residues re-present deeper forces. Thus the internality of the self is a constant source of energized images wherein self and social form are transmuted into a dramatic structure—the dream. In this sense, transference mythologizes the self and its history. But there is compromise or reduction as well. Although depth is given expression, it is also concealed; although surface is enriched, it undergoes distortion.

Transference is defined, of course, in contrast to another psychic mode, one free from distortions so that depth is, so to speak, transparent to surface. The famous formula "where id was let ego be" refers to this second mode by which the conflictual relation between depth and surface is transformed and corrected. A now well-established inventory of psychoanalytic terms—integration, reality, insight—refer to the introduction of meaning into an apparently arbitrary and meaningless psychic situation.

The transference relation between analyst and patient is

simply the interpersonal, relational correlate of transference understood internally. Here Freud's thoughts and admonitions fall into two types of consideration: the transference relation as disease and as cure.[10] This double-edged principle is crucial for an understanding of our critique of the theological notion of transcendence. For theology denies the deeper interconnection of disease and cure and thereby places its own constructs and methods beyond psychological clarification.

The transference relation as disease involves that aspect of the doctor-patient relation in which excessive—and therefore inappropriate—feelings and attitudes of affection and hostility are expressed by the patient toward the physician. This relation shows all the marks of psychic life psychoanalytically understood. On the surface there are the conventional amenities and formalities of a professional relationship, but underlying these are excessive feelings and attitudes that ultimately emerge. Transference feelings are sustained in their current state by memories repressed during childhood. Once appropriate, they are, in the context of the present, inappropriate—they are carried over from the past to the present, thereby providing the physician with yet another opportunity to discern depth and intention.

In this relation, social history and psychic inwardness intersect in a symbolic reconstruction of the past, and the therapeutic relationship gradually becomes itself the disease. Unlike other forms of psychic life, however, the transference relation is not simply a symbolic system, but actually *becomes* the disease. Psychic alienation receives social embodiment, and it is this that makes it accessible to change. Freud was convinced that this new relation, which he called the "transference neurosis," is the prerequisite and basis of all successful analysis.

Analytic therapy is often criticized for creating interpersonal isolation. Yet it can be argued that the transference situation is one in which conventional distinctions—such as personal versus

[10] See Freud, "The Dynamics of the Transference," and "Recollection, Repetition and Working Through," *Collected Papers,* II.

impersonal, familial versus social role, personal versus professional—collapse around a deeper concern common to both parties, namely, an encounter characterized by the immediacy of the confrontation in which the inward, erotic energies of the self and its images are clarified in a social context that repeats the original paradigm of growth and alienation. This "descent into immediacy" is protected by the "professional" side of the physician's self-understanding—that is, by his mastery of his own growth paradigms—and the interpretations he brings keep the descent from becoming too precipitous.

How can the disease be the cure? That, of course, is the point. The transference relation functions as the medium for the cure, representing heightened potentiality for both illness and health. Cure occurs neither through the abolition nor the denial of this relation, nor through ignoring it or preserving it, but through "recollection" and "working through." The interpretations—addressed as they are to all forms of psychic life—provide understanding (insight) or the inner appropriation of just that meaning that transforms a transference relation between depth and surface into an integrative, progressive one. Depth and surface, past and present, each becomes increasingly transparent to the other.

Freud turned from his analysis of individual dynamics directly to that of group psychology, history, culture, and religion. If our argument is correct, then transference should be especially helpful in understanding his view of religion, the most formidable of those institutions that comprise culture. More than any other institution of culture, religion opposes the developmental premises of psychoanalysis—the methodological style of continuity. In the language of our discussion, religion is finally and always a transference phenomenon—without, however, providing the means for recognizing it as such.

Like so much of his thought, Freud's thought on religion underwent change, depending on the particular problem under discussion and what readers he had in mind when writing, as well as the period of theoretical development. Religion was sometimes understood as obsession, then as wish-fulfillment, then as illusion, and finally as the return of the repressed.[11] However, there is something common to all of these interpretations: Each may be understood as a transference phenomenon. Both the contents of religion—the beliefs about the divine or supreme being or beings —and the dynamics underlying their formation and maintenance are the result of transference. Freud saw religion as doctrine, a theory of divine objects, a theory, moreover, competitive with his own. Religious belief and the motives for it are, therefore, interpreted along psychoanalytic lines: Religion is a world-historical error of speech, dream symptom, or transference. It too goes back to the fundamental and enduring problem of hidden meaning.

Freud's critique of religion is entirely dependent on his own descriptive understanding of it. Religion means the conviction or belief that an omniscient and omnipotent being exists in space and time for the purposes of informing, protecting, and guiding men in their lives on earth.[12] Religion further defines the kind of relations men might have with this being, what thoughts and actions please him, and how his nature might be most authoritatively and completely known. Religion is, therefore, a theory of the external life, just as psychoanalysis is a theory of the internal life. In his more official moments, then, Freud associated religion with what we have called surface and psychoanalysis with what we have called depth.[13]

At bottom, the varieties of religion—its doctrinal, institutional, and moral forms—all serve a single purpose, that of making bearable an essentially unbearable infantile situation. What

[11] For illustrations of these four basic approaches, see, respectively, Freud, "Obsessive Acts and Religious Practices," *Collected Papers,* II; "A Philosophy of Life," *New Introductory Lectures; The Future of an Illusion,* trans. W. D. Robson-Scott (Garden City, N.Y.: Doubleday, 1957); and *Moses and Monotheism,* trans. Katherine Jones (New York: Vintage Books, 1955).

[12] See Freud, "A Philosophy of Life," *New Introductory Lectures,* pp. 216–224; see also *Civilization and Its Discontents,* p. 13.

[13] See *Moses and Monotheism,* pp. 164–169, for Freud's distinction between "historical" and "material" truth, which we have referred to as the distinction between depth and surface.

is unbearable is the universal fate of childhood, the task of integrating the instinctual life (internal) with sociohistorical reality (external). As already noted, anxiety has its developmentally specific contents. But these contents all retain the same dynamic meaning. They refer to separation, loss, and longing for return and reunion. Religion, then, is nostalgia, consolation for the lost parent. The garden becomes the nursery—or, rather, in religious imagination the nursery becomes the garden, because it is easier to think about it that way. Transference is nostalgia, yearning; religion provides this nostalgia with its form and object. Religion is the answer that "the very undeveloped creature" provides for his own most basic problem: What am I to do with my longing?

Religion as transference receives interpersonal embellishment in the father-son aspect of the oedipal relation, with its characteristic ambivalence between submission and rebellion. The former assures protection and favor, whereas the latter, in risking independence, exchanges the advantages of submission for the sadder but wiser fate of aloneness. The "sense of relatedness to God" is transference all over again; it reintroduces childhood dependency, this time in relation to a cosmic image the functional meaning of which is to bind unresolved transference phenomena and thereby make difficult any working through. Thus it does permit a measure of freedom from the only father one really ever had although it creates a new and different state of submission, one that is more social than familial, more unconscious than conscious.

Religion is therefore "from the beginning." It binds the anxious longing that accompanies separation, and this anxiety is permanently organized in the oedipal period and its subsequent historical projections. Religion, therefore, is also cultural—that is, it possesses dynamic meaning at the point of the self's transition to society and away from the family. In fact, religion, more than any other institution, binds anxiety at *all three points*— internal, interpersonal, and sociohistorical. When men say that they believe in God, their utterances both consummate and legiti-

mate the failure of each individual to integrate distortions between surface and depth. One of Freud's letters to Oskar Pfister
summarizes quite succinctly this entire matter and also shows
with equal clarity the sense of irony that the subject of religion
so often evoked in him:

> I note with satisfaction what a long way we are able to go to-
> gether in analysis. The rift, not in analytic, but in scientific
> thinking which one comes on when the subject of God and Christ
> is touched on I accept as one of the logically untenable but psy-
> chologically only too intelligible irrationalities of life. . . . In
> contrast to utterances as psychologically profound as "Thy sins
> are forgiven thee; arise and walk" there are a large number of
> others . . . useless for our lives. Besides, the above statement
> calls for analysis. If the sick man had asked: "How knowest
> thou that my sins are forgiven?" the answer could only have
> been: "I, the Son of God, forgive thee." In other words, a call
> for *unlimited transference* [italics mine]. And now, just sup-
> pose I said to a patient: "I, Professor Sigmund Freud, forgive
> thee thy sins." What a fool I should make of myself. To the
> former case the principle applies that analysis is not satisfied with
> success produced by suggestion, but investigates the origin of
> and justification for the transference.[14]

Therefore it seems correct, although Freud himself did not
do so, to suggest the term "transference-God" to designate his
psychological understanding of religion. In the paraphernalia of
religion we see cosmic, world-historical images drawing together
morals, doctrines, and credos. Although remote from their origins
and a distortion of these origins, these images do give statement
to that which is most deeply unlived, incomplete, and unacknowledged in human life. In religion the secrets and failures of civilization, the family, and the person are subtly explicated, deliber-
ately legitimated, and fervently celebrated.

But there is another side to it. Religion guards its secrets

---

[14] *Psychoanalysis and Faith: The Letters of Sigmund Freud and Oskar Pfister,* ed. Heinrich Meng and Ernst L. Freud; trans. Eric Mosbacher (New York: Basic Books, 1963), pp. 125–126.

well—so well, in fact, that only a science that formulates its definition precisely in opposition to religion can penetrate them. Naturally science will oppose religion, for, in commending the transference-God, religion reenforces and recreates those very distortions between surface and depth that therapy seeks to heal. The cure of civilization—a foolishness for Freud, but that is another problem—lies in the ever-steady interpretation of religion by science, especially the science of psychoanalytic psychology. What gets interpreted in psychoanalytic psychology is, above all else, transference.

The psychological dimension of the
subject-object dichotomy

WE now turn to some of the theological notions of Paul Tillich that bear directly on these psychoanalytic discussions. But we must do so in a manner protective of the inner integrity of that theological system. That is, we must not reduce the theological constructs or the reality they affirm in the interests of the argument. Thus we momentarily suspend our own interpretive schema in favor of the more immediate interests of understanding the constructs at hand. But, given this suspension, we may also entertain our bias: that the theological injunction to transcend the subject-object relation intersects with the psychological notion of overcoming repression and that transference is central to this overcoming.

We have already suggested that the subject-object relation is a crucial methodological construct for theological existentialism. Theological discussions generally take up this construct in the language either of their own religious tradition, their contemporary intellectual commitments, or both, but agreement among different discussions can usually be found at two points.

First, we are likely to be told that there is a kind of personal existence and relatedness that, because it bears the mark of the subject-object relation, is nontheological or nonreligious. Secondly, it is often suggested that the presence of this kind of relatedness, in and of itself, is precisely what constitutes man's moral and religious plight. What is problematic for man is his capacity and need for a kind of personal relatedness that goes beyond subject-object relatedness. If man's life is to become religious, the subject-object quality must be transformed and must acquire a quality of transcendence. The subject-object relation must be transcended.

Easily the most familiar and most influential instance of this type of argument is Martin Buber's distinction between the two attitudes, I-It and I-Thou.[15] The attitude of I-It is precisely what characterizes the subject-object relation. Here the reference is, of course, as much epistemological as it is personal and dynamic. In the I-It relation, the subject characteristically views the object from the perspective of its own ideality and centeredness. But, in the I-Thou relation, meeting replaces knowledge, the existential replaces the merely epistemological, and, therefore, subject and object coexist in unanalyzable integrity and wholeness. The subject-object relation can be and is overcome ("overcome" is Buber's preferred term) from time to time by the emergence of real meeting and betweenness, and it is this overcoming—or, more

---

[15] See Martin Buber, *I and Thou*, trans. Ronald Gregor Smith (Edinburgh: T. & T. Clark, 1937), and *Between Man and Man*, trans. Ronald Gregor Smith (Boston: Beacon Press, 1955). On the one hand, Buber's emphasis on religion and on the concrete in personal existence, his disavowal of institutionalism and of theology (see, for example, *Two Types of Faith*, trans. Norman P. Goldhawk [London: Routledge & Kegan Paul, 1951]), and his strong criticism of Kierkegaard's understanding of individuality—all dissociate his thought rather clearly from that of the theological existentialism under discussion here. Consider, for example, Maurice Friedman's distinction between Buber, the "existentialist of dialogue" and Tillich, the "theological existentialist" *(To Deny Our Nothingness* [New York: Delacorte Press, 1967], pp. 262–306). On the other hand, these objections have not prevented theological existentialists from a thoroughgoing appropriation of Buber's formulation of the two fundamental human attitudes. But because Buber's criticism of Freud is so similar to that of Niebuhr and Tillich, it would seem that theological existentialism is not entirely mistaken in its approval of Buber's I-Thou and I-It distinction.

precisely, the rhythmic alteration of *both* modes of relatedness—
that makes personal relatedness religious.

On the extreme left of the theological scene, Karl Barth
denies to the subject-object schema any Christian theological
validity.[16] Barth's way is a radical *via negativa* with respect to
the subject-object schema; God is "indissolubly subject,"[17] and
therefore the subject-object schema is transformed through its
very obliteration. In Emil Brunner's familiar delineation of the
divine-human encounter, we are told that, although psychology
can comprehend dislocations within the self, only theology can
speak of their unity. Thus the subject-object schema, the I-It
relation, precludes a personal encounter between self and God.
Consequently, Brunner speaks of the resolution in faith of the
object-subject antithesis.[18] Tillich gives a more balanced view:
the subject-objection relation must be transcended without, however, being destroyed.[19] As we have seen in some detail, Reinhold
Niebuhr's notions of self and spirit have meaning only in relation
to the vital coherence and predictable sequences of nature. Spirit
transcends the mechanistic objectivity of science and the vital
subjectivity of romanticism just as God transcends vitality and
form. We might say that, for Niebuhr, the subject-object relation must be dramatized or "spiritized." Much of the force of

---

[16] See Karl Barth, *Church Dogmatics* (Edinburgh: T. & T. Clark, 1936–
1962), I, Part I (1936), 438; I, Part II (1956), 280–297; II, Part I (1957),
13–23, 56, 61; III, Part II (1960), 22–27. See also *Prayer: According to the
Catechisms of the Reformation,* trans. Sara Terrien (Philadelphia: Westminster Press, 1952), p. 36.

[17] See James Brown, *Subject and Object in Modern Theology* (New York:
Macmillan, 1955), chap. vi.

[18] See Emil Brunner, *Truth As Encounter* (Philadelphia: Westminster
Press, 1964), pp. 111–118.

[19] Tillich's discussions of the subject-object structure are numerous, and he
uses the term in a variety of different contexts and associated meanings.
References are noticeably more frequent in the third volume of his *Systematic Theology* (3 vols.; Chicago: University of Chicago Press, 1951–1963)
than in the first two volumes. In Volume I the most concise discussion is
logical and ontological. (See I, 171–174; II, 62–66.) In Volume III the discussions are more sustained, and the index includes a listing for "subject
and object." (For particularly illustrative instances, see III, 68–76, 252–262.)
See also *The Dynamics of Faith* (New York: Harper, 1957), pp. 109–110.

Bultmann's work lies here, for his "world seen from the outside" is a subject-object attitude that he believes stands in contrast to faith.[20]

Therefore, we now attempt a stereotypical, synoptic picture of the subject-object relation as it is said to qualify the nature of personal existence in order that we may examine its possibly psychological form. According to these discussions, it is said that the subject-object relation, if permitted to prevail, falsifies personal existence on two accounts. On the one hand, one may wish to view the other person "objectively." If so, the relation between subject and object is generally said to have one or more of at least three characteristics: detachment, manipulation, and generalization. Detachment suggests attempting the removal or suspension of all private (that is, subjective) feelings, attitudes, and thoughts—whatever does not entirely emerge in direct and specifiable response to the reality resident in the other person. There can be no passion, involvement, or participation. Detachment, then, means rational control with respect to inner vitalities. In manipulation, one uses the other person, fitting him into a means-end schema in the interest of the subject and not primarily for purposes referable to the internal nature and direction of the other person. Through manipulation one ignores the inherent intentionality in the other person by reducing him to a function of

[20] In this regard consider Schubert M. Ogden's discussion in the essay, "Myth and Truth," *McCormick Quarterly*, XVIII (January 1965), Special Supplement, 57–76. In this discussion Ogden establishes connections between Bultmann's view of myth and Niebuhr's distinction between primitive and permanent myth. In doing so he notes that Bultmann, like Niebuhr, seeks to locate faith as a third reality in relation to mechanistic objectification and subjective fantasy. Bultmann says: "We only acknowledge as actual in the world what can be demonstrated to have a place in this lawful continuum, and we consider assertions that do not allow themselves to be controlled by this idea to be fantasies" (quoted in Schubert M. Ogden, *Christ Without Myth* [New York: Harper, 1961], p. 32). Note how Bultmann's remarks are reminiscent of our first and second readings of Freud, polarizing as they do the objective and subjective, the mechanistic and the dynamic. A "higher" reading of the meaning of fantasy would transform Bultmann's construction, opening it to a psychology of myth. But as such Bultmann's theory of myth is, of course, thoroughly inaccessible to any psychological consideration. His methodology stands as a barrier to any higher psychology of transcendence and myth.

one's own will. Generalization is a more cognitive and epistemological characteristic of the subject-object schema. In this case, the other person is recognized only insofar as he shares certain marks, traits, or characteristics with others. Nothing interior and private can be of concern except as it is part of a larger scheme of things. To generalize is to make the person a member of a series, to type him. Such are the vices to which objectivity is heir.

On the other hand, one may also err on the side of subjectivity; the internal and private dimensions of the person as subject obscure the objective reality of the other and even of the subject's capacity to know himself. Subjectivity may take the form of surplus vitality and emotional overinvolvement in relation to another person. Or, it may take the form of self-surrender (the opposite of manipulation), in which case the intentionality of the subject is obliterated in deference to that of the other as object. Here, the subject assumes a posture of unwholesome passivity in which the other person as object dominates and tyrannizes the subject. Thirdly, subjectivity overemphasizes uniqueness and individuality in relation to the collectivities of life. Individual differences seem to make generalization impossible. The radically subjective cannot be objectified.

Both subjectivity and objectivity, therefore, are finally insufficient, partial, and incomplete as relational attitudes or postures. Neither one nor both together are structurally capable of leading to full and genuine relatedness with another person. Something must occur, some event must take place, if the partialities of the subject-object relation are to be transformed.

According to our theologians, the source of such transformation lies beyond partiality. The most regularly recurrent term is "transcendence." Whatever the term, the idea is to indicate the manner in which the new situation does and does not resemble the old. So we are told that, for transcendence to occur, there must be a union of subject and object; but it is a union that includes both detachment and emotional participation while at the same time going beyond these. We are told that there must be mutuality; but it is a mutuality in which manipulation and domination are somehow reconciled with surrender without either being totally denied or abrogated. And we are told that there must be centeredness; but this must include both generalizing and individualizing tendencies, such that general characteristics and personal uniqueness coexist, each in some way supporting and being supported by the other. In such fashion is the subject-object relation said to be transformed, and precisely at this point personal relatedness becomes a theological possibility.

Descriptions of this sort and the sources from which they are drawn are helpful only up to a point, for they do not provide a clear picture of what is supposed to happen. We are told not to expect an experiential—that is, a dynamic-psychological—description of that which by definition transcends the experiential and psychological. But is it really asking too much to insist on an experiential description of what gets transcended?

At this point Tillich's work is helpful, for he has been willing to discuss this theme from time to time in more concrete and dynamic terminology, although these descriptions are infrequent. This motif is of such importance to his thought that it is Tillich as much as or more than any other theologian today who urges that we transcend the subject-object relation in order that genuine personal life and relatedness emerge, both individually and socially. How does he describe, theologically, the subject-object relation and its transcendence?

> The God of theological theism is a being beside others and as such a part of the whole of reality. He certainly is considered its most important part, but as a part and therefore as subjected to the structure of the whole. He is supposed to be beyond the ontological elements and categories which constitute reality. But every statement subjects him to them. He is seen as a self which has a world, as an ego which is related to a thou, as a cause which is separated from its effect, as having a definite space and an endless time. He is a being, not being-itself. As such he is bound to the subject-object structure of reality, he is an object for us as subjects. At the same time we are objects for him as a

subject. And this is decisive for the necessity of transcending theological theism.[21]

So far so good; this is what anyone who reads Tillich has learned to expect. However, his understanding of precisely *what* is wrong with all of this and *why* it is wrong is very much more illuminating for our concern. What does it mean and why is it wrong to make God or the other person an object for which one is oneself the subject, and what does it mean and why is it wrong to be merely an object to God or to another subject? Tillich continues:

> For God as a subject makes me into an object which is nothing more than an object. He deprives me of my subjectivity because he is all-powerful and all-knowing. I revolt and try to make *him* into an object, but the revolt fails and becomes desperate. God appears as the invincible tyrant, the being in contrast with whom all other beings are without freedom and subjectivity. He is equated with the recent tyrants who with the help of terror try to transform everything into a mere object, a thing among things, a cog in the machine they control. He becomes the model of everything against which Existentialism revolted. This is the God Nietzsche said had to be killed because nobody can tolerate being made into a mere object of absolute knowledge and absolute control. This is the deepest root of atheism.[22]

The implicit psychological assumptions of this description are especially transparent. Tillich suggests that the subject-object relation is also a transference relation, in the full sense in which that term has been explicated; and the transcendence of this relation, therefore, is a working through of the transference. What we have called Freud's transference-God is also Tillich's God of theological theism. It is also, as we shall see, the God of the "death of God" theology. Here Tillich shares Freud's psychodynamic critique of religion.

---

[21] Tillich, *The Courage to Be* (New Haven: Yale University Press, 1952), pp. 184–185.
[22] *Ibid.*, p. 185.

The point can be further strengthened by calling attention to the dynamic tone of Tillich's use of the word "bound": the God of theological theism "is bound to the subject-object structure of reality." Recall, too, the way psychoanalytic psychology speaks of the binding of anxiety or the binding of cathexes. This dynamic tone characterizes many of Tillich's discussions of the subject-object structure in the third volume of *Systematic Theology*. For example: "The 'search for identity' which is a genuine problem of the present generation is actually the search for the Spiritual Presence, because the split of the self into a controlling subject and a controlled object can be overcome only from the vertical direction, out of which reunion is given and not commanded. The self which has found its identity is the self of him who is 'accepted' as a unity in spite of this disunity."[23]

Is not the transference-God a "being beside others"; is he not seen as a "self which has a world"; and is he not subject to the categories of time and space? The transference-God, therefore, is "bound to the subject-object structure of reality." One of the crucial marks of transference is its enforced dependency and corresponding "mythologizing" of the analyst into a destructive and authoritarian father—a token individual memory of the archaic and terrible primal father. Tillich's description of the desperate revolt against the God who makes man into "nothing more than an object," who denies all "freedom and subjectivity," the God who *"had to be killed"* (my italics) is identical with Freud's analysis of fathers, both primal and personal. "Nothing more than an object" is a theological statement, but it is unmistakably psychoanalytically psychological as well; it is really the ontologizing of the sadomasochistic relation between the retaliatory father and the fearful son. Tillich as much as says it himself; he says, "He is equated with the recent tyrants . . . " and this could just as well be rendered, "He is a transference from recent tyrants. . . ." To put our conclusion entirely in the language of

---

[23] Tillich, *Systematic Theology*, III, 260.

Tillich and Freud, the God above God emerges only when and insofar as the transference-God is destroyed, and the destruction of the transference-God occurs only when and insofar as the subject-object relation is transcended. Transference, and especially the transference-God, is the link between psychological repression and theological transcendence.

Tillich, in fact, discusses the notion of transference explicitly:

> One of the great achievements of psychoanalytic theory is its insight into the depersonalizing consequences of the phenomenon of transference, not only on the patient, but also on the analyst, and into the attempts to overcome this situation by methods finally removing the transference in the healing process. However, this can be successful only if the ambiguity of working for personal growth is overcome. And this is possible only if the subject-object scheme is conquered. Unambiguous life is impossible wherever the subject-object scheme is unbroken.[24]

The notion of transference, when placed alongside the Tillichian construction of the subject-object relation, not only lends it psychological clarity, but also exposes the deep congeniality between psychoanalytic psychology and the roots of Tillich's own theological existentialism. For those marks of personal existence that theology so often characterizes as "subject-object"—detachment, manipulation, and generalization—are also the marks of repression, of mechanistic objectivity. Their matching polar opposites—the subjectivity side of the subject-object dichotomy—are also characteristics of the transference experience. Heightened subjectivity and the insight it makes possible must be an ingredient of theological analysis if transcendence is to become something more than simply a repressive stance toward repression, a mechanistic transcendence of mechanism, a "subject-object" kind of transcendence of the subject-object relation. The imperative to transcendence is an imperative to objectivity—but only of the sort that is grounded in and embodied by the richly

[24] *Ibid.*, III, 76.

subjective, immanental, and immediate in human life. Therefore, it is in "working through" the transference that the reality of transcendence is to be found.

At this point Freud and Tillich—and in many ways psychoanalysis and theological existentialism—agree, at least with regard to the delineation of what is problematic for the self and the incipient direction of its fulfillment. Tillich rejects the God of theological theism on the grounds of the Protestant principle; Freud rejects the transference-God on grounds very different from those of Tillich, although these grounds are no less an equally prior intuition regarding the structure of human nature and destiny.[25] Both are concerned with the formulating human possibility "beyond" mutually agreed upon "images of destructive power," Tillich's theological interpretation of the superego.[26]

However, the resulting formulations differ. For Tillich, like Niebuhr, proposes in the final moments of his analysis a methodological style of the gaps. The courage to be, as moral possibility, Tillich says, consists in "the accepting of the acceptance *without* somebody or something that accepts. It is the power of being-itself that accepts and gives the courage to be (my italics)."[27] On the one hand, Tillich seems to be saying that, if

[25] That this discussion is fundamentally in accord with Tillich's understanding of his own theology can be seen in his rejoinder to a paper of mine stating some of these ideas. Tillich finds the connection between his God of theological theism and what I have called Freud's transference-God quite correct. But he adds, ". . . in Freud the idea of healing is exclusively related to temporal existence and the horizontal meaning of time and, consequently, cannot overcome the tragic character of life, while the Christian faith (which I try to interpret) adds the vertical line, transtemporal being and participation in it, and expresses a hope 'beyond tragedy,' though in a non-objectifying, symbolic language" (Paul Tillich, "Rejoinder," *Journal of Religion,* XLVI, No. 1, Pt. II [January 1966], 194–196). Tillich's rejoinder also speaks of objectifying, which "makes God only into an object of knowledge, not into an object of control." What I have called a third reading of Freud —one that goes beyond the distinction between mechanism and dynamics makes possible a higher, psychological reading of Tillich's theological epistemology.

[26] Paul Tillich, "Existentialism and Psychotherapy," *Psychoanalysis and Existential Philosophy,* ed. Hendrick M. Ruitenbeek (New York: E. P. Dutton, 1962), p. 14.

[27] Tillich, *The Courage to Be,* p. 185.

human courage is to be grounded in the power of being, an act of personal disengagement from all forms of social participation is required. Thus absolute faith, as the religious correlate of the (moral) courage to be, requires transcending socialization processes, just as, theologically, the God above God transcends the God of theism. For the God above God is a distant God and, in his abysmal nature, is rich in aseity.

On the other hand, the Tillichian virtue of centeredness and the balance he commends between individuation and participation, for example, suggest that overcoming the God of theological theism releases the self for a more clearly ontic form of relatedness. This form of sociality should in turn be reflected, one would think, in a more immanental understanding of the divine—a God whose "aboveness," if you will, is matched by his "withinness" or internality in the life of man. It is difficult to reconcile this ontic sociality with the God above God, if only because of the imagery employed. The God above God, so suggestive of extreme distance and externality, in this sense inadvertently reconstitutes the oppressive—and as our argument now permits us to say, repressive—qualities of the God of theological theism.

Do the deepest intentions of Tillich's thought run in the direction of an ontic sociality in which objectifying and subjectifying modes of relatedness are grounded in a vision of a transformed sense of individuality and participation?[28] Does the desig-

[28] This implies that objectivity and subjectivity are the means of their own transcendence. See Tillich's discussion of the transition from the dimension of self-awareness to the dimension of the spirit, *Systematic Theology,* III, 27–28.

This discussion of Tillich's thought has certain affinities with a recent interpretation of Tillich's theological method as self-transcending naturalism rather than self-transcending realism. Guyton B. Hammond discusses ontologically the point we are discussing theologically and psychologically. Hammond says: "On the level of the divine life, it would appear that self-estrangement must be conceptualized as the separation of 'subject' and 'object,' the separation of the self-which-transcends from the self-which-is-transcended. On the other hand . . . on the finite level Tillich does not consider the separation of subject and object to be the primary estrangement; and the naturalist view has been criticized for understanding estrangement as the subject-object split. Does Tillich reinstate on the divine level what he has rejected on the finite level? Does Tillich break with reductionist naturalism only to reinstate a 'self-transcending' naturalism?"

nation "God above God" originate in a dynamic intention that really runs counter to that suggested by its special imagery of extreme distance and external relation? These questions focus the issues between theology and psychoanalysis concretely and problematically.

Our discussions of Freud's thought do not permit an answer in the affirmative. We see that the theological imperative to transcendence is based on a specifiable and particular infrastructure of psychological processes—superego, repression, transference, and interpretation. The theological view presupposes a gap between these processes and the higher reality of transcendence at the expense of an immanental and dynamic approach to the superego and all that it represents. The more dynamic approach suggests that these psychological processes may be more a medium through which understanding must pass if it is to reach the reality of which theology speaks. This is the possibility of a higher psychology of self-transcendence, the new question toward which our theological and psychological discussions now point us.

Further discussion of this problem is reserved for Part Two. By way of preparation for that discussion, we will first examine the bearing of the argument thus far on the early psychology of religion and pastoral psychology.

Hammond continues: "Since this is a new form of naturalism (one might question the use of the term at all), it cannot be viewed as necessarily inadequate for an expression of the Christian world-view. It is, however, clearly in conflict with traditional theism (which Tillich calls supernaturalism). Tillich's rejection of supernaturalism suggests a reconsideration on the part of Christian theology of its relation to various types of humanistic naturalism" (*Man in Estrangement: A Comparison of the Thought of Paul Tillich and Erich Fromm* [Nashville, Tenn.: Vanderbilt University Press, 1965], pp. 177–179).

Four: A retrospective

interlude

Introduction

WE have examined in some detail two major theological responses to Freud and taken them to be representative of theological existentialism. Weaving our way in and out, we have fashioned a thoroughgoing criticism of these two theologies. We have argued that each has proposed an anthropological and methodological style of discontinuity; as a result certain psychological considerations, given theological expression only through the notion of immanence, are ignored.

We were able to interpret these theological discussions in terms of psychoanalytic categories in a way that, although they are not employed by the theologians themselves, nevertheless seems not to distort their intentions. For example, what Niebuhr and Tillich consider problematic about self-understanding can be rendered in psychoanalytic terms as well. In fact, psychoanalytic psychology itself, contrary to theological readings of it, has proposed a very similar analysis of what is problematic for the self. Psychoanalysis casts its proposals into a nucleus of interrelated constructs—Oedipus complex, superego, repression, transference and its understanding and interpretation. We were able to conclude that the theological meaning of transcendence is adduced by theology in a way that is precisely analogous to those life processes that this nucleus of psychoanalytic concepts seeks to describe.

Anthropologically, theology commends transcending the superego (structurally), repression (dynamically), and developmentally earlier and lower processes (socially). In Tillich's methodological discussions of the subject-object relation we see reflected the psychological understanding and interpretation of transference, suggesting that transcendence of the subject-object relation is also overcoming or transcending the psychological processes of transference. Such concepts as superego, repression, mechanistic knowing, and the like are interchangeable in Freud's psychology with the notion of transference. Transference is a retrograde process of going back into the dynamics of repression and the formation of the harsh superego. But all of these terms are finally referable to the problematic side of human life, which, according to theological analysis, requires transcendence. Through the notions of transference and transcendence, then, we are able to draw Freud's thought into a direct encounter with the intentions of theology.

These conclusions do not, however, simplify or resolve our understanding of what has taken place in these theological responses to Freud. Rather, they generate a new question, that of whether there is a higher reading of Freud that is richer than that offered by the theologians and that may, for that reason, be theological in form. From Niebuhr's thought we are able to develop a mechanistic-scientific reading of Freud. Tillich's thought provides a more dynamic understanding. Freud's dynamic view of religion, in turn, implies resources for a third or iconic reading of Freud, directed first and foremost to the problems of myth and symbol. The clinical phenomenon of transference cannot be separated from its cultural and religious implications.

These last concerns, we argue, are prior to metapsychological theorizing, prior even to the strictly clinical-dynamic orientation of Freud's thought. The means by which one may transcend or surpass the superego may have more to do with imagination than with rational choice—human or divine. Is there, for example, a fantasy, myth, or symbol system particular to all we have said about the superego? Two post-Protestant interpretations of Freud argue that the religious image of the Devil is closely associated with the superego, on the one hand, and the spiritual dilemmas of Protestant thought and life, on the other hand. This suggests that Niebuhr has dissociated primitive myth from permanent myth, reducing the former and elevating the latter while denying any continuity between the two. Perhaps a higher psychology of symbols can not only clarify the roots of theological objection to such continuity, but can also serve to mediate between primitive and permanent myth and those many gaps of which this distinction is but one instance.

However, the relationship between Freud and theology needs to be pursued in a retrospective direction as well. We need to know whether or not these discussions and questions are characteristic only of theological existentialism and psychoanalysis or whether they occur in other contexts. If the latter, then some discussion of these contexts will give additional breadth to our problem. We have already noted that theological and psychological considerations are not easily separated. Because of this, we are led to wonder what relation there might be between theological existentialism and two movements in psychology to which it has by and large remained indifferent or else critical. These are the early psychology of religion, which emphasized a pietistic form of conversion, and pastoral psychology, which has attended to the work of Freud more than to his thought or person. We are also led to wonder about the relation between psychoanalysis and the psychology of religion and pastoral psychology. For the decline of structuralism and the appearance of behaviorism subsequently produced a polarization of much American psychology into behaviorism and psychoanalysis, an objective and a subjective psychology.

In this chapter, I will argue that theological existentialism, and behaviorism and psychoanalysis in psychology do bear some relation to the early psychology of religion and that this relation is clarified by considering it in the context of the thought of Freud.

The psychology of religion and the thought of Freud

WE have already spoken of Erikson's analysis of the origins of psychoanalysis and his delineation of the three interlocking dimensions of psychological discovery—the crisis in therapeutic technique, clinical conceptualization, and personal identity. I suggested above that, when expanded more generally to "work," "thought," and "person," these categories are helpful for an understanding of Freud. Their use can be extended further. When these three dimensions of discovery are brought together in the life of an individual person or an intellectual movement, they constitute a model for the discipline in question. Thus the model can be used to understand the interrelations between religion and theology, on the one hand, and psychology, on the other hand.

The psychology of religion was a movement within the then newly emergent discipline of psychology and was conceived of far more as a branch of psychology than as an interdisciplinary effort. For these psychologists,[1] there was no discipline in addition to psychology called "religion"—for religion, or "religious experience" (the preferred term), was conceived of entirely as a phenomenon to be interpreted by other disciplines. It could be described and analyzed in many ways, only one of which is psychological, where the emphasis is on the psychological function of religion. We have here an important methodological point regard-

[1] Of the many names that come to mind, I am alluding primarily to James, Starbuck, Coe, Leuba, and Hall. However, this discussion is directed primarily to William James's study, *The Varieties of Religious Experience* (New York: Modern Library, 1902).

ing the work of the psychologists of religion: a close and mutually determinate relation between understanding the nature and purpose of psychology, on the one hand, and the psychological nature and meaning of religion, on the other hand. The kind of psychology available to the psychologists of religion determined their interpretation of religion. By means of the functional psychology of Hall and James, a particular understanding of religious experience was given credence.

James and Hall led in the appearance and establishment of American psychology, each man presenting a broadly functional-adaptive psychological point of view,[2] and they brought this psychological perspective to bear on their understanding of religion. Both James and Hall completed substantive work in the psychology of religion,[3] and at certain points in their lives both were personally involved in the kind of experiences that had interested them as psychologists—James from time to time through his own private quest and Hall through his early career first as a student at Union Theological Seminary and later for a brief period as a minister.[4]

For the psychologists of religion, the referent for the word "religious" pertained to a power, force, energy, presence, or the like, always experienced initially as phenomenologically other to one's own immediate perceptive awareness. The task of the

[2] William James, *The Principles of Psychology* (2 vols.; New York: Dover, 1950).

[3] See for example, G. S. Hall, *Jesus, the Christ, in the Light of Psychology* (2 vols.; Garden City, N. Y.: Doubleday, Page, 1917). Hall also founded the *Journal of Religious Psychology, Including Its Anthropological and Sociological Aspects.*

[4] I am referring to James's own description of his personal struggles, which he describes in *Varieties.* For reference to these, see R. B. Perry, *The Thought and Character of William James* (briefer version; New York: Harper & Row, 1964), chap. xxxviii. Boring describes Hall's first year of theological study: "He took his philosophy with him to the Union Theological Seminary in New York City, and so much the philosopher and so little the theologian was he that, after his trial sermon, the member of the faculty whose custom it was to criticize, despairing of mere criticism, knelt and prayed for his soul. Henry Ward Beecher was more sympathetic; he advised Hall to go to Germany to study philosophy" (Boring, *History,* p. 518).

psychologist lay in describing and analyzing the effects and meaning of this "religious" referent. They argued that its effects and meaning consist in its dynamic and functional facilitation of both psychic and social adaptation and adjustment—although the former outweigh the latter. It is, therefore, what theological existentialism would perhaps prefer to call today a subject-object type of experience: The religious experience occurs simply and objectively to consciousness and is described and analyzed on this basis. Or, to use Tillich's categories, these psychologists made religious experience the source and not the medium of religious knowledge.

This methodological stance toward religion is intimately related to probably the most notable and memorable feature of the psychology of religion, namely, its special fascination with the conversion experience. For the conversion experience, they argued, is clearly the paradigm of the religious. The psychologists of religion had available to them a great deal of anthropological and historical data, yet they seemed mysteriously drawn to and preoccupied with those conversion experiences that were so much a part of the religious institutional life of their times.[5]

The conversion experience is really "an experience"—it has a beginning, a middle, and an end. There was a time in the individual's life when it wasn't, then it occurred, and then it was over. And, although testimony abounds to the effect that the experience remains memorable in the life of the person, it also remains just as clearly an event in the past, one in which he no longer participates actively. Typically, how do these psychologists describe the occurrence of the experience?

For the most part such experiences occur when the individual is alone, quite often in some sort of natural setting. He

---

[5] See, for example, the chapters on conversion in James, *Varieties*; in G. S. Hall, *Adolescence* (2 vols.; New York: D. Appleton, 1904); and in E. D. Starbuck, *Psychology of Religion* (New York: Scribner's, 1903). A typical "case" in James's study begins as follows: "One morning, while I was walking in a solitary place as usual, I at once saw that all my contrivances and projects to effect or procure deliverance and salvation for myself were utterly in vain" *(Varieties, p. 209).*

is characteristically unaware of and does not anticipate any impending psychic crisis. Sometimes, in fact, the very opposite is often the case. Sometimes the individual is rather well in control of things, although sometimes a sense of uneasiness or troublesomeness may hover on the periphery of awareness. It is quite often reported that the person has begun to pursue some solitary activity that does not require the presence of others—reading a book, writing a letter, making an entry in a diary or book of personal thoughts, taking a walk, or perhaps simply meditating about a previous incident, event, person, or the like.

The onset of the crisis is most often sudden. What was before simply quiet musing, muted reverie, or simply a moment of inattentiveness or vagueness suddenly becomes focused and overwhelming in the individual's consciousness. Often a single phrase or sentence or idea receives great affective intensification. This produces the dominant affective tone of the crisis, that of guilt, as it is perceived to be rooted in prior acts, omitted or committed, in relationships, or in particular experiences. Most often, the guilt is conceived less in terms of specific behavior and more in terms of a pervasive, painful, and nonspecific sense of worthlessness and remorse.

From the point of view of the psychologists of religion, the force of the conversion experience as a whole is always dynamically away from isolation, conflict, and guilt and in the direction of resolution and adjustment, in relation to other persons but more immediately and dramatically in relation to the inner, psychic demands and imperatives of the experience itself. The resolution occurs, like the onset, abruptly and in isolation. Through it, one achieves a sense of restoration and renewal such that the precise occasions of remorse and feelings of worthlessness are removed. In some cases, the individual simply feels that he has been allowed to return to his former life rhythms. In others, there is a clear sense that the resolution has created a new, higher, and more satisfying stance toward life.

But the conversion experience is always "an experience," something one "goes through." It can be likened, at least in its minimal effectiveness, to a psychic thunderstorm that appears suddenly, asserts itself violently, and then as quickly disappears. The experience, then, is more a homeostatic stabilizing of psychic pressures than a transformation the effects of which continue to stimulate novelty in conscious awareness and in social relatedness.

Our previous discussions have some bearing on the conversion experiences as described by the psychologists of religion. Although their technical vocabulary, as they described and then moralized about the conversion experience, does not employ such terms, the experience that so fascinated them may also be characterized as a superego crisis, for guilt and loss of self-esteem are the predominant characteristics. The psychological function of the conversion experience is to resolve the crisis. This religious experience therefore has something in common with the theological doctrine of transcendence, which, as we have seen, also involves transcending harsh superego processes and their isolating, guilt-producing effects. And, as noted, the subject-object relation with which theology is so concerned, and which we have linked to the problematic processes of repression and the harsh superego, underlies the methodological thinking of the psychologists of religion. The absence of any emphasis on religious symbols and a preference for focusing on the conversion experience itself distinguish the psychology of religion both from depth psychology, which separates conscious or surface processes from unconscious or depth processes, and from theological existentialism, which separates religion from revelation.

The psychology of religion as a discipline and the conversion experience as the discipline's special object of study constitute a model or synthesis for understanding the relation between religion and psychology. In addition, the discipline was characterized by a professional sense of workmanship in the face of common problems, for these men were by and large either psychologists or else educators concerned with psychology. Thus they were not professionally concerned with institutional forms of Christianity or with theology, except as these were understood to be the proper object of psychological analysis. To some extent, this is true also of the religious education movement, which, despite its formal identification with institutional, Protestant Christianity, made considerable use of psychological materials and was integrated into the theological community more at the administrative rather than the intellectual level.

Why is the psychology of religion today so uninteresting to both theologians and to depth psychologists? The reasons for its quick and thoroughly undramatic decline are far more interesting and important than the work of the movement itself. For the beginning of this indifference coincided with the beginnings of both theological existentialism and psychoanalysis. It has often been noted that the nineteenth century, as an ideological synthesis, "ended" at the time of the First World War. The decline of the psychology of religion, which also occurred at this time, was due in part, one would suspect, to the same shift in cultural modes of self-understanding that produced existentialism and psychoanalysis. For the kind of religion that so intrigued psychologists of religion is precisely the kind of religion that psychoanalysis and theological existentialism exclude and argue against. Thus both theological existentialism and psychoanalysis may be seen as attempts to solve a similar problem, albeit in different ways. Again, the notion of the superego serves as a connecting term.

The changes undergone in American psychology during the first decades of this century can be understood in terms of the relation between functional psychology on the one hand and behaviorism on the other hand. James's functional psychology articulated well with the approach taken by the other psychologists of religion. Although James and others were critical of the structuralist program, James nevertheless retained the possibility of introspection as a fundamental methodological premise, and the problem of consciousness remained for him real and important.[6] Although it is perhaps more correct to note that both functional-

---

[6] See James, *Principles,* I, 185.

ism and behaviorism took form in critical protest against the structuralists' willingness to combine both introspection and exact science, we are concerned as well to note the extent to which behaviorism defined itself in opposition to functionalism. Watson, at least, saw in James's approach to psychology the very obstacle that above all others needed to be removed.[7]

In Watson's behaviorism consciousness and introspection are considered to be pseudoproblems that prevent psychology from moving ahead.[8] They were linked in his mind with religious moralism and pietism, and he was convinced that both were a kind of spurious or defective emotionality. Hence he posited the need for an "objective psychology" that would ignore the problems of the nature and function of inwardness and the internality of the self as variables in psychological study. His work must certainly be understood on the level of its expressed intention, a thoroughgoing reformulation of the problems and methods of psychology.[9]

Yet Watson's writings may also be considered from a more programmatic and ideological perspective, and in this regard they bear some relation to the piety already noticed in the psychology of religion. Watson's personal life and career have been interpreted as an attempt to break away from the ideology of pious and rural America, and his psychology has been understood in part as a response to these origins.

[7] See John B. Watson, *Behaviorism* (Chicago: University of Chicago Press, 1924), pp. 1–5.

[8] *Ibid.*, pp. 1–19.

[9] In one sense, Watson's methodological innovation is a permanent dissociation of subject from object; on the other hand, it is also a step that permits a subsequent return from subject to object. Consider Merleau-Ponty's remark about Watson's behaviorism: "What is healthy and profound in this intuition of behavior—that is, the vision of man as perpetual debate and 'explanation' with a physical and social world—found itself compromised by an impoverished philosophy. . . . When Watson spoke of behavior he had in mind what others have called *existence*" (*Structure of Behavior*, p. 226, n. 3). Behaviorism is a psychology of otherness, a notion of interest to theologies of the secular: "By grace and otherness I wish to indicate the theological concern which is with men as having to do with what is not themselves" (R. G. Smith, "A Theological Perspective of the Secular," *The Christian Scholar*, XLII, No. 1 [March 1960], 11–24).

Bakan describes the interrelation between the formation of behaviorism as a viable definition of psychology, certain features in the personal development of Watson, and the social context of both—in this case the social process of urbanization. He points out that Watson "was born and raised in a very religious family, and was slated for the ministry," that, as an adolescent in a rural, Southern town, he was semidelinquent. Bakan describes the psychological problems that accompany a transition from a rural environment in which there is a relatively simple harmony between the inner and outer world, to the impersonality and alienation of a complex, urban society. He argues that behaviorism and psychoanalysis appeared as attractive theoretical options in American psychology in part because the presence of urbanization created both the need to master an increasingly complex interpersonal environment—the prediction and control of strangers —and the opposite urge to rescue the individual from the anonymity of mass society. The emphasis on prediction and control was created because urbanization interrupted the possibility of developing intimate personal relations. This "called for a kind of ruthless suppression of affective responses," and Bakan concludes that this in turn created a type of attitudinal orientation through which only the external environment is given validity.[10]

Watson's psychology also served as a rallying point for a

[10] See David Bakan, "Behaviorism and American Urbanization," *Journal of the History of the Behavioral Sciences*, II, No. 1 (January 1966), 5–28. It is interesting to speculate on whether or not the early thought of Reinhold Niebuhr could be approached in a similar way, thereby adding a psychosocial dimension to our discussion of the theoretical interrelation between behaviorism, psychoanalysis, and theology. Niebuhr's *Leaves from the Notebook of a Tamed Cynic* (Chicago: Willett, Clark & Colby, 1929), are the reflections of a young man who, like Watson, after spending his adolescence in a rural, preurban environment, also moved to an urban-industrial situation, in his case Detroit. Niebuhr's "diary" reflects his moral and spiritual struggles during the period 1913–1928. On the basis of the experiences of this period of pastoral ministry, Niebuhr wrote *Moral Man and Immoral Society,* in which he discussed the ineffectiveness of a social ethic based on the assumptions of family life. The Gifford Lectures, in which there is a shift in emphasis from the problem of self and society to the doctrine of transcendence, were published in 1939, after Niebuhr had lived at Union Theological Seminary in New York City for more than ten years.

new sense of professional identity[11] for psychologists whose personal lives were no longer organized by the pieties and imperatives of declining religious institutions. The last paragraph of *Behaviorism* indicates the way in which his psychology depended on a rejection of pietism and moralism.

> Behaviorism ought to be a science that prepares men and women for understanding the principles of their own behavior. It ought to make men and women eager to rearrange their own lives, and especially eager to prepare themselves to bring up their own children in a healthy way. I wish I could picture for you what a rich and wonderful individual we should make of every healthy child if only we could let it shape itself properly and then provide for it a universe in which it could exercise that organization—a universe unshackled by legendary folk-lore of happenings thousands of years ago; unhampered by disgraceful political history; free of foolish customs and conventions which have no significance in themselves, yet which hem the individual in like taut steel bands. . . . The universe will change if you bring up your children, not in the freedom of the libertine, but in behavioristic freedom. . . . Will not these children in turn, with their better ways of living and thinking, replace us as society and in turn bring up their children in a still more scientific way, until the world finally becomes a place fit for human habitation?[12]

Might not such programmatic and ideological—one should really say eschatological—rhetoric be seen as an attempt to break out of the kind of psychic and moral bewilderment ("taut steel bands") created by a declining pietistic ethos?[13] Watson's

[11] Boring says that prior to Watson's work, American psychology had developed in three areas—experimental human psychology, animal psychology, and mental tests—and that it was beginning to read Freud. Of Watson's effect on this development he says: "Then Watson touched a match to this mixture, there was an explosion, and behaviorism was left. Watson founded behaviorism because everything was all ready for the founding" *(History,* p. 506).

[12] Watson, *Behaviorism,* pp. 303–304.

[13] Bakan notes that behaviorism and psychoanalysis emerged in a social context of rebellion against religious-ideological restraints and that both are theories that emphasize sexuality ("Behaviorism and American Urbanization," p. 24). We add that both psychoanalysis and behaviorism also emphasize childhood and early development, whereas theological existentialism, as noted over and over again, emphasizes a kind of self-understanding that is said to lie "beyond" the developmentally early.

rather domestic Nietzscheanism, his rejection of religion, although in the context and concerns of scientific psychology, are really a flight from that particular kind of religious consciousness that was the object of study for the psychologists of religion. In commending what is, in theological language, a "kenotic" evacuation of the psyche in favor of the behavioral field, Watson sought a methodological solution to the psychic problem that religious piety seeks to resolve through the experience of conversion. In this sense, behaviorism may be seen as a methodological flight from the superego.

Psychoanalysis puts forth a similar and far more powerful critique of the psychology of religion and the moral and religious sensibilities that it represented. Watson effects a methodological strategy that renders irrelevant the subjective or psychic, and with it the possibility of religious experience. In doing so, he rejects the internality of the self as a psychological problem; behaviorism recognizes only that aspect of experience that is outwardly observable. On the other hand, Freud recognized two internal levels of psychic reality, but he assigned religious experience (along with a number of other phenomena) to the repressed or dynamic unconscious; like Watson he thereby eliminated it as a factor in any normative understanding of psychic life. In advocating a restoration of strength to the ego in its struggles with the superego, Freud attempted to depotentiate the binding power of the harsh superego.

There are notable similarities between the work of James and Freud and between functional psychology and psychoanalysis generally.[14] James was sympathetic to many notions basic to psychoanalysis, as the following discussion of sexuality surely illustrates:

> The fondness of the ancients and of modern Orientals for forms of unnatural vice, of which the notion affects us with horror, is probably a mere case of the way in which this instinct may be inhibited by habit. We can hardly suppose that the ancients had

[14] See, for example, H. D. Lasswell, "Approaches to Human Personality: William James and Sigmund Freud," *Psychoanalysis and Psychoanalytic Review*, XLVII, No. 3 (1960), 52–68.

by gift of Nature a propensity of which we are devoid, and were all victims of what is now a pathological aberration limited to individuals. It is more probable that with them the instinct of physical aversion toward a certain class of objects was inhibited early in life by *habits,* formed under the influence of *example;* and that then a kind of sexual appetite, of which very likely most men possess the germinal possibility, developed itself in an unrestricted way.[15]

Shakow and Rapaport note that this passage and its context anticipate Freud—presumably in its suggestion of libido, identification, and sublimation. They also note a formal anticipation in the fact that "James recognized the importance of the faint, the fleeting, and the devious, which are so frequently the primary data of psychoanalysis."[16] And there is the personal aspect: James's almost wistful remark to Jones, who accompanied Freud during his 1909 visit to the United States: "the future of psychology belongs to your work" and Freud's admiration of James's courage in the face of physical infirmity.[17]

Valuable as such comparisons are, however, they obscure a point of difference between James and Freud, one that is exposed by considering their respective understandings of religious experience. We need carry the discussion only as far as a brief paper by Freud entitled "A Religious Experience,"[18] in which he cites a letter received from an American physician who had read a published interview in which Freud expressed a "lack of religious faith." The author of the letter attempted to persuade Freud of the validity of religious faith by reporting a religious

---

[15] James, *Principles,* II, 438–439; quoted by Shakow and Rapaport, *The Influence of Freud,* pp. 38–39.

[16] *Ibid.,* p. 39.

[17] Quoted in Jones, *Freud,* II, 57; See also Freud, *An Autobiographical Study,* p. 99.

[18] Freud, *Collected Papers,* V, 243–246. We wish only to remark that at the point of their psychological understanding of religion James and Freud take fundamentally different approaches. We do wish, however, to remain open to the possibility that this difference might carry through to their psychologies as well, that the definitions of religion that a psychology assumes may bear an intrinsic relation to that psychology itself.

experience of his own. This experience bears a remarkable similarity, in both ideas and style, to the conversion experiences discussed above. An exchange of correspondence ensued in which Freud remarked that he himself had not had such an experience and furthermore that he was a Jew; the physician replied that neither of these objections was an obstacle and that prayers were being offered for his "faith to believe."

Freud commented, first in an ironic but nevertheless friendly way: "I am still awaiting the outcome of this intercession";[19] and then, more seriously, he remarked that unlike his correspondent he was "accustomed to regard men's internal experiences and actions analytically."[20] James never felt it necessary to take such an analytic stance with its characteristic rhythm of participative immediacy and subsequent imaginative distance from the immediacy of experience. This imaginative distance, or insight, permits immersion and reimmersion in unconscious processes. Analytic distance undercuts the immediacy of the conversion experience and objectifies it. However, the analytic distance does not necessarily thereby invalidate the experience. But it does create a different interpretive approach.

It is in this sense that we find in psychoanalytic psychology a revolution in psychological method that, like Watson's programmatic behaviorism, directs its criticism against the manner of normatively conceiving psychic organization and function legitimated by the psychologists of religion. Although both behaviorism and psychoanalysis are first and foremost methodological reformulations within psychology, there is also a more subtle connection with the conversion experience. They are two different attempts to solve the same problem, to cope with those processes that go by the name of the superego.

Psychoanalysis and behaviorism are instances of a peculiar polarization of the dominant options in American psychology. This polarization has vexed methodological discussions in psy-

---

[19] *Ibid.*, V, 244.
[20] *Ibid.*, V, 245.

chology and is at the root of much dissension. The "objective" point of view has been carried on by learning theory, stimulus response theory, and animal psychology. The "subjective" appears in the psychotherapeutic and dynamic stream. It appears metaphysically in the controversy between idealism and naturalism and sociologically in the arguments between those who oppose the inner creativity of the self to the adjustments of the socialization process.[21]

Theological existentialism shares at certain points a methodological pattern in relation to the psychology of religion similar to that of behaviorism and psychoanalysis. For theological existentialism is also an attempt to break away from the pietistic and moralistic ethos that the psychology of religion represents in its studies of the causes and revolution of conversion experiences. Schleiermacher was the only theological figure whom the psychologists of religion used in a positive or constructive manner. Barth's critique of Schleiermacher—like Watson's and Freud's critiques of religion—was precisely at this point, that of religious feeling.[22] In addition to the importance of guilt and self-evaluation in the conversion experience, these experiences are also characterized by strong feelings of dependency. Concern with the psychological phenomena of emotion, dependency, and conversion are all features of liberal theology that roused Barth, to reverse the Kantian cliché, from his undogmatic slumbers. It is on grounds such as these that theological existentialism rejects "religious experience" in favor of what could be called "theological existence." The motives for doing so lie in a desire to transcend the pieties of mere religion. Theological existentialism seeks to go beyond the subjective and the psychological, to an objectivity that is not, however, the objectivity of science. Here

[21] The following distinctions quickly come to mind: ideographic and nomothetic (Allport), scientific and experiential (Rogers), B and D cognition (Maslow). These distinctions all contain corollary understandings of socialization.

[22] Consider, for example, Barth's understanding of revelation as the abolition of religion. See Barth, *Church Dogmatics*, I, Part II, 280–361.

Barth and Wieman, so different in so many ways, seem to agree.[23] Thus theological existentialism in its own way also seeks a way out of the psychic bewilderment that we have called a superego crisis and that is given a religious resolution in the conversion experience.

The decline of the psychology of religion and the appearance of theology and psychology, considered as separate disciplines, is associated with the appearance of pastoral psychology.

Pastoral psychology
and the thought of Freud

PASTORAL psychologists[24] have achieved a workable relation between theory, personal identity, and professional technique. That is, they have produced a body of literature in which religious, theological, and psychological notions are discussed; there is

[23] Wieman's work encompasses both the early psychology of religion and the later theological existentialism. It is perhaps the more bold in contrast to other theological existentialists because he attempted to draw scientific method into the very center of his thought. However, the conception of science that Wieman adopts is very similar to what Allport has called the Lockean tradition in American psychology. (See, for example, Henry Nelson Wieman, "Knowledge, Religious and Otherwise," *Journal of Religion,* XXXVIII, No. 1 [1958], 12–28.) Wieman's thought is drawn to the protection from bias that science appears to have, such that scientific method seems to occupy the same position in his thought that the doctrine of transcendence does, e.g., in Niebuhr and Barth. But it is mistaken, I think, to view Wieman's efforts to draw scientific method into the Protestant theological tradition as simply an effort to apply it to religious data. In another sense, science for Wieman has also been a metaphor for "imaginative distance," through which he could articulate his sensitivity to the theological meaning of transcendence without having to recur to substantive, static, and supernatural meanings of transcendence. The metaphor of science enabled Wieman to reflect on the rich immediacy of the processes of creative interchange. In this sense, Wieman's work is a more sensitive and effective attempt to break out of the mechanism/transcendence-of-mechanism dichotomy.

[24] I am referring primarily to the work of Carroll Wise, Seward Hiltner, Wayne Oates, and Paul Johnson.

special emphasis on the professional role and interprofessional relations; and there is a good deal of concern in this movement for the pastor's personal identity. Pastoral psychology has, since its inception, always been included, at least administratively, in most theological curricula although a deeper integration is still wanting, recalling the earlier plight of the religious education movement. Since it is a praxis rather than an academic discipline, its associations with psychology are more in terms of clinical psychology. That is to say, its uses of Freud are cast first and foremost in terms of the work of Freud and only secondarily in terms of his thought; Freud's person as a source of either psychological or religious understanding remains for the most part untouched.

Given the predominantly clinical, ministerial, and pastoral concerns with psychology and the variety of religious organizations and traditions this movement represents, pastoral psychology has remained nevertheless deeply committed to what is fundamentally a dynamic, psychoanalytically oriented psychology, one sufficiently broad to include the so-called neo-Freudian and even Rogerian perspectives. From theological existentialism—and in some few cases from liberal and neo-liberal religious thought—the pastoral psychologists have acquired their concern with the more classically theological implications of the pastoral role and its origins in the life of the church and their often direct employment of Christian theological and Biblical symbols and images and their bearing on a doctrine of man.

Perhaps most distinctive of the several emphases within pastoral psychology is the very regular and insistent way in which psychological principles and insights are employed to clarify and then eliminate moralistic and idealistic distortions of Christian faith. A corollary to this, or perhaps simply a more specific form of it, is the effort made in much of the pastoral psychology literature to mitigate compulsive imperatives to perfection and self-control. Pastoral psychologists regularly warn against and criticize moralistic coercion, especially in the pastor's work as counselor. Through the clarification of moralistic and idealistic distortions of faith, the pastoral counselor believes that he is in fact assisting in that process whereby the power of the Gospel is released into the lives of his parishioners. Consequently, the pastoral psychologist insists on the clarification of the motives and attitudes of the counselor, in order not to be drawn into or reenforce distorted aspects of his parishioners' faith.

In the moralistic and idealistic claims to which pastoral psychology is so sensitive we may detect residues of that same piety manifest in the religious conversion experience so carefully and thoroughly analyzed by the psychologists of religion. However, in lieu of religious experience, pastoral psychology substitutes— or found that its clientele had substituted—the psychotherapeutic experience; and, for the inner demands and apparently autonomous and *sui generis* nature of the religious experience, pastoral psychology substitutes the psychotherapeutic relationship, the strategies of psychotherapeutic technique, and a dynamic, psychological understanding of human development. Pastoral psychology, in Freud's words, regards men's internal experiences and actions analytically.[25]

For this reason the earlier notion of religious experience, understood as an event with a beginning, middle, and end, was submitted to critical psychological analysis and related to the entire developmental life-span of the individual. The pastoral counseling process, claimed as a theological reality by its practitioners, is the most recognizable heir to the conversion experiences of the psychology of religion. Pastoral counseling moved psychological studies of religion one step further toward a theology of the secular.

Pastoral psychology was able to dissolve this understanding of religious experience into the psychological and developmental modalities of the dynamic psychotherapies only because it be-

---

[25] I do not suggest that the psychology of religion and pastoral psychology are incompatible. It is important to note that Hiltner, Oates, and Johnson have all written books in the psychology of religion and that they do not conceive their work as fundamentally different from it. The work of Anton Boisen, however, is an important link in the relation between the psychology of religion and pastoral psychology. See Anton T. Boisen, *Exploration of the Inner World* (New York: Harper, 1936).

lieved its practice and theory to be anchored in an extremely crucial theological presupposition, namely, that faith ultimately transcends all forms of (so-called) religious experience and all forms of developmental process as well. It assumes in effect that the process of conversion, at best, could lead to faith and, at its worst, could come to constitute and, in that sense, substitute for faith.

By and large, however, pastoral psychology has remained satisfied to focus on the critical and clarifying power of dynamic psychology in its operational dimensions and has not concerned itself with systematic theological formulations of the problem of understanding faith in relation to developmental and psycho-therapeutic modes of experience. This task it has allowed to remain in the hands of the systematic and dogmatic theologians. This no doubt accounts for much of the mistrust and dissatisfaction that sometimes exists between these two groups, and it has often produced a fruitless series of mutual indictments: the theologians inducing guilt in the pastoral psychologists for not being sufficiently "theological" and the pastoral psychologists protesting against the operational isolation ("ivory tower") of the theologians.

Summary

IN this brief review I have attempted to establish some continuity between the earlier discussions of theology and psychology and two other efforts to deal with the same general areas of thought. There are many, many differences between the theological material, the psychology of religion, and pastoral psychology. But, despite the many important differences, there is a point of similarity between them—a general structure of experience, in particular, a structure of guilt, that at some points is considered by each to be the fundamental problem to which each gives its own special solution.

At least at this point, things are a bit more of a piece than they seem, especially from within a particular discipline. Perhaps this accounts in part for the singular inability of theology and psychology, for example, to locate a ground of common concern around which to think through their respective functions and relations. Perhaps one of the reasons for the apparent magnitude of the alleged differences between them lies in the desire to define this ground in terms of conclusions and the failure to see that, in fact, what they share most of all is a common question, a common problem—a common perception of "what is wrong."

Returning momentarily to those struggles between the pastoral psychologists and the theologians, we conclude in a fanciful manner. In those reciprocally accusatory gestures between the pastoral psychologists and the theologians, do we not have a reenactment, in a theological context, of a scenario already noted in some of the more obvious ideological infighting between the objective and the subjective psychologies? Here, the pastoral psychologists play the role of the psychoanalysts, speaking of personal life, interpersonal encounters, the importance of "nondefensive" attitudes, and the like. And the theologians play the role of the behaviorists who, fearful of the enigmas and ambiguities of subjectivity and with less of an obligation to demonstrate a sense of professional identity, seek a realm of cognitive objectivity that they endow with a special priority, removing that realm permanently from any of the more immanental motions of the self.

Perhaps these two scenarios are only subplots in a more general drama: the behaviorists with their objectivity, the psychoanalysts with their subjectivity, and the theologians who nod in a friendly way to each en route to their own reality that transcends both. Do we have anything more than a romantic triangle, a family romance, displaced to the level of method? Perhaps it is really only a family quarrel, the father and mother arguing late at night: the detached, objective husband-theologians and/or behaviorists arguing with their participative, intuitive psychoanalytic wives.

But it may not be an entirely facetious notion. For theological existentialism defines the methodological relation between theology and psychology by placing the polarity of behaviorism and psychoanalysis in a triangular relation to its own work. As noted, when these theologians speak of psychology, they generally identify psychology with the subject-object schema; and they find it epistemologically defective for this reason, at least as a resource for the theological task of defining faith. The psychologies that are most likely to be cited are usually behaviorism and psychoanalysis. Faith transcends those experiential processes most accessible to empirical and dynamic psychologies.

A still more sober notation may be possible. Both behaviorism and theological existentialism share a consistently mechanistic reading of Freud, in addition to their common quest for a realm of objective certainty the status of which will not be contaminated by subjective, dynamic, or affective elements. Does this mean that behaviorism and theological existentialism share certain dynamic features? If the former is an effort to predict and control the external environment, might not theological existentialism, whenever its doctrine of transcendence acquires mechanistic overtones, be an attempt to predict and control the internal environment? Both avoid a direct encounter with the internal environment—Watson through his critique of James (the rejection of consciousness and introspection) and Barth through his critique of Schleiermacher (the rejection of feelings of dependency).

Yet this attempt to master the inner and outer world can take the form of repression—the repressive mastery of the perceptual field or of what we have called the dynamic dimension of the self. Here the theological doctrine of transcendence bears on our discussion of the superego. In asserting a radical transcendence of the superego rather than its contextual transformation, theological existentialism initiates a therapeutic encounter with the superego and, at the same time, denies this encounter. This approach to the psychological materials, raising as it does an alternative reading of Freud, returns us to the mainstream of the argument. Is there a way to approach the internality of the self through understanding and interpretation rather than through a voluntaristic approach? Freud's thought makes possible such understanding; and despite theological readings of Freud, it is Freud's work that makes possible a re-understanding of the notion of transcendence.

We now turn to these issues directly and ask: How can we further open up the meaning of transcendence in relation to these psychological processes? Is there a third reading of Freud that gives us clues to the dynamics of self-transcendence? We will allow this reading to emerge by discussing three recent responses to Freud that reinterpret psychoanalysis in relation to theological meanings.

Part Two

---

*Post-Protestant theological
experimentation with Freud*

Five: Three post-Protestant
interpretations of Freud

Introduction

A THIRD, iconic reading of Freud has far-reaching consequences for theological existentialism, consequences that cannot be met by simply adjusting the doctrine of transcendence to psychological insights and findings—as if, in Kierkegaard's words, China could be assigned to another place. The very status and viability of the doctrine of transcendence becomes questionable.

A third reading breaks down the methodological segregation of theology and psychology so characteristic of theological existentialism. It may well be that theology once again can become a "discipline"—but not until it comes to terms with the difficulties in its own house. It is, for example, no longer feasible to speak of anthropological questions and theological answers (Tillich) or of testing the tenets of Christian faith in the crucible of historical analysis (Niebuhr). Such extremely definite separations between faith and culture are no longer possible. On the other hand, the very suspension of these programs may be a creative resource heretofore obscured by the very loyalty to them. There is some precedent for this in theological tradition; after all, Staupitz was really on Luther's side when he tried to help him be a little less religious.

One of the specific consequences of a third reading is that the initial categories drawing together theological and psychological assertions into dialogue no longer serve simply as heuristic guidelines for organizing statements about the self. Instead, in what follows, the categories—structure, dynamics, self and society, and methodology—become focal points in terms of which the problems resulting from an iconic reading of Freud acquire special clarity. Until now only the instruments of dialogue and of psychological criticism, they now become questions in themselves or, as I prefer to put it, dilemmas. They are dilemmas occasioned by the at first heuristic but subsequently more binding introduction of a psychological perspective on theological understanding of the self. Further discussion of these dilemmas is now necessary in order to pursue the meaning of transcendence beyond that given it by theological existentialism.

Our starting point, then, will be with the question of dynamics. Posing this problem leads directly to a group of writers whose work I wish to describe, unfortunately in rather cumbersome fashion, as post-Protestant theological experimentation with Freud—Norman O. Brown, David Bakan, and Philip Rieff.[1] The dilemmas created by an expanded psychoanalytic critique of theology are precisely the issues with which this group is centrally concerned. Their writings carry forward and make explicit both the theological concerns and the implicit psychological assumptions of theological existentialism. These men have been drawn to an exceptionally profound appreciation of Freud's thought and work (and, perhaps, his person as well), even though their discussions do not arise from a professional interest in psychoanalysis. They are concerned instead with the impact of Freud's thought and work on current moral and existential understanding, and they find this double concern intersecting with the meaning of religion and its decline. Stimulated by Freud to draw

[1] Norman O. Brown, *Life Against Death: The Psychoanalytical Meaning of History* (New York: Random House, 1959), and *Love's Body* (New York: Random House, 1966); Bakan, *Freud, and The Duality of Human Existence* (Chicago: Rand McNally, 1966); and Rieff, *Freud, and The Triumph of the Therapeutic: Uses of Faith after Freud* (New York: Harper & Row, 1966).

certain irrefutable conclusions about the inadequacy of precisely those theological formulations that I have been examining, they are nonetheless equally unwilling to pursue the problem along lines already set forth by so many interpretations of Freud. The result has been a number of highly idiosyncratic, brilliant analyses of the problem of Freud and theology in its most advanced and extreme phases.

The writings of Brown and Bakan emphasize the religious image of the Devil as a link between theological definitions of transcendence and the psychological constructs that we have been discussing. The work of Philip Rieff raises the question of a collapse of transcendence into the immanental modes of mass society; it also gives us a first glimpse into what is substantially the argument of the final chapter, that psychoanalysis can become a hermeneutic for cultural and religious self-understanding.

Transcendence, fantasy,
and the psychology of repression

THUS far we have concluded that, anthropologically, transcendence means going beyond repression and a predominantly harsh superego orientation; and, methodologically, it means finding a means of self-understanding that is neither entirely objective nor subjective—going beyond the subject-object dichotomy, if you will. From the perspective of psychology, repression, the harsh superego, and the bifurcation of knowing into rigid objectivity and subjectivity are all of a piece. Together they constitute the psychological form of the human problematic to which theological existentialism is addressed.

"Transference" is another connecting term for these psychological and theological considerations. On the one hand, it is a generic term organizing various aspects of Freud's thought, especially those pertaining to such regressive psychological processes as repression and the harsh superego; on the other hand, it has also come to mean, by way of our third reading of Freud's psychology, that immediacy and subjectivity that is never "merely psychological" and that theology implicitly speaks of in its discussions of immanence.

Central to all of this is a very simple question. On the one hand, theology in effect urges the overcoming of repression. On the other hand, we also know that repression is overcome through a particular kind of participation in those processes and materials from which it originates—that is, through examination of the phenomenon of transference. Therefore, we need to ask, What psychological consequences follow when the theological imperative to transcend repression is carried forward dynamically? This question, which theological existentialism does not ask, is the basis of all post-Protestant analyses of Freud. Their answer to this question, like the question itself, begins with dynamic, rather than structural, social, or methodological considerations.

The first consequence, in a psychodynamic but also in a formal sense, is a release of image and fantasy. A dynamic implementation of the theological imperative to transcendence calls for an imaginative immersion in the materials of repression that make their appearance through the transference relation, symptoms and dreams, but especially dreams. Dreams indicate that repression has not yet won the day. Dream and fantasy are the new materials of transcendence. Perhaps a better formulation for all of this might be that immersion in the materials of repression produces a capacity to appreciate the presence and significance of fantasy and image or, better still, an awareness of their close and perhaps even reciprocal relation and interconnectedness with the higher processes of theological thinking. What is clearly not in question here is whether the theology of the sort under discussion is a defense against the experience of fantasy and image. Theological doctrines may or may not serve as defenses against deeper aspects of affectivity and their accompanying imaginative forms; the point is, rather, the manner in which fantasy is imaginatively received and subsequently understood.

Reductive readings of psychoanalysis typically polarize this problem into reality and a restricted view of fantasy; in this single methodological gesture, they often overlook the wider implications of fantasy itself. The mechanistic view asserts that the reality principle governs an adjustment of the inner life to the everyday world, in which case the pleasure principle contrasts permanently with the reality principle, for it is the latter that regulates the inner world of fantasy, reducing it to reality. Fantasy is thereby conceived as "the merely psychological" activities of daydreaming or, as the vernacular has it, an "escape mechanism." This polarization of fantasy and reality corresponds to what our theologians have called the subject-object dichotomy, and they rightly urge its transcendence. However, such transcendence must come from a deepening of our appreciation of fantasy and not through a theological "third" dimension that simply hovers above the processes of fantasy formation and fantasy analysis. I will speak below of a religious or expanded view of fantasy and inquire whether or not it is the deepest and most appropriate source for what eventually becomes theological statement.

In preparation for that question, let us briefly turn to the work of Herbert Marcuse,[2] for fantasy is the point at which he develops his critique of Freud and in so doing introduces his recommendation of a nonrepressive reality principle. Marcuse first sketches the historical development of the notion of reason as Logos in the formation of modern, Western, scientific rationality. In its psychological implications, Logos presupposes an ego-self that intends the progressively rational transformation of the human and natural environment. The ego "experiences being as 'provocation,' as 'project' . . . the ego becomes preconditioned for mastering action."[3] It is an aggressive ego intending the sort of knowledge that best facilitates domination and achievement.

Whatever the implications of the original Greek conception of Logos as the essence of being, since the canonization of the

[2] Herbert Marcuse, *Eros and Civilization: A Philosophical Inquiry into Freud* (New York: Vintage Books, 1962).

[3] *Ibid.*, p. 100.

Aristotelian logic, the term merges with the idea of ordering, classifying, mastering reason. And this idea of reason becomes increasingly antagonistic to those faculties and attitudes which are receptive rather than productive, which tend toward gratification rather than transcendence—which remain strongly committed to the pleasure principle. They appear as the unreasonable and irrational that must be conquered and contained in order to serve the progress of reason.

But the logic of domination does not triumph unchallenged. The philosophy which epitomizes the antagonistic relation between subject and object also retains the image of their reconciliation. The restless labor of the transcending subject terminates in the ultimate unity of subject and object: the idea of "being-in-and-for-itself," existing in its own fulfillment. The Logos of gratification contradicts the Logos of alienation: the effort to harmonize the two animates the inner history of Western metaphysics.[4]

These psychical effects of scientific rationality appear in the social sphere to produce domination and servitude, the relation of master to slave. Epistemologically the logic of domination "reduces the units of thought to signs and symbols," and "the laws of thought have finally become techniques of calculation and manipulation."[5]

In its most advanced positions, Marcuse argues, Freud's thought partakes of this "philosophical dynamic," especially at the point of the crucial distinction between the reality principle and the pleasure principle. Therefore, in its most advanced positions Freud's psychology also articulates with the epistemological pattern so prevalent in theological existentialism, the subject-object relation. Marcuse then points out that, in the notion of fantasy, Freud came upon one kind of mental activity that retains a high degree of freedom from the reality principle—or, as we have said, from the subject-object schema. Again the logic of domination asserts itself.

[4] *Ibid.*, p. 101.
[5] *Ibid.*

The establishment of the reality principle causes a division and mutilation of the mind which fatefully determines its entire development. The mental process formerly unified in the pleasure ego is now split: its main stream is channeled into the domain of the reality principle and brought into line with its requirements. Thus conditioned, this part of the mind obtains the monopoly of interpreting, manipulating, and altering reality—of governing remembrance and oblivion, even of defining what reality is and how it should be used and altered.[6]

As a result, "reason prevails: it becomes unpleasant but useful and correct; fantasy remains pleasant but becomes useless, untrue—a mere play, daydreaming."[7] Or, as we have said, fantasy becomes "merely psychological."

However, Marcuse also argues that Freud made possible a reunderstanding of reality and pleasure, one that takes cognizance of "the image of the immediate unity between the universal and the particular under the rule of the pleasure principle."[8] In such a reinterpretation of Freud as this, fantasy becomes the medium whereby the imperative to transcendence can be realized. Fantasy remains the last outpost to prevail against what Tillich has called the bourgeois principle.[9] Marcuse concludes:

Freud's metapsychology here restores imagination to its rights. As a fundamental, independent mental process, fantasy has a truth of its own, which corresponds to an experience of its own —namely, the surmounting of the antagonistic human reality. Imagination envisions the reconciliation of the individual with the whole, of desire with realization, of happiness with reason.

[6] *Ibid.*, p. 128.

[7] *Ibid.*, p. 129.

[8] *Ibid.*

[9] Of Tillich's use of the phrase "the bourgeois principle," James Luther Adams says: ". . . The characteristic positive preoccupation following from the bourgeois principle has been the creation of means of objective control; and this preoccupation has displaced the intuitive grasping of intrinsic values" ("Tillich's Concept of the Protestant Era," in Paul Tillich, *The Protestant Era* [Chicago: University of Chicago Press, 1948], p. 282). The Freudian term that corresponds to Tillich's bourgeois principle is the reality principle.

While this harmony has been removed into utopia by the established reality principle, fantasy insists that it must and can become real, that behind the illusion lies *knowledge.* The truths of imagination are first realized when fantasy itself takes form, when it creates a universe of perception and comprehension— a subjective and at the same time objective universe.[10]

On the basis of this restoration of the imagination, Marcuse then speaks of an erotic imagination. Although he pursues the possibility of nonrepressive social forms primarily at the point of the artistic imagination, we wish to speak of fantasy in such a way as to at least assume the possibility of a religious imagination. We do not have to discuss art and religion, nor need we side with or against Marcuse's moral outrage at the brutality of the Western theological formulation of transcendence in order now to ask a second question regarding the theological imperative to transcend repression: Precisely what kind of images are released when the doctrine of transcendence is permitted to include the possibility of such an understanding of fantasy?

We have in fact already approached this problem in discussing the dynamic and methodological aspects of Freud's personal relationship with Wilhelm Fliess. Through that largely regressive relationship, Freud acquired sufficient personal support and integration to discover the oedipal features of his own life and to explore this discovery in conjunction with the lives of his patients. From a psychodynamic point of view, it is correct to say that he also encountered the superego, thereby successfully countering its repressive energies. This dynamic advance coincided with shifts in his methodology, especially a disenchantment with prevailing mechanistic modes of scientific work; and disenchantment produced a search for a new psychological method, one appropriate to the newly recognized clinical reality —the method of free association and interpretation, as these take form in relation to transference. As several observers have noted, the developmental significance of this discovery consisted in part

[10] Marcuse, *Eros,* p. 130.

in an integration of anal, psychosexual components into the newly discovered, wider genital organization. For our purposes, it is also important to note that the discovery of the Oedipus complex is also a rediscovery of the significance of the mother and the feminine in the entire psychic life of the self. The superego—which Freud called the heir to the Oedipus complex—is an internationalization of the struggle of the son with the father, and behind this struggle lies the presence of the mother.

As Erik Erikson, Norman Brown, and David Bakan have pointed out,[11] the figure of the Devil is a religious image embodying significant anal features. In psychoanalytic psychology, it seems, anality covers a multitude of sins, linked as it is with the death instinct, the harsh superego, and repression; the death instinct energizes the repressive process, that loop of destructive energy that the superego redirects back from the environment and into the ego. So we have a duality of processes: on the one hand, repression, the harsh superego, and the death instinct, which together I have called transference; and, on the other hand, the overcoming of repression, the overcoming of the harshness of the superego, and the life instinct, which theology by implication refers to as transcendence. The logic of these interconnections suggests that the image of the Devil and its peculiar psychodynamics is closely related to theological formulations of transcendence.

These considerations lend further support to an earlier observation, that both theology and Watsonian behaviorism find mechanistic considerations central to Freud's psychology. In so doing, both pursue what Marcuse calls "the logic of domination" while attempting to be critically alert to precisely this problem. If we were to say that behaviorism, as a methodological stance, is an attempt in its psychological aspects to dominate the external environment of the individual, then it would follow that theology is an attempt to dominate the internal, intrapsychic environ-

[11] Erik H. Erikson, *Young Man Luther: A Study in Psychoanalysis and History* (New York: W. W. Norton, 1958), pp. 60–74, 243–250; Brown and Bakan are cited above, n. 1.

ment of the individual. A third reading of Freud and an expanded understanding of fantasy complicate this simplistic polarization. To read Freud's psychology as merely mechanistic is, in effect, to call him the Devil. Yet it is precisely psychoanalytic psychology that, when properly expanded, provides a therapeutic perspective on this dilemma. Without this perspective, theology becomes demonic. With it, however, doctrine discovers its true datum and object. Theology's true object is not the religious experience of the early psychologists of religion, nor is it the theological existence of theological existentialism. It is the religious image that unites the predominant affectivity of the experience of conversion with the predominantly cognitive features of faith and belief.

The three theological readings of Freud now to be considered attempt to offer solutions to what I have called the dynamic dilemma as this has been derived from psychological discussion of theological existentialism. In this respect, the work of Brown, Bakan, and Rieff is markedly similar. It is their respective responses to the problems of structure and socialization that distinguish them. Each proposes a thoroughly different way out of the dynamics dilemma, and through their work the problem of theological response to Freud is carried forward to its extreme conclusion. At that point, the analytic force of psychoanalytic psychology is exhausted.

In his relentless criticism of Freud's "genital organization," Norman O. Brown conceives a way out that is really a way back, a regressive reappropriation of the primary dynamics of the psyche and an eschatological dissolution of the superego, creating, in Susan Sontag's phrase, an "eschatology of immanence."[12] David Bakan's position is more qualified. According to him, the superego is suspended through "beholding" the religious images that it represses; through this beholding, the superego becomes a link rather than a barrier between the self and its wider social, historical, and futuric emotional investments. Philip Rieff's argu-

[12] Susan Sontag, *Against Interpretation* (New York: Farrar, Straus & Giroux, 1966), p. 262.

ment for the appearance of "psychological man" at the hands of psychoanalytic psychology presupposes the "decline of the super-ego" and its permanent erosion in the context of mass society. In this articulate and compelling reading of Freud, theological dis-cussions of the collapse of the transcendent—most notably those of the "death of God" group—articulate directly with the psy-chological literature on the decline of the superego.

Perhaps this group has earned the title "neo-Freudian" even more than the neo-Freudians themselves, for, in a spirit that always remains fundamentally appreciative, they attempt to pen-etrate the deepest strands of Freud's thought, isolating there something that they regard to be fundamentally positive regard-ing the nature of self-understanding. They are students of Freud caught between the claims of his thought and the crisis in theo-logical meaning. So caught, they have willingly settled for the difficult and perhaps impossible task of working their way out—not by making revisions, but by refusing to allow closure to re-place a deepening sense of ambiguity. Their work is the more pro-found and, as it happens, of its own necessity eventuates in what can only be called a religious appreciation of Freud's work. That turn of events is, of course, the argument of this study.

Norman O. Brown:
Transcendence as regression
to infantile delight

THE work of Norman O. Brown is incomprehensible apart from the theological materials that we have been discussing. Although Brown's work is clearly post-Protestant in the sense that he re-jects reductive, mechanistic readings of Freud, his work also re-tains close connections with the Protestant tradition, perhaps even more so than the work of Thomas Altizer or other death-of-

God theologians who make use of the thought of Freud. Brown has undertaken a thoroughgoing and systematic reinterpretation of Freud, but his solution does not lie in collapsing the Protestant notion of transcendence into immanental and psychological categories and modes of experience; rather, he inverts transcendence to create a radical, immanental eschatology. He converts the structural focus of theological existentialism into sheer, primary dynamics. Brown romanticizes Freud's naturalism to give us an eschatological psychoanalysis of history that, for all its primary mysticism, remains under the control of the Protestant view of the meaning of transcendence. Of all the theological reinterpretations of Freud, Brown's is the one that most vigorously attempts to remain faithful to the premises of both. In the long run, however, it is psychoanalysis that gives ground. His final conclusions remain eschatological and, as such, are inaccessible to psychodynamic, developmental, and moral considerations. But that is the way Brown wants it.

Brown's first step is to enter Freud's world at the point of religion, noting that his psychology of religion must be understood first of all as an extension of his psychology of the person and only secondarily as an attack on religion. Neurosis is the universal condition of man and not an occasional aberration of a few individuals. The nucleus of constructs already discussed—repression, superego, Oedipus complex, transference—is therefore the conceptual equipment of the historian: "The pattern of history exhibits a dialectic not hitherto recognized by historians, the dialectic of neurosis."[13] These constructs are also the equipment of the theologian, for "the link between the theory of neurosis and the theory of history is the theory of religion."[14] Freud's psychology of religion is also a psychology of history, and neurosis is the "psychoanalytical analogue" of the theological doctrine of original sin.

It is the doctrine of repression that makes possible a theory

[13] Brown, *Life Against Death,* p. 12.
[14] *Ibid.*

of religion as a crucial aspect of human behavior. Like dreams, symptoms, and slips of the tongue, religion is an "expression, distorted by repression, of the immortal desires of the human heart." It is the "heart of the mystery of the human heart."

> Psychoanalysis is equipped to study the mystery of the human heart, and must recognize religion to be the heart of the mystery. But psychoanalysis can go beyond religion only if it sees itself as completing what religion tries to do, namely, make the unconscious conscious; then psychoanalysis would be the science of original sin. Psychoanalysis is in a position to define the error in religion only after it has recognized its truth.[15]

At this point, then, psychoanalysis and Christian theology share a common understanding of the enemy of man—it is religion, the universal neurosis of mankind, the transference-God. It is what Tillich has called the God of theological theism and what Niebuhr means by the Christ who *was* expected.

At this same point, however, theology and psychoanalysis also cease to resemble each other. Like Christian theology, psychoanalysis lies inside the neurosis. The cure that it offers and the theory that it advances are both at many points no less "the disease" than is theology. But Brown finally concludes that psychoanalytical consciousness is a higher stage in the general consciousness of mankind and that it is, therefore, better equipped to provide the means for stepping outside the neurosis.

> Christian theology, or at least Augustinian theology, recognizes human restlessness and discontent, the *cor irrequietum,* as the psychological source of the historical process. But Christian theology, to account for the origin of human discontent and to indicate a solution, has to take man out of this real world, out of the animal kingdom, and inculcate into him delusions of grandeur. And thus Christian theology commits its own worst sin, the sin of pride.[16]

The difference between Christian theology and psychoanalysis

[15] *Ibid.*, pp. 13–14.
[16] *Ibid.*, p. 16.

lies not in their understandings of the human condition, but in their respective strategies of reparation. In particular, the difference lies in their approaches to the dynamics of the universal neurosis—repression and the superego. And that means, theologically, the dynamics of immanence. Psychoanalysis insists on immanence through its proposal that one begins to step outside the neurosis by stepping more deeply inside it. This strategy underlies Brown's second methodological step, a dynamic analysis of the image of the Devil.

If religion links neurosis to history and psychoanalysis to society, what is the link between religion and its deepest psychological roots? When Brown speaks of religion in this context, he means Protestantism and, when he speaks of psychoanalysis, he means the theory of infantile sexuality. The link or connecting term between infantile sexuality and Protestantism is the image of the Devil. Thus Brown has made two absolutely crucial modifications in psychoanalytic theory. First, he distinguishes between the clinical method of orthodox or classical psychoanalysis, on the one hand, and historical studies, on the other.

> Vulgar psychoanalytical dogmatists—those for whom psychoanalysis is a closed system rather than a problem—seem to believe that the adult anal character is to be understood as a fixation to a trauma occurring in the process of infantile toilet training. . . .
> But whatever the merits this theory may have as a working hypothesis in dealing with neurotically abnormal individuals, when confronted with the anal character as a socio-historical phenomenon it is useless.[17]

In attempting to correct a reductive, "diagnostic" understanding of psychoanalytic categories, Brown in effect rejects a mechanistic reading of Freud. In so doing, he transposes psychoanalytic categories into historical and finally (as we shall see) eschatological ones. Brown elevates psychological categories into the

[17] *Ibid.,* pp. 204–205.

status of theological ones. The image of the Devil becomes an historical and not a clinical problem.

This does not, however, prevent him from brilliant psychoanalytic speculations—speculations so brilliant that no doubt Freud himself would have been pleased with them. For Brown's second modification is a critical revision of psychoanalytic studies of the Devil. Such studies, he argues, have emphasized the oedipal nature of the Devil to the neglect of certain anal features. Brown examines the anal imagery in Luther's writings about the Devil, noting that Protestantism experienced the Devil with peculiar immediacy, power, and pervasiveness, concluding that Luther is therefore in this respect the most representative man of his age. "It is Luther's grossly concrete image of the anal character of the Devil that made the privy the appropriate scene for his critical religious experience." Or, again: "Protestantism was born in the temple of the Devil, and it found God again in extremest alienation from God."[18] The image of the Devil is the clue to the psychodynamics of Protestantism.

Brown's analysis, at least at this point, might be characterized as an incipiently dynamic phenomenology of the religious image, a psychoanalytic hermeneutic, one, however, that quickly gives way to psychoanalytic demythologizing. So the image of the Devil is a mythical archetype that says something that we cannot say in any other way. Brown then tries to say it in other ways. The main features of the Devil are his restlessness, his mastery of all techniques, and the association of both of these with death. The image of the Devil covers a multitude of sins, and Brown detects its dynamic equivalent in such places as Aristotelian and Thomistic understandings of natural virtue and natural reason, which make reason and mastery guides to the moral life. He also detects the Devil in the deeper psychological forces behind the formation of capitalism and science and in Protestant theological rejections of justification by works. The

[18] *Ibid.*, p. 209.

desire to effect good works receives projective elaboration in the restlessness and mastery of the Devil.

Brown argues, first, that much of Protestantism's psychological meaning lies in an especially courageous and fearless encounter with anality, and, secondly, that its constructive solutions retain anal overtones. But a theological doctrine of the demonic, as a statement of the experience of the Devil, is also an attempt to respond to the developmental problem of anality. What relation does this theological problem have to the doctrine of God and God's transcendence? For Luther, as for the neo-Reformation theological tradition, God's mercy lies beyond his wrath. The Protestant experience of evil was so intense and pervasive that it required an image of God as exceedingly transcendent, for only such a God could comprehend the pervasiveness of evil in this world. Brown points out that for Luther the drama of redemption was not conceived as a struggle between man and God, but rather as a struggle between God and the Devil over the will of man. If God is so conceived to be prior to, or above, or beyond the sphere of the demonic, we must ask, developmentally, what is beyond anality?

Brown's most dynamic point, the anality of the image of the Devil, bears on the Oedipus complex and the developmentally subsequent formation of the superego. The death instinct energizes the sadism of the superego toward the masochistic ego. The image of the Devil is, therefore, also an image of the harsh superego. However, the harsh superego functions dynamically to keep the ego from "seeing" more deeply into its own dynamics: the Devil, it would seem, is also an image of repression, of psychological blindness. Furthermore, the purpose of oedipal repression lies not only in reducing conflict between father and son, but also in obscuring the original occasion of this conflict, which is a struggle over possession of the mother. The Devil, therefore, is also a symbol for deflecting the attention of the ego from the feminine sectors of the ego's relationships. To successfully encounter the Devil is to successfully counter repression; and it is also to discover the Oedipus complex, which means the discovery of the image of the mother. It is the image of the mother, then, that lies beyond anality.

This dynamic analysis generates the problem of structure, and for Brown structure means "genital organization" or genital tyranny, the touchstone for his systematic rereading of Freud and the point at which his work both continues and departs from theological existentialism. Brown argues that in Freud's understanding of the genital organization—that is, the conclusive instinctual organization authenticated by the formation of the superego—the component or partial instincts consisting of oral, anal, and phallic libido are

> . . . narrowed in range, concentrated on one particular (the genital) organ, and subordinated to an aim derived not from the pleasure-principle but from the reality-principle, namely, propagation (in Freudian terminology, the genital function). Then the pattern of normal adult sexuality (in Freud's terminology, genital organization) is a tyranny of one component in infantile sexuality, a tyranny which suppresses some of the other components altogether and subordinates the rest to itself.[19]

This tyranny is the result of repression, for it permits pregenital components to exist only in repressed condition alongside the conscious genital organization. It is the victory of one part over the whole. Brown's call for the abolition of repression is therefore an imperative to recover the infantile delight of infantile play. Developmentally, this means that Brown handles the structural problem by a principle of radical negation, of radical regression. However, the kind of regression he commends is not clinically observable. It is no regression in the service of the ego, a point of view that simply perpetuates the problem of organization at a different level. Indeed, like theological existentialism, Brown rejects the very notion of development itself. For if the problem of history is the problem of repression, then to personalize and to psychologize history by means of the notion of development simply reestablishes repressive history in a more

[19] *Ibid.*, p. 27.

subtle, internalized way. That, in fact, is precisely what Freud "officially" did in proposing the notion of the superego.

Starting at this point, Brown systematically and exhaustively reinterprets Freud. "Instinctual dialectics" are preferred to "instinctual dualism," the latter imply reintroducing the genital organization in a manner dissociated from infantile sexuality. The psychoanalytic distinction between object-choice and identification and its notion of ego boundaries suggests a firm distinction between ego and external reality, between internal and external. Brown reformulates these by means of the position of the mother in the eschatological regression. For the object of infantile delight is the mother—an image lying even more deeply in the unconscious than that of the father. Through the suggestion of a regressive reunion behind or beyond the genital organization, we find Brown attempting to present in psychoanalytic terms the theological imperative to transcend the subject-object relation. For the subject-object relation, either as an epistemological or ontological formulation, presupposes the firm distinction and separation of ego and reality that Freud called the reality principle and that theology insists must be transcended. It presupposes a firm ego "over against" reality and existence. In this sense, Brown's notions of infantile delight and magical body—and, more recently, his emphasis on fusion and participation—are eschatological images that connote the deeper, underlying unity in human experience which theology has defined as the hope of resurrection. Only subject-object thinking construes the superego as an "introject," as tyranny. And yet it is psychoanalysis and not theology that has developed a vocabulary and a manner of exploring these deeper experiential elements.

The way out, therefore, is finally the dialectical imagination —or, more recently, symbolical consciousness. Only this kind of thinking can discern infantile delight behind the genital organization, a dialectic of instincts beneath instinctual dualism, and an erotic sense of reality behind the aggressive interpositions of the Devil. "By 'dialectical' I mean an activity of consciousness struggling to circumvent the limitations imposed by the formal-

logical law of contradiction."[20] Contrary to mechanistic readings
of Freud, in which a dream symbol is the functional equivalent
of an infantile wish, Brown finds in such psychoanalytic notions
as free association and overdetermination grounds for concluding
that the basic structure of Freud's thought is committed to dialectics—a mode of consciousness in which a plurality of images is
permitted to intersect simultaneously without being considered
meaningless. The dialectical imagination makes it possible to
step outside the neurosis. It is Brown's third reading of Freud.

In an important sense, Protestant theology has mounted a
strong imperative to do just this, to step outside the neurosis, to
transcend repression, to transform the superego structure of human guilt. It appears in Reinhold Niebuhr's attempt to develop
a theory of myth that transcends the univocal tendencies of science and rationalistic philosophy. His notion of the dramas of
history anticipates a dialectic imagination, and his shattering of
the self can be seen as a preliminary attack on the genital organization. Tillich's struggle to protect a theory of symbolism
from controlling reason also anticipates Brown's argument for a
symbolical consciousness. Brown does not collapse transcendence
into immanence, nor does he psychologize theology. What he
has done instead is to translate the imperative to transcendence
without essential modification into the immanental-eschatologi-
cal imagery of infantile sexuality. He draws the human condition back, first along the developmental axis and then subsequently out of it entirely, in an effort to transform those modes
of thought that insist on distinctions (the methodological equivalence of ego boundaries)—the developmental as opposed to the
existential, the psychological as opposed to the theological, the
ultimate as opposed to the preliminary. Brown starts where
theology starts—with the problem of the transcendence of the
superego—and then attempts to go beyond by going back.

Yet Brown's eschatology is one of immanence and not transcendence. In his rhetoric a dynamically opaque Reformation

[20] *Ibid.*, pp. 318–319.

piety at last becomes luminous. He lifts the veil to expose what Protestantism knew all the time but simply could not say. In Reinhold Niebuhr's discussions of God as personality and in Tillich's manner of thinking about the kerygma (a thing to be interpreted) we see what Brown calls "literalism."

> The return to symbolism would be the end of the Protestant era, the end of Protestant literalism. Symbolism in its pre-Protestant form consisted of typological, figural, allegorical interpretations, of both scripture and liturgy. But the great Protestant Reformers were very explicit in their condemnation of the typological method: "the literal sense of Scripture alone is the whole essence of faith and of Christian theology." *Sola fide, sola litera:* faith is faith in the letter.[21]

In a sense, Brown truly proposes a therapeutic for both theological method and theological anthropology. Compare these remarks by Reinhold Niebuhr:

> The hope of the resurrection nevertheless embodies the very genius of the Christian idea of the historical. On the one hand it implies that eternity will fulfill and not annul the richness and variety which the temporal process has elaborated. On the other it implies that the condition of finiteness in freedom . . . is a problem for which there is no solution by any human power. Only God can solve this problem. From the human perspective it can only be solved by faith. All structures of meaning and realms of coherence, which human reason constructs, face the chasm of meaninglessness when men discover that the tangents of meaning transcend the limits of existence. Only faith has an answer for this problem.[22]

with this statement by Norman Brown:

> Symbolical consciousness begins with the perception of the invisible reality of our present situation: we are dead and our life is hid. Real life is life after death, or resurrection. The deadness

[21] Brown, *Love's Body*, pp. 191–192.
[22] Niebuhr, *Nature and Destiny of Man*, II, 295.

with which we are dead here now is the real death; of which
literal death is only a shadow. . . .[23]

Finally, however, Brown's way out is no different from that
of his Protestant theological forebears, for his critique of the
genital organization is as much a flight from the superego as is
the Protestant transcendence of it. Nor does Brown have any
need to concern himself with either development or therapy, two
of the central contributions of psychoanalytic psychology. Because he ignores the therapeutic force of Freud's work and
thought, things that Brown has brilliantly drawn together are
followed by new divisions. It is all genital organization or magical
body, all literalism or symbolical consciousness, all detachment
or participation. Brown's debt to a structural transcendent forces
him, as it does theological existentialism, to understand immanence eschatologically but not psychologically; again like the
theological existentialists, he is more concerned with the end-
states that must remain opaque to the ongoing vicissitudes of personal existence. Brown returns us to the initial problem: How
can image and thought bring transcendence to psychic depth?

David Bakan: Transcendence
as transgenerational ego identification

Two books by David Bakan show deep concern with the life and
thought of Freud and their bearing on religion generally, but
especially on Protestantism in its historical, institutional, and
also theological aspects.[24] Like Brown and Erikson, to whom
Bakan is indebted, he is fascinated with Protestantism and finds
in the psychology of its leadership and its primary spiritual perceptions lessons for contemporary self-understanding. Like them,

[23] Brown, *Love's Body*, p. 207.
[24] See note 1, above.

he commends an expanded reading of Freud that depends on the by now common set of nuclear considerations—the image of the Devil, the psychoanalytic understanding of anality, and certain stereotypical conceptions of science. In so doing, however, Bakan creates a unique reading of Freud; he retains through a consideration of transference just that dynamic perspective that Brown rejects, and, most important of all, by insisting on a permanent status for female sexuality in religious understanding, he introduces a methodological innovation of exceptional importance for the Protestant theological categories of immanence and transcendence.

The first book, *Sigmund Freud and the Jewish Mystical Tradition,* is a closely argued and carefully documented effort to discover the roots of psychoanalysis in eastern European Jewish mysticism. The core of this argument contains a discussion of three closely related phenomena: the experience of the Devil, the function of the superego, and Freud's discovery of transference. In a section entitled "The Devil as Suspended Superego," Bakan notes that the clinical relationship, because it permits and encourages the appearance of repressed feelings, attitudes, and thoughts, is likely to be perceived by those unfamiliar with its purposes as diabolical, and the physician is therefore likely to be perceived as a tempter. Seen from the outside, the physician appears to have the power to make people think and behave in ways contrary to the moral structure of their personality. The dynamic meaning of transference is therefore identical with the dynamic meaning of the image of the Devil. Bakan argues that Freud himself underwent a personal crisis, and in the midst of it he made a pact with the Devil—that is, he immersed himself in the metaphor of the Devil; in so doing he immersed himself in a psychologically meaningful way in the alienated portions of his own inner experience.

> In order to understand how it is possible for the suppressed material to rise to consciousness, let us consider how this is conceived in the framework of psychoanalytical theory. The reason for the suppression is the action of forces associated with the

superego. If God is identified with the superego, then the corresponding antagonistic image is the Devil, who dwells in hell. . . . In a psychoanalytic relationship the analyst is at one and the same time the representative of the superego as well as a tolerant, understanding father figure. Now what is the Devil, psychologically? The answer is eminently simple, on one level. *The Devil is the suspended superego.* He is the permissive superego. The Devil is that part of the person which permits him to violate the precepts of the superego.[25]

Bakan provides us with what is at once a hermeneutic of the image of the Devil and a therapeutic for the superego. He also in effect provides a means for transcending the superego, thereby linking his work with Brown's and with theological existentialism. However, Bakan understands Freud to be calling for a "lifting" or suspension of the superego, whereas Brown finds Freud urging a radical regression from the genital organization of the superego. Bakan sees something inherently therapeutic in the Devil and in demonic energies. Brown, like his theological forebears, also wishes to interpret the Devil psychologically, but his normative solution does not depend on or include a reformation of demonic energies. Which proposal is the Freudian one?

This contrast appears even more clearly in the two theological interpretations of the Oedipus complex and its origins. For Brown the Oedipus complex is the beginning of all things tyrannical, and its theological meaning lies in radical regression to a pretyrannical plurality of instincts. Bakan would agree with Brown that the Oedipus complex is an internalization of the individual's own original situation; it is an internalization of an image constructed out of the search for one's own origins. A therapeutic for the Oedipus complex, however, lies in apprehending this and not in an abrogating regression. In discussing Freud's notion of the primal scene, Bakan in effect develops a theology of separation.

As the child's self-consciousness develops, as he begins to wonder and seek answers to questions concerning the origin of things

[25] Bakan, *Freud*, pp. 210–211.

he asks also about his own origins. This question is perhaps more universal among children than the Oedipus complex in the particulars as sometimes outlined by Freud. But with the metaphor of the Oedipus complex, Freud was able to seize upon the much more critical question that is in the life history of each person, the question "Where did I come from?" If the Oedipus complex does not exist cross-culturally in its limited form, it exists cross-culturally in the more general form of the sense of wonder at one's own being. The Oedipus complex is a profound metaphor which catches at the deep mystery of human existence. . . .

The mystery of the Oedipus complex is the mystery of the story of genesis, creation. . . . What the child wants to know is how he was created; and the secret which he discovers is that the moment of his creation was the moment in which his father and mother were having sexual intercourse. There is thus a sense in which the essential feature of the Oedipal wish is the wish to have been present to witness the act of one's own creation. This wish is transformed into the fantasy of the primal scene, and the urge to replace the father in the act of creation.[26]

Thus the oedipal wish is and remains ontological, although it is "transformed into the fantasy of the primal scene." Recall now Freud's discussion of anxiety, separation, and the "ultimate, the underlying principle" of neurosis: as if the "still undeveloped creature did not know what else to do with his longing." What I have referred to again and again as a third reading of Freud is here strikingly clear. Like Freud, but then so very different from Freud, Bakan answers that the "poor creature" creates the Oedipus complex and all that it implies in order to do something with his longing. This, of course, is exactly what Freud said: the Oedipus complex organizes the earlier anxiety of separation, and the superego is heir to the Oedipus complex. Psychoanalytic therapy is an attempt to remedy this state of affairs. What distinguishes the approaches of Brown and Bakan from that of Freud is the way in which the theological imagination permits them to gain distance from the problem, to see it both as a ques-

[26] *Ibid.*, pp. 275–276.

tion and as a means to the solution of that question—that is, to see it in a wider moral, imaginative, and even implicitly ontological context.

A second book, *The Duality of Human Existence,* expands this nuclear association of superego, image of the Devil, and transference into a comprehensive proposal that draws together religious imagery and developmental stages in the life of the self. Bakan proposes four stages in the "natural history of Satanism": separation, mastery, denial, and beholding that which is denied.[27] The result, what he calls a psychotheological interpretation of sexuality and religion, is remarkably free from reductionism of any kind. It is an explication of the latent psychological content of theological existentialism.

In the phenomenon of separation lies the genesis of the image of Satan, for all that is peculiarly satanic stems from Satan's refusal to remain with the other angels and his urge to establish himself as independent being. This division of the religious imagination into God and the Devil is reflected in another kind of division, that found in the origins of repression; for repression is also a defense against separation. Separation creates its own universal developmental solution, the formation of the Oedipus complex. The Oedipus complex is formed to overcome the sense of separation and the anxiety that accompanies the awareness that one must become an independent other. Repression, the harsh superego, and the possibility of transference all coalesce around the problem of separation.

> A major crisis of life is associated with the fact that the organism must develop the ego and must commit itself to the ego. But, in the development of the ego, one is already committed to personal death. To break the shell of tragic existence, one must undermine the superego, which one allowed for the sake of the ego, as a step in mitigating the ego itself in order to permit the communion feature in the psyche to function. To do this, one projects the image of Satan as a step toward the refusion of the two fathers, the father who is master with the father who is

[27] Bakan, *Duality,* chap. iii.

generative of life. And one must further fuse the separation of father from son, in order to become a father in turn.[28]

Separation, which is the occasion of the formation of the superego, also sets the task of religion as well: to undermine the superego—or, as theology would have it, to transcend the superego.

Because the formation of the Oedipus complex is occasioned by anxiety, continuous mastery of its current organization is necessary; therefore, mastery is the second stage in the history of Satanism. Indeed, the superego is a form of inner mastery. It is clear that mastery, both of inner, psychic and outer, environmental reality, is what our theologians have referred to in their critiques of manipulation, generalization, and domination. We note again the close interrelation between superego considerations in depth psychology and theology's epistemological subject-object considerations. The final goal of Satan's work is to become master of the entire world. The Devil, then, is the remythologization of what theology calls the subject-object relationship; or rather, the subject-object relation is a demythologization of the image of the Devil.

Mastery as a form of psychic activity gives way finally to denial, wherein repression is maintained by more strenuous willpower. Denial, "the nub of neurosis," is an activity of mind that seeks to "convert the flow of existence into things which are of an unchanging nature."[29] Theology and religious existentialism have repeatedly commented on this psychological condition in their endless perusal of modernity's loss of surprise, novelty, mystery, and transcendence. This condition is, in classical Protestantism, the bondage of the will, and it reappears in Niebuhr's analysis of the circularity of pride as well as in Tillich's analysis of the anxiety of guilt and condemnation and his discussions of heteronomy. It has also inadvertently insinuated itself into much of the "answer" side of Protestant theology, notably so in the case

[28] *Ibid.,* p. 53.
[29] *Ibid.,* p. 88.

of Tillich's conception of the God above God and in Niebuhr's conception of the principle of comprehension beyond comprehension.

The final stage, "beholding what has been denied," proposes a resolution of the superego dilemma through courageous immersion of the self in the denied elements. The individual runs the risk of appearing and even becoming diabolical. Yet this is so only from "inside the neurosis." From outside, it is the process of repression that is considered evil and not the specific contents of the unconscious. Just as, in religious imagery, God stands over and precedes the Devil, so does the divine stand for or represent a movement of the self from inside the neurosis to the outside. Bakan writes:

> The major difficulty associated with this stage is that it *appears* to be diabolical. . . . Thus, we have the paradox that to behold what was denied appears to be diabolical. . . . "Playing the Devil" enables one to overcome the evil consequences of repression. . . . To "play the Devil" means to allow thought to go as it will . . . we enter into the deepest portions of the psyche . . . to behold that which is "behind" for, as we saw in the discussion of anality, the fear of beholding is associated with the projection of the Devil.[30]

To "behold" is to move from inside the neurosis to outside the neurosis. In this movement, the image of Satan as a dynamic necessity is surrendered, for the ego surrenders to an awareness of the portions of reality that lie beyond its mastery. The superego, the author of separation, is no longer able to separate the ego either from its own depths or from a kind of sociohistorical depth that Bakan refers to as the formation of a transgenerational ego identification. In surrendering its opacity, the superego itself becomes the link, rather than the barrier, between the individual's sense of self and his wider ranges of organic social attachments and solidarity. Transference gives way to transcendence. The Devil is the vivid connecting term that is at once religious and deeply psychological and that links transference, the superego,

[30] *Ibid.*, pp. 90–91.

anality, and repression to transcendence. Bakan clearly believes that transference is integral to his own argument.

> Since from the very beginning of the development of the ego the separations which took place within also entailed the separation of the person from other persons, in the healing relationship the separation between the two people is overcome as the paradigm of the overcoming of all other separations. This is the meaning of the transference in psychoanalytic psychotherapy.[31]

Unlike Brown and Rieff, Bakan undertakes theoretical discussion of theological and psychological categories, and it is his methodological style that is of importance here. Characteristic of this style is the attempt to draw theological and psychological categories together around a third set and to exemplify these by religious images rather than simply analytically discernible processes. His most important contribution is to anchor the third set of categories firmly in human sexuality. Even more important, however, is the introduction of female sexuality into theological understanding, and this distinguishes his work from that of Brown and Rieff, and from theological existentialism as well.

There is an assumption common to both theology and psychology that human functioning is best understood by means of levels—biological, psychological, and theological, for example. Bakan prefers moral and ontological modes, which pertain to all levels of functioning. The first he calls "agency," referring it to the impulse to mastery, separation, isolation, independence—to everything pertaining to the organism "as an individual." The second mode, called "communion," characterizes the participation of the individual organism in a wider context. The "communal feature" serves to mitigate and mollify the individualistic tendencies of the organism by drawing the individual into a wider communal context. Consequently, communion is characterized by openness and inclusiveness, cooperation without regard for reciprocity, and by union with that which is "other." Agency is clearly a distinctive aspect of male sexuality, and communion is a distinctive aspect of female sexuality.

[31] *Ibid.,* pp. 100–101.

In theology agency is easily recognized, for example, in such notions as idolatry and pride. Tillich's extensive and often intricate discussions of estrangement and his analysis of the self's tendency to elevate preliminary concerns into the status of ultimate concerns also refer to the "agentic feature" of the self. This feature is discussed by Bultmann as man's tendency to construe God as "an object of thought towards which I can take a position."[32] On the basis of this particular style, it is possible to cross over from theological to psychological processes. In psychoanalysis, the process of repression is agentic; through it the individual separates what will be forgotten from what will be remembered and separates himself from aspects of both in the very act of discrimination. The oedipal situation, in its repressed form, also separates, for the superego keeps the ego from forming nonrepressive attachments. Psychologically, communion refers to all those processes whereby separations are overcome—insight, integration, the transgenerational—all of which render the superego transparent.

Because these categories are said to be embodied in images and rooted in human sexuality, the figure of Satan is at once an image of agency as well as a figure embodying alienated male sexuality—that is, male sexuality separated from the limitations that female sexuality imposes on it.

The theological categories of transcendence and immanence and the psychological categories of repression and understanding are thus transformed into a third set of categories that is at once deeply dynamic, erotic, and moral. Consider for a moment the possible methodological implications of this. Schubert Ogden, for example, in his *Christ Without Myth,* has argued that there is in Bultmann's work a structural inconsistency, an inconsistency in the logic of his insistence that both the kerygma and the demythologized statements be radical. This structural inconsistency might also be called a psychological inconsistency as well in that there is methodologically no possible way to render the kerygma dynamically. In speaking of the longing of modern man for an

---

[32] See Rudolf Bultmann, "What Sense Is There To Speak of God?" trans. Franklin H. Littell, *Christian Scholar,* XLIII, No. 3 (Fall 1960), 215–219.

ideology that omits considerations of his own existence, Bultmann says: "Precisely in the moment when his existence is shaken
and problematical he declines to take this moment seriously, [he
understands] it rather as one case among others. . . ." Man wants
to objectify this longing, thereby to "free himself from his own
existence," and Bultmann adds, "Precisely this is the arch-de-
ception." Or again: "When I seek after myself—looking backwards and forwards—then I have at the same time split my ego
. . . and the existential ego which is concerned about myself, which
quests, shows itself in this very questioning, in this self-concern
to be godless."[33] The implications of these remarks for psychology are clear. If psychology is concerned with this longing, Bultmann's position declares, it must necessarily objectify it and in so
doing enters the circularity of longing and self-deception. A
higher reading of Freud's psychology, however, does not submit
to this interpretation, but instead suggests possibilities and conditions under which this yearning can be investigated in a manner
at once dynamic and existential, in which subjectivity and objectivity may coexist. But Bultmann's point is itself more dynamic
than it may appear. He says, in effect, that objectification distorts
awareness of the "shaken and problematic" nature of existence.
To distinguish so radically between kerygma and interpretation is
to separate religious documents from their dynamic, human
meaning. One of the implications of our critique of theology is
that its hermeneutical work has been grounded in a deep and pervasive bifurcation of conscious and unconscious, of myth and
interpretation, of kerygma and self-understanding.

It would be foolish, of course, to offer such considerations as
these as the basis for a constructive theology. But if overcoming
repression is a theological imperative, it does suggest that theology, with a sense of its own authority, could attend those dynamic
processes that underlie a release of images in the psyche, regard-
less of their particular content. If such a proposal could be dignified with the fashionable phrase, "a rebirth of images," then it

[33] *Ibid.*, pp. 215–217.

also suggests a rebirth of the theological imagination itself, a rebirth that is not a negation of the materials we have been examining. The appearance of images is, of course, an immanental
process, although their function is that of creating transcendence.
This function need not deny their immanental beginnings.

Mechanistic readings of Freud do imply that psychoanalysis is inadvertently demonic, that it provides a false mastery of
emotionality and of the moral life, and that psychoanalytic
therapy is a process in which deeper sectors of human inwardness
are either mechanized or else collapsed into mere vitalistic and
subjective fantasy. Denis de Rougemont, who speaks more elo-
quently than most for this point of view, has said: "There is no
Devil in the eyes of the Freudians, but only a belief in the Devil
resulting from the 'projection' of a feeling of guilt. Cure this
feeling and you will no longer have a belief in the Devil, nor consequently a Devil. The Demon, then, is nothing but an image of
neurosis. . . ."[34] No doubt much psychoanalytic work has proceeded and does proceed in this manner. However, we have come
to learn that such phrases as "nothing but" are characteristic of a
genre of theology inadvertently caught up in the subject-object
dilemmas of projection and the transcendence of projection.

In point of fact, however, Bakan does not discuss the consequences of beholding. The moral consequences are clear, but
what takes place, theologically, once the act of beholding occurs?
Two alternatives seem to be suggested. On the one hand, Bakan
tells us that the image of Satan re-fuses with the image of God
resulting in the "motherized" God of the Old Testament. He interprets Biblical injunctions against polytheism as injunctions
against the splitting of agency and communion in the psyche.
Such a conclusion bespeaks, in a sense, a return to Biblical faith;
it calls for the recovery of a religious dimension in modern life,
and it necessitates psychologically active religious images in the
moral life of the self.

---

[34] Denis de Rougemont, *The Devil's Share: An Essay on the Diabolic in
Modern Society,* trans. Haakon Chevalier (New York: Meridian Books,
1956), p. 52.

On the other hand, Bakan agrees with Brown that psycho-analysis is a higher stage of consciousness, "the proper successor to the more classical form of the Judeo-Christian tradition." So one is also led to conclude that the dynamics of beholding, when pursued to their conclusion, release the individual from all classical forms of religion. Bakan says:

> If God is the guilt-producing imago, then the Devil is the counter-force. But the Devil's very permissiveness is the cause of his own destruction. Having permitted all to become open, the infantile character of both imagos is revealed and "distance" with respect to each is won.[35]

This conclusion implies not only that the projection of the image of Satan is agentic, but also that projection itself, the very presence of a sense of the "phenomenological otherness" of a religious image, is agentic. In this case, the religious imagination is itself eliminated, and the reality of the image is returned to its origins in the inner life of the self—as in the case, for example, of Jung's "withdrawal of projections."

The first alternative allies Bakan with the work of Thomas Altizer and others, who employ a broadly psychoanalytic critique of the Christian doctrine of transcendence in order to open up the possibility of religious images as these are understood by comparative religion. The second alternative allies Bakan with the "religionless" Christianity motif in modern theology, with its characteristic moral emphasis on responsibility, commitment, and servanthood. These are, in fact, two possible resolutions to the dilemmas of theological response to Freud.

Underlying these two alternatives—and perhaps of some value in clarifying them—is a consideration still unexplored, a reading of Freud that begins and ends with the sociological consequences of his psychology not for the restoration of the religious and the theological, but instead for the permanent decline in the power of religious institutions and leadership to integrate personal and social life. In the work of Norman Brown and of the

[35] Bakan, *Freud,* p. 233.

death-of-God theologians as well, Freud is not considered to be
a psychologist of secularization, one for whom the phrase "the
end of the Protestant Era" is an inevitable psychological conclusion. Yet if it is true that the structure of Protestant moral experience has been, as it is in theological existentialism, of the
superego sort, then this question becomes crucial. In the work of
Philip Rieff theological discussions of the "collapse of the transcendent" and psychological discussions of the "decline of the
superego" intersect.

*Philip Rieff: The collapse
of transcendence into mass society*

THE writings of Philip Rieff raise the question of mass society
and in so doing pursue the negative features of Freud's thought
to their negative conclusions. Other interpreters, albeit anguished
and struggling, bring their study of Freud and their search for
religious meaning to a happy issue; by comparison, their conclusions are sanguine and irenic. Rieff sees Freud as forcing the
psyche reluctantly along the developmental axis. Development
is not outward into a disclosure of deeper forms of social relatedness and not backward into deeper erotic depth, but rather
forward into a largely structureless, anomic, and morally indifferent mode of social existence. Rieff finds no "hidden" trend in
Freud's thought to relieve this dreary picture, nor is there any
value in such distinctions as being "inside" and "outside" the
neurosis. To be outside the neurosis is to be outside that form of
psychosocial organization known as Christian faith and ethics.
The triumph of the therapeutic is clearly in the ironic mode. The
most obviously Protestant of our interpreters, Rieff has called
attention to exactly those social consequences of psychoanalysis
most dreaded by theological existentialism, with its characteristic

fear of adjustment psychology and consequent reduction of human being and transcendence to lower psychological and sociological processes.

The power of Rieff's work lies in its style as well as in its content, and the two are deeply consistent. His message is that psychoanalytic morality and its resultant therapeutic character type have created a permanent fissure between contemporary inwardness and ancient faith; his rhetoric is one of consolation. In a sense, one should not "discuss"—and least of all analyze—Rieff's ideas; one should rather simply suffer with him. As he points out: "These preliminary studies in the psychohistorical process are not aimed primarily at fellow theorists interested in the problem, but at those troubled readers in whose minds and hearts one culture is dying while no other gains enough power to be born."[36] The power of his work lies in a churning and restless elaboration and reelaboration of this single and central insight, his own "spiritual perception." For this reason, his work is itself very much in the psychoanalytic mode, in which a single percept is reworked again and again—and again—but always in a new context and always because there is more to it than one had previously realized.

The meaning of Christian faith, Rieff argues, lies in its having produced a controlling ethic whereby the deepest impulses of life and their social consequences are organized into images, symbols, doctrines, and precepts. The function of faith is to provide a system of "interdicts" and "remissions" that pattern internal energies in the direction of moral passion and social cohesion. This process whereby faith "superintends" personality organization and social relatedness is for the most part unconscious. Rieff is fond of Sullivan's remark that sublimation is unwitting. What is taken away by the interdictory symbolic (through instinctual renunciation) is given back better, or, as Rieff prefers to say, in religion one does not choose but is chosen. Preaching, evangelism, care, and casuistry—all serve, in a com-

[36] Rieff, *Triumph*, p. 2.

pulsive and authoritarian manner, as a therapy of commitment, to generate means for instinctual limitation in the interests of the freedom and integrity of one's neighbor. All surplus aggression and surplus sexuality which might create psychological stress and social disorder are transformed into the actions and symbols of liturgy, devotion, and ethics.

Psychoanalysis, however, in Kierkegaard's words, plays the music backwards, it breaks the spell and creates disenchantment. For psychoanalysis is "deconversion," a spiritual perception calculated to unravel in the fashion of parody the formation of those very erotic illusions that bind men together and give them the assurance that control, delay, and renunciation are all really worth the effort. Psychoanalysis thus produces the "analytic attitude," characterized by interdictory neutrality. The good patient learns to view his faith—or really, the faith of his parents—with ethical distance, imposing a permanent tentativeness on all ecclesiastical and devotional compulsions. This is a doctrine of antidoctrine in which the patient takes a scientific stance toward himself and "does not attach himself too passionately to any one particular meaning or object." The rhetoric abounds with lyrical irony.

> In a highly differentiated democratic culture, truly and for the first time, there arose the possibility of every man standing for himself, each at last leading a truly private life, trained to understand rather than love (or hate) his neighbor.
>
> . . .
>
> Crowded more and more together, we are learning to live more distantly from one another . . . rather than in the oppressive warmth of family and a few friends.[37]

A remissive psychotherapy, Rieff muses, may become "a kind of secular methodism for those who remain obstinately uncomfortable in their pleasures."[38]

The analytic attitude, since it reverses those processes that

[37] *Ibid.*, pp. 70, 243.
[38] *Ibid.*, pp. 238–239.

generate commitment, produces a new ideal type, "the therapeutic," whose inwardness is transparent to himself and who
therefore can make the inwardness of others transparent to himself as well. Well-being, understood as the pursuit of dynamic
self-understanding, replaces moral passion and social commitment, both of which require a barrier, an opacity between intention and self-understanding. Under such conditions there can
be no point of psychic vulnerability—no unconscious guilt or
sense of sin—by which institutions may gain leverage in the coercive manipulation of prescribed behavior. Indeed, the persist-
ence of such vulnerability is now a sign of illness, the failure to
recognize that sacrally rooted moral energies are really symptoms. Therapeutics live, therefore, in a "negative community" in
which each new sense of impulse remission yields to yet another,
rather than being caught up abruptly by a new sense of inner control or obligation. Society becomes a mosaic of therapeutics,
each warding off, with analytic skill, residual claims to organic
solidarity.

Rieff has called Freud a moralist in that he cut psychology
away from the physical sciences. Thus he distinguishes clearly
between a moral science of the psychic, intentional, and volitional
aspects of the person, on the one hand, and the mechanistic science of the nineteenth century, on the other hand. And in so doing, Rieff affirms the Protestant theological distinction between
nature and history, a distinction that, as we have seen, has made
it methodologically difficult for the theologian to admit dynamic,
psychological considerations into his theological work. However,
Rieff places Freud on the voluntaristic rather than the mechanistic side—psychoanalysis is a "crisis psychology." It follows
that Rieff's understanding of psychodynamics remains one of
control and discontrol, of "impulses" that are controlled by self-
conscious rational willing. Like Brown, he retains the presuppositional equipment of theological existentialism, although he re-
locates Freud within that schema.

Rieff therefore interprets Freud to have retained the subject-
object dichotomy, and this dichotomy and its various forms un-

derlie his own psychology of deconversion, which is a psychology of the gaps and resembles what I have called a theology of the gaps. Rieff understands psychic structure as the simple juxtaposition of an authoritarian superego and an anarchic id; he understands socialization as the juxtaposition of the harsh superego of primary group passion (the Oedipus complex) and the negative community of the therapeutic; and dynamically he juxtaposes repression and a form of insight that, because it is morally neutral, brings about a mechanistic, detached consciousness of self. In each case, Rieff understands Freud to approve that association of superego, repression, and the subject-object relation that we have already discussed.

Theology and religion are simple superego phenomena. The task of the Christian mission has been to nuture the cultural superego. Little wonder that Rieff is impatient with the Tillichian kind of theological interest in depth psychology and with the pastoral psychology movement. For Rieff, all theological notions of transcendence are compulsive and authoritarian. There is no God above God, no revelation that transcends religion. Nor is there any distinction between developmental limitation and existential commitment. The tragedy of the modern church is not, as Tillich would say, that faith was misinterpreted to the modern self as authoritarian; the tragedy lies in the fact that Freud figured it out and gave the game away. Rieff's reading, therefore, although it supports a good deal of our own critique of theology, is unnecessarily closed to a possible reformulation of a psychology of transcendence, a possibility that, we have been arguing, is not inconsistent with the deepest intentions of the Freudian canon.

Let us return to the notion of transference and its meaning. That endlessly remissive quality of the therapeutic's emotions and imagination, the emptying of inwardness, so to speak, is clearly a transference phenomenon. Rollo May, who more than any other existential psychologist has sensed the theological meanings of Freud's thought, argues that the phenomenon of transference must be understood as a distortion of "encounter" in personal relationships.[39] He speaks of encounter dynamically, as the "going out" of energies from one's own centeredness in order to participate in the reality of other beings. May points out that there is the risk of "going out too far," which can result in a loss of centeredness and identity. Such distortion of the proper form of personal encounter can result in "dispersing one's self in participation and identification with others until one's own being is emptied." He writes:

> Patients will say, "If I love somebody, it's as though all of me flows out like water out of a river, and there'll be nothing left." I think this is a very accurate statement of *transference*. That is, if one's love is something that does not belong there of its own right, then obviously it will be emptied. . . .[40]

The point is simply whether sublimation is an unconscious process the dynamics of which can be submitted to a naturalistic determinism, or whether it "goes through decision." And, if the latter, how are we to understand that process? Tillich says, in describing the meaning of sublimation: "This explains that fact to which Rollo May drew my attention, that in so many of his patients' dreams there appears the necessity of deciding. His patients have not yet lost the awareness that sublimation goes through decision, and that the power of deciding makes men human. . . . The centered act of the centered self is the source of sublimation."[41] Rieff recognizes this distinction, for he quotes with approval Scheler's description of Christian asceticism, the purpose of which was, according to Scheler, "not the suppression or even extirpation of natural drives, but rather their *control* and complete *spiritualization*. It is positive, not negative asceticism— aimed fundamentally at a liberation of the highest powers of personality from blockage by the automism of the lower drives."[42] Freud's thought, we only argue, makes possible and even favors

[39] See Rollo May, "On the Phenomenological Bases of Psychotherapy," *Phenomenology: Pure and Applied,* ed. Erwin W. Strauss (Pittsburgh: Duquesne University Press, 1964).

[40] *Ibid.,* p. 177, n. 3.

[41] Tillich, "Existentialism and Psychotherapy," p. 12.

[42] Quoted in Rieff, *Triumph,* p. 18.

both this higher asceticism as well as a lower anti-asceticism that Rieff calls interdictory neutrality.

So May proposes a moral psychology of personal encounter in which the mode of personal relatedness is not only distinguished from but also can even emerge therapeutically from precisely that remissive transference experience that so concerns Rieff. However, the presence of encounter rather than of transference does not consist, as Rieff seems to indicate, in a simple restoration of the harsh superego and all the paraphernalia that Rieff lumps under the term "organizing symbolic." In this regard, Rieff's assertion that psychoanalysis is a parody of Christian faith could be reversed: Christian faith, if merely of the interdictory sort, is a subtle parody of transference and therefore of encounter and transcendence, which the proper interpretation of transference can evoke.

It is possible to discuss Rieff's rendition of insight in much the same way. The "analytic attitude," characterized by interdictory neutrality, lacks moral passion and direction for it interposes a barrier of tentativeness or distance between occasion and moral action. Thus, the ego of the therapeutic gains a vantage point on the superego—both its own and the cultural superego. More correctly, the attitude of the therapeutic is in effect one of detachment of the individual ego from the cultural superego. A therapeutic for the superego, far from creating deeper, communal attachments by luring the isolated ego toward that which lies beyond its own immediate developmental loyalties, creates the opposite effect.

Again the final pages of the case of little Hans are important. There Freud paused to reflect on the moral consequences of insight into the dynamics of the Oedipus complex. After noting that, at least in this case, there seemed to be no adverse moral effects, he concluded that:

> . . . the only results of the analysis were that Hans recovered. . . . For analysis does not undo the *effects* of repression. The instincts which were formerly suppressed remained suppressed; but the same effect is produced in a different way. Analysis replaces

the process of repression, which is an automatic and excessive one, by a temperate and purposeful control on the part of the highest mental faculties. In a word, *analysis replaces repression by condemnation.*[43]

Insight is therefore both dynamic and moral, and, as a perspective on transference, it does not encourage moral neutrality but rather reorganizes energies under the auspices of a higher moral center. Repression, therefore, pertains both to a moral center as well as to the objective content of the oedipal drive. Transference is not neutralized or depotentiated; it becomes the substance of transcendence, as other readings of the meaning of psychoanalytic insight, such as Norman Brown's "symbolical consciousness" and Bakan's "beholding that which is denied," both suggest.

But there is another sense in which Rieff's work is, I think, a good deal more sympathetic to an expanded reading of Freud than much of his discussion for the most part suggests. Here Rieff almost contradicts his major argument and briefly develops an iconic reading of Freud. Contrast his remarks on Freud's views of religion with those on interpretation.[44] Perhaps somewhat in the sense in which Freud's own work on religion is of less value to theologians than his general writings, Rieff's discussion of interpretation is richer and of more value than his discussions of Freud's views on religion.

Although Rieff argues insistently that there can be nothing mutually supportive between Christian faith and psychoanalytic psychology, he does admit that there are curious similarities. The instinct for aggression, for example, has some "formal" similarity to the role that Christian psychology assigns to free will: just as aggression enables man to rebel against authority (the primal father), so free will enables man, in the religious account, to rebel against God. Again, introjection formally resembles the religious idea of the free act of faith: in both cases, the subject is reconciled to authority. But theologians who may be tempted to

[43] Freud, *Collected Papers,* III, 285.
[44] See Rieff, *Freud,* chaps. iv and viii.

see their own doctrines reflected in psychoanalytic psychology are mistaken.

> But Freud's view does not invite this response, for what the religious think of as moral evil—these aggressive feelings and the reaction to them—he discusses as entirely natural. His remedy, too, is far from a religiously acceptable one. To reduce human aggressiveness he recommends that we reduce our overextended moral aspirations, since aggression is, in part at least, a reaction against too fervent a desire for personal virtue.[45]

In such fashion Rieff continues the approach to Freud taken by theological existentialism.

Rieff's discussions of Freud's "tactics of interpretation" display single-minded appreciation (the word "interpretation" does not occur in the chapter on religion). Freud's methods, Rieff notes, press beyond the clinical case and beyond an examination of emotions in any shallow, empirical-rational sense. The opacity that obtains between emotion and mind, and that therefore requires interpretation, likens psychoanalysis more to a religious hermeneutic than to any other form of understanding; for, just as religious hermeneutics presupposes opacity between experience and expression, so psychoanalysis presupposes that the dream cannot be simply equated with its affective origins. Yet the hermeneutic of psychoanalysis remains a parody of religious hermeneutics (of course), which sees as hidden what is "high" whereas psychoanalysis sees what is "low" to be hidden.

Nevertheless, Rieff wishes us to understand that there is a sense in which Freud's hermeneutic is appropriate to higher processes as well. His method is "astonishingly fertile and ingenious" and no more so than in its suggestiveness regarding the relation between language, the unconscious, and the body. Psychoanalysis as a therapy starts with talk and ends with it; its theory is never directed toward considerations beyond that reality that it approaches immediately and directly. However, it is the unconscious that mediates between talk and the body. The psychopathology of everyday life may be an attempt to reduce

[45] *Ibid.*, p. 274.

everything to a base motive; but is Rieff implicitly suggesting that it may also be a hermeneutic of the body and its modes of transcendence? In his concluding paragraphs Rieff goes so far as to propose looking "beyond the interior logic of his interpretive method," a method that "need not imply base meanings at all"; and, in so proposing, he registers his approval of Freud's well-known remark to Binswanger: "Mankind has always known that there is spirituality. I have to show that there are also instincts."

Rieff concludes with a formula of his own for what is truly distinctive about Freud's thought. It is that "the quality of humiliation in his interpretive method is designed not merely to lower what was once elevated, but, more subtly, to elevate what was once lowered. . . ."[46]

This remark recalls the problem that Rieff has raised again and again: the juxtaposition of interdictory neutrality and a compulsive, authoritarian faith—the inner dynamic of crisis psychology. Freud concluded the above remark to Binswanger by adding: "But men are always discontented, they cannot wait, they always want something whole and ready-made; however, one must begin somewhere and one progresses only slowly."[47] On hearing this, Binswanger reports that he went "one step further" in the conversation and pressed on Freud an argument for "something like a fundamental religious category in man." This suggestion aroused Freud's opposition, and, to dramatize his reluctance, he presented the completed manuscript of *The Future of an Illusion,* stating its argument and concluding: "I am sorry I cannot satisfy your religious needs."[48]

Why did Binswanger's argument for a "religious category" arouse Freud's opposition? Was it because his view of religion and the psyche was ultimately reductive? Or was it because he believed that he had sensed (correctly or incorrectly—that is not the point here) in Binswanger's own remarks the need for "something whole and ready-made"? Like Freud, Rieff, too, has

[46] *Ibid.,* p. 146.
[47] Ludwig Binswanger, *Sigmund Freud: Reminiscences of a Friendship,* trans. Norbert Guterman (New York: Grune and Stratton, 1957), p. 81.
[48] *Ibid.,* pp. 81-82.

sensed the need for something whole and ready-made in much of today's rapprochement between theology and psychotherapy. That is precisely the analytic point.

But Freud also said, "One must begin somewhere," and he added to that, "One progresses only slowly." In so saying Freud betrayed not the virtues of Rieff's therapeutic, but a steady moral and epistemological passion in the service of which and in the protection of which he was forced from time to time to adopt the analytic attitude. It is important to note that behind the irony of the merely analytic lies the impulse "to begin somewhere," and "to progress only slowly." That is the impulse we have attempted to free from the theological readings of Freud.

Rieff, in his pursuit of the analytic attitude and its consequences, has made his own analytic point, one that undercuts all the attempts to disguise the terrifying ignorance that obtains between contemporary inwardness and ancient faith. In doing so, he has found it necessary to establish a fundamental connection between the meaning of Freud's work, the future of Christian faith, and the status of the personal in mass society: they are all of a piece. His work challenges all theological encouragements that speak of "pregnant void," "waiting," and "eclipse"—and, as we shall see, "the death of God," too.

Rieff's moral indignation with psychological theologians is reminiscent of the impatience Freud once expressed with Pfister, a remark Rieff himself uses in defense of the analytic attitude. Commenting on one of Pfister's cases he said:

> Your analysis suffers from the hereditary weakness of virtue. . . . One has to become a bad fellow, transcend the rules, sacrifice oneself, betray, and behave like the artist who buys paints with his wife's household money, or burns the furniture to warm the room for his model. Without some such criminality there is no real achievement.[49]

Rieff argues that this criminality, this "creative egoism," has passed to others outside the profession of psychoanalysis. It also has passed to these more recent interpreters of Freud, especially Rieff himself.

[49] Quoted in Rieff, *Triumph*, p. 107.

Six: Transcendence, mass culture,

and the psychology of distance:

an interpretation

---

*The fate of transcendence
in mass society*

THREE very different interpreters of Freud carry forward to their extreme conclusions the central issues in theological response to Freud. Unlike theological existentialism, these analyses explicitly set forth the now familiar nuclear set of psychological terms (repression, superego, Oedipus complex, transference), and in this regard each must be characterized as post-Protestant. Yet each in its own way also claims to have found in the thought of Freud something deeply reminiscent of what is central to theology itself, and in this sense each remains just as clearly theological. What these discussions do is to make explicit the implicit psychological form of Protestant thought; at the same time, they reject mechanistic and dynamic views of Freud's thought.

The interpretations of Brown, Bakan, and Rieff all begin with the same dynamic point; once that point has been made, however, no one of these interpretations really lends much support to the others. Instead, taken together they seem to destroy permanently the possibility of a unified reading of Freud's psychology and its implications for theological method and anthropology, especially for the theological conception of transcendence. The considerations that divide these interpretations are related to one another, however, if only by negation. Brown's eschatology of immanence neglects psychodynamics and the problem of mass society. Bakan's hermeneutic of religious images and the pivotal notion of beholding lack a certain kind of sociological realism in that he ignores the decline of the superego. Rieff's work turns on the erosion of the Protestant construction of the centered self; yet, his sociological urgencies must be kept in some kind of fluid relation to the deeper, interpretive possibilities of psychoanalytic psychology. What one omits remains central to the other.

These different interpretations of the fate of transcendence when confronted with psychoanalytic psychology are of importance because they are also suggestive of the mutations that theology undergoes as a workable discipline, again at the hands of psychoanalytic psychology. For the meaning of transcendence as a theological concept cannot be separated from the viability of theology. A position such as that of Norman Brown suggests that theology, *qua* theology of culture (Tillich), is no longer workable but that it is still possible to speak of a "theological dimension," more dynamic than structural, but which nevertheless endures and to which the word "theological" can rightly be attached. Bakan's work can be taken to propose that the proper work of theology is the analysis of religious images, images that are no longer believed to "exist" (that is, to be dynamically operative) in a scientific culture. Theology is really the correlation of images (and not of clear and distinct questions and answers). These images, once conscious to individuals during religious periods of history, are in a sense unconscious in modern thought and life. Analyses such as those of Philip Rieff propose that whatever remains after the collapse of the transcendent should be given over to a moral psychology of mass society. There is the implication that such a psychology could eventually be expanded to become a theology once new forms of commitment become possible. With regard to contemporary trends in theological studies, the first approach suggests a theology of culture extended to become what could be called a "culture theology"; the second suggests the recent concern of theology with comparative religion; and the third supports current studies in a theology of the secular.

Different readings of Freud do make possible different proposals. But is there a sense in which the distinctiveness and mutual exclusiveness of these proposals is more apparent than real? Is it possible that psychoanalysis could become, with proper qualification, a hermeneutic of images, images that could well be at once "theological," "religious," and deeply contemporary? Is it, perhaps, the case that the deepest meaning of the thought of Freud for theology does not lie in its helpful "scientific" testimony in the courts of doctrinal reconstruction (the mechanistic reading of Freud) and not in its prophetic and purgative power, as a kind of negative theology (the dynamic reading of Freud)? Perhaps the theological importance of Freud's thought lies in its hermeneutical resourcefulness in binding together the residues of theological tradition, the images (both high and degraded) of the religions, and the collective imaginings of mass society.

That there is some validity and propriety to raising this question is one of the conclusions of this essay, for the logic of the question lies within the already discussed psychological and theological materials themselves; however, these materials give even greater priority to a group of thinkers whose concerns are also not only post-Protestant and theological, but are psychoanalytically psychological as well. The death-of-God theology has deep affinities with the thought of Freud and with the particular dynamic intuitions that underlie its criticism of theology. An important aspect of these theological writings is the way in which they carry forward the dilemmas occasioned by the psychoanalytic critique of theological existentialism. The death-of-God theology also tries to go "beyond" theological existentialism and Freud, and it should not be too difficult to integrate it into the main stream of our argument.

In this chapter I shall develop an interpretive overview, what is really an interpretive recapitulation, that will express the sense in which there is a common problem and solution characteristic of all these materials, despite the many differences between them. I shall try to link together theological existentialism, its psychoanalytic criticism, the post-Protestant uses of Freud, and the death-of-God theology. Following some of the implications of Rieff's argument, I argue that both the central focus of these theological discussions and the final conclusion of Freud's analysis of religion lie in the collapse of transcendence into the immanental modes of mass society. Just as the superego is heir to the Oedipus complex, mass culture is heir to the superego.

To explore this notion I find it necessary to introduce a consideration seemingly external both to the materials and to the argument thus far: the psychology of distance and the interrelations that obtain between a sense of distance and a sense of guilt. Although the meaning of distance is not overtly explicated in the theological and psychological materials discussed in Part I above, it is implicit in those discussions; it is explicitly treated in the materials just reviewed; and it is even more germane to the death-of-God theology. Distance is the connecting term between what appears in theological discussions as transcendence and in psychoanalytic thought as insight, recollection, understanding, and the like. That it is progressively more in evidence as the Freud-and-theology question is debated is in itself some grounds for taking it into consideration. The validity of this procedure lies in whether or not, once the construct has been adduced, it seems to have been resident in the materials all along.

I also suggest that a second way to understand the collapse of transcendence is to see it as a shift in the way in which self-understanding is fundamentally conceived. This shift is a movement away from self-understanding conceived primarily as self-limitation and in the direction of self-understanding conceived primarily as self-completion. Is the structure of Christian anthropology inherently that of self-limitation, or can Christian theology just as appropriately open itself to the ethics of self-completion so much in evidence today? Is it possible for the modern self to enter upon the processes of self-completion without entirely abandoning that structure of limitation that underlies Protestant theological anthropology? In this regard I propose that in the problem of distance lies the permanent psychological contribution of Protestantism to contemporary self-understanding and that the "recovery of distance" is one of its contemporary tasks. I shall not attempt to formulate what such a recovery might require, but only to carry the discussion to the point where such a formulation seems necessary, given the nature of these theological and psychological materials.

The argument of this chapter proceeds in a manner somewhat different from the previous discussions. It consists of a series of somewhat self-contained proposals, which, for this reason, might just as well be called "vignettes." Their purpose is neither to describe further nor to persuade. Instead, they are rather self-contained, highly synoptic, and hopefully precise, figures that serve to draw together into a single and unified perception much of what has gone before. It is in this sense that the term "interpretation" is used. These proposals recapitulate previous discussions in an attempt to achieve closure.

Transcendent God and
anguished conscience: a synopsis
of the Protestant experience

THERE is a not too broken line of progressive psychic narrowing extending from the Reformation experience of justification by faith, and its paradigmatic exemplification in Luther's spirituality, to the present ambiguities of selfhood now under discussion. Its complex pathway connects most obviously with the inner turmoil of distressed souls caught up in the Great Awakening and in revivalism everywhere, and it settles finally on those very conversion experiences that, as noted, so fascinated the early psychologists of religion. Even more precisely, perhaps, the line ends in the conversations that William James had with Jones in 1909 in which James told Jones that the future of psychology lay in his work, and in Freud's admiration of James's courage in the face of physical infirmity.

Freud, however, was convinced that the future of religion lay in his hands as well, a conclusion James did not share, and here the line splits into two lines, the one going in the direction of neo-Reformation theology, the other into depth psychology. One reaffirms the problematic of self-understanding to be primarily that of self-limitation. The other, no longer under the control of transcendent legitimation, grimly but rebelliously affirms the inherent priority of self-completion.

Paul Tillich has taken Luther's spirituality to be in an important sense normative for his own psychological understanding of Protestantism and the Protestant era, and he has I think associated himself quite deeply with it. His threefold typology of Western man's anxiety turns on the Protestant experience of guilt and justification, and it is his interpretation of Luther that gives the distinctive and definitive tone to his own theological piety. Luther's spirituality lies at the root of the Protestant Christian's sense of God's transcendence. In this "spiritual perception," to use Rieff's term, coalesce psychological, social, and existential-theological factors to form a total image of the self and its world. I wish only to note here this experience synoptically in terms of its image of God and the theological consequence of this image of God, the Christian's image of himself.

In describing Luther's "tremors," which occurred during the saying of his first mass, Roland Bainton summarizes in a helpful way the objective referent of this experience.

> Luther's tremor was augmented by the recognition of unworthiness. "I am dust and ashes and full of sin." Creatureliness and imperfection alike oppressed him. Toward God he was at once attracted and repelled. Only in harmony with the Ultimate could he find peace. But how could a pygmy stand before divine Majesty; how could a transgressor confront divine Holiness? Be-

fore God the high and God the holy Luther was stupefied. For such an experience he had a word which has as much right to be carried over into English as *Blitzkrieg*. The word he used was *Anfechtung,* for which there is no English equivalent. It may be a trial sent by God to test man, or an assault by the Devil to destroy man. It is all the doubt, turmoil, pang, tremor, panic, despair, desolation, and desperation which invade the spirit of man.[1]

The spiritual referent for the Protestant experience is, in Bainton's terms, "God the high and God the holy." It is the God who is the contrary of man, whose abysmal nature, so rich in aseity, internality, and self-relatedness, appears to the Christian only as he moves beyond the fringes of his own immediately given self-consciousness, his own immediate and "merely psychological" forms of self-understanding, both in will and imagination, in knowledge and action.

This spiritual perception receives dogmatic and systematic theological expression in the doctrine of transcendence—first as the transcendence of God, but also as the self's capacity and incapacity to transcend itself. As a ground for theological anthropology, this spiritual perception asserts a divine reality that lies beyond those meanings that occur simply within self-awareness or within the compass of one's relations to others; it is therefore with reference to this transcendent reality that the self ultimately organizes its relation to itself and to others. Protestant theology, especially neo-Reformation theology, always speaks of immanence in some kind of dialectical relation to transcendence; nonetheless, it is the transcendence of God that has been such a powerful attraction for the Protestant theological imagination. The immanence of God, his nurturing presence, and the integration of this into an understanding of his otherness appear experientially to the Christian only on the other side of the crisis of faith.

The Christian's experience of God the high as the object of his faith articulates inwardly and subjectively with what we here call "the anguished conscience." Again, Luther's *Anfechtung,* his

[1] Roland H. Bainton, *Here I Stand: A Life of Martin Luther* (New York: New American Library, 1955), p. 31.

"tremor," is representative. Clearly, this crisis is one of *total* self-understanding and cannot be defined by reference to localized acts, attitudes, feelings, or special experiences. It is the whole man who is "stupefied" before God the high, who says of himself, "I am dirt and ashes and full of sin," and who thereby calls into question his final meaning and worth. It is the whole existence of the whole man that is under question. Nor is it possible to separate the object of faith from the inward, subjective response. We must not attempt to understand God the high as the cause of the anguished conscience any more than we should attempt to construe the spiritual perception of God the high as a "projection" of the crisis of an anguished conscience.

Although the inner dynamics of this crisis of conscience drive toward resolution in the form of self-fulfillment or self-completion, the inner structure of the experience has for the most part been described and understood by theologians in terms of its crisis side. That is, the inner crisis of conscience that is so immediately real to the believer points toward a form of self-validation that remains by contrast for the most part eschatological. It appears to the Christian and is received by him as promise, such that the total meaning of the experience itself is weighted more on the side of self-limitation than self-completion. This emphasis on struggle rather than fulfillment has created those characteristic Protestant polarities between law, justice, wrath, and sin, on the one hand, and gospel, mercy, forgiveness, love, and grace, on the other hand.

It is the law-and-wrath side of the experience that is associated with what Bainton describes as the experience of "God the high." The apparent irreconcilability of these moral attributes of God and His attitude toward the believer is resolved in the experience of justification, as a result of which the apparently paradoxical nature of God's attitude toward man is resolved in the mind of the Christian. Here Christological meaning and psychological function fuse.

This polarity has a social or interpersonal aspect as well. For the crisis of conscience and its associated appreciation of the unapproachable nature of God together create social isolation; the resolution of the crisis has the opposite effect. As Luther remarked, "I have my worst temptations when I am by myself," and one of his antidotes for temptation was the company of others, especially the company of a woman.[2] The Protestant Christian, at the apex of his encounter with God the high, has found his psychic energies, relational capacities, and wider perceptions and commitments all turned in upon himself, as if the problematic of total self-evaluation in the presence of his Lord could only be solved by means of some utterly interiorized and introcathected spiritual gesture.

This spiritual conclusion has acquired special contemporaneity in the hands of Protestant theological existentialism, which has recast the crisis of conscience and total self-evaluation into its own special vocabulary under the general term "self-understanding": pride, estrangement, I-certainty, self-concern—all are intended to suggest the Reformation rendition of the crisis of conscience. The objective referent, God the high, appears in Niebuhr's principle of comprehension beyond comprehension and in Tillich's God above God. In this regard, theological existentialism is a celebration of the primacy of self-limitation and its logic —both theological and psychological—which insists that self-completion has an eschatological and nonetheless highly dynamic status in the economy of Christian self-understanding.

It is precisely against this style of theological formulation that the death-of-God theology has lodged its protest and done its work. The meaning of the death-of-God theology has been formulated in many ways—as profoundly anti-Christian; as the appropriate result of the inner, historical logic of Christianity; and as simply the inevitable exhaustion of Christian culture and the intellectual and social forms that have embodied it. I will attempt to understand it here under the rubric of "the collapse of the transcendent" in the following manner: the collapse of the self-authenticating giveness of the spiritual reality of God the high;

[2] Quoted in *ibid.*, pp. 284–285.

the collapse of the doctrine of transcendence as a workable theological construct; the collapse of theology as a workable discipline, at least insofar as its work is grounded in such a primary spiritual perception; and the collapse of the anguished conscience as the problematic ground for all theological self-understanding. The modern self can no longer reflect upon itself and derive its sense of deepest validation from an appointed encounter with God the high. The doctrine of transcendence gives way to a doctrine of immanence, and the crisis of conscience and its eschatological conclusion no longer organizes the self and its inner imagining and social behavior.

Different figures in the death-of-God complex have formulated in different ways the consequences of this alleged collapse for the problem of self-understanding. But each in his own way exemplifies the same dynamic. Altizer proclaims a mystical and romantic liberation of latent potential within the self, a potential long bound up within the structure of the transcendent. The collapse of the transcendent transforms "paradox" into "coincidentia." Hamilton's documentation is sociological and moral rather than eschatological and mystical: the death of the God who is the "meeter of needs and solver of problems" releases the self for relational and moral commitments heretofore impossible Van Buren's work may seem least amenable to such discussion. However, in collapsing the transcendent into language analysis methodologically, and into the ethics of interpersonal relations anthropologically, Van Buren proposes a form of self-understanding and moral behavior that is recognizably psychological. Standing uneasily at the edge of the cliff over which the others have tumbled, Gabriel Vahanian ruminates about the horrors of radical immanentism.

At this point the death-of-God theology articulates directly with the concerns of this book. With the collapse of the transcendent as the final referent for the Protestant Christian's organizing spiritual perception, the crisis in conscience thereby receives a new imperative at the hands of Freud's "analytic" of the superego. The death-of-God theology transports us with horrifying rapidity down the aforementioned line of progressive psychic narrowing, forcing in a single imaginative gesture a confrontation between Luther's violently positive affirmation, "God does not lie," and Freud's grim counsel, "Analyze the transference." What direction will a resolution of this confrontation take?

Transcendence and
the psychology of distance

It would be helpful, I think, briefly to consider what we have called the Protestant experience *more indirectly* and *more formally* and with less regard simply for its stated contents. This can be done through an analysis of its imagery. The imagery of transcendence is primarily spatial, and therefore much of the meaning that belongs to this concept depends in particular on the sense of distance that it suggests and that it communicates. It is through a sense of distance and through alterations in a sense of distance that the Protestant ego is able to grasp its distinctive spiritual orientation and validity. In particular, it is the shifting sense of proximity and distance with regard to "God the high," both as the object of faith and as the occasion of unfaith, that lies close to the root of this experience. The sense of distance that separates the Christian from his God is intimately related to the crisis in self-evaluation. What precisely is implied in this association between conscience or guilt and a sense of distance?

It is worth recalling that the principal argument against the usefulness and validity of psychological discussions of religion and especially of theology is that, because of its methodological orientation, psychology must inevitably view religion as a projection and that much of Freud's criticism of religion was in fact based on a psychology of projection. The phenomenon of projection is really the point at which *both* theology and depth psychology so often register their objections each to the other. Those objections, as noted, appear in the form of interpretations; psychologists argue that religious experience and the data of theological statement are projections of developmental needs and the like, and theologians, inverting the procedure, argue that it is revelation, grace, and so on, that determine the self or the "I" in its deepest motivations and behavior. Thus theologians interpret psychological processes as introjection or internalization of the divine.

Consider, for example, this statement by Karl Barth:

> Jesus Christ is the donor and the warrant of the divine Fatherhood and of our filiality. It is the reason for which this Fatherhood and this filiality are incomparably superior to any other, to any relationship suggested to us by the words "father," "son," "children." These human bonds are not the original, of which the other would be a symbol. The original, the true fatherhood, the true filiality are in these ties which God has created between himself and us. Everything which exists among us is merely the image of this original filiality. When we call God our Father, we do not fall into symbolism; on the contrary, we are in the full reality of these two words: "father" and "son."[3]

All such discussions, to transpose John Wisdom's well-known remark, die the death of a thousand interpretations.

This fruitless debate, whether it is in the form of simple bickering or assault and counterassault, reflects what we have come to recognize as the dilemma of the subject-object dichotomy: the methodological impasse between an object-oriented psyche and the subjectivity that it projects onto objective reality. In an effort to move beyond this impasse I have already proposed discussing theological statements at the point of their psychological form and then returning to the original theological in-

[3] Barth, *Prayer*, p. 36. Barth juxtaposes a reductive view of symbolism to faith and dogma and then argues in behalf of the latter. But the success of his argument depends on his prior estimate of the limits of symbolism. A different, more generous estimate of the function of symbols embarrasses Barth's position, raising valid higher psychological questions about the relation between "the original" and the "symbol."

tention. Now I propose that the imagery of distance, as contained in the psychology of projection, gives psychological form to the collapse of transcendence. For the psychology of projection, like, if you will, the theology of transcendence, also presupposes the imagery of distance.

To do this I turn to that part of clinical psychology concerned with projective devices, in particular the materials of the Rorschach test, for it is the best available exemplification of the psychology of projection and its bearing on the imagery of distance. Although the intrusion once again of apparently unrelated considerations—in this case didactic and psychological—may well appear *ad hoc,* I introduce them here only to be able to extrapolate from the clinical materials in the direction of cultural and existential understanding. This procedure is consistent with a third reading of Freud, one that attempts to avoid the subject-object dichotomy as it undergirds and sustains the debate between projection and a reality that allegedly transcends projection.

Although there is a rather precipitous gap between the more fundamental and general principles of the Rorschach test and the actual details and intricacies of the test itself, we can nevertheless quickly pick out those materials that bear on our argument in a manner that, although oversimplified, will not distort their intent.[4] One set of materials is of particular value here and is especially amenable to cultural and theological materials. I refer to a particular type of response usually known as "vista responses." In Rorschach interpretation, all responses are described and analyzed according to the special psychological processes that a stimulus evokes in the subject. Responses or associations classified as vista responses characteristically indicate a sense of height and depth, but more especially of distance. The subject, in responding to the ink blot, constructs a sense of perspective and distance. According to Beck, vista responses indicate the projection of a differential perspective between objects and their ad-

[4] This discussion is drawn from Samuel J. Beck, Anne G. Beck, Eugene E. Levitt, and Herman B. Molish, *Rorschach's Test, Vol. I: Basic Processes* (New York: Grune and Stratton, 1961), pp. 109–125.

jacent area in the stimulus card.[5] A recent discussion of vista responses states that they add a transcendental quality of expansiveness or distance to the entire percept.[6] Clearly, vista responses are one point at which projective psychology bears on discussions of transcendence, for both presuppose the imagery of distance.

Vista responses belong to a larger group of responses all of which are determined by the effects of shading and light and these together stand in contrast to those responses determined by color. Color responses in general pertain psychologically to the "lively affects," to impulse sensitivity and gratification and to social pleasure—provided of course that they are appropriately modulated by form and that the form is adequate. On the other hand, the shading responses suggest painful emotionality—anxiety, depressed attitudes, and especially, feelings of inadequacy. Therefore, vista responses are especially associated with the psychological processes of self-evaluation, self-esteem, and the adequacy of self-control. Their psychological meaning is neither good nor bad—that is, they can refer to destructive feelings of inadequacy or they may just as well indicate that a total self-evaluative process is under way in the subject. It is clear, however, that the sensing or construction of distance as a psychological act is intimately related to inner, self-evaluative processes. Vista responses and their underlying meaning therefore give still further psychological form to what Protestant theology means by transcendence.

We can move beyond the immediate considerations of clinical insight and closer to theological and existential concerns by way of the psychology of Alfred Adler, whose writings on the problem of distance are often adduced to clarify the inner, psychological processes associated with vista responses on the Rorschach.[7] According to Adler, the construction of distance is to be

---

[5] Beck *et al., Rorschach's Test,* I, 109.

[6] Robert M. Allen, *Student's Rorschach Manual* (New York: International Universities Press, 1966), p. 90, n. 2.

[7] Alfred Adler, "The Problem of Distance," *The Practice and Theory of Individual Psychology* (New Haven: Harcourt, 1924).

properly understood only in the context of the wider range of
processes that together compose man's full psychological nature.
Distance is understood as a function of the overall thrust of the
self toward its own self-completion. The presence of references
to distance in the language and imagery of the subject signifies
the presence of an obstacle to self-completion.[8] We may take
Adler's notion of "the obstacle" to signify inner division and also
social alienation. Therefore, the imagery of distance indicates
that the inner movement of the self toward its own completion
—as regards its instinctual trends, its social propensities, and its
desire for forms of meaning and understanding that encompass
these—has not yet been centered into a higher, wider source of
unification. In this regard, Adler has spoken of those patients
whose therapeutic plight is summarized in the synoptic com-
plaint, "if only." If only I had this ability, if only that had not
happened, if only things were thus and so. Or, as Luther might
just as well have said, if only God were both just and merciful, if
only I were not sin and ashes.

Brief and simplistic as these psychological notations are,
they do encourage the conclusion that the "collapse of the transcendent" signifies a rather thorough-going alteration in the
internal organization of self-restraint or self-limitation. The ap-

[8] Adler's remarks on distance resemble Denis de Rougemont's discussion
of romantic love. De Rougemont speaks of "the obstruction" that creates
distance between passion and its possibilities for completion in faith. This
dynamic is the subject of his attempt to disclose the deeper, theological
meanings behind the erotic myths of the West. The pervasiveness and
tenacity of this dynamic require his conclusion that the marriage relation
must be brought under the control of faith if it is to survive the assaults of
passion. (See Denis de Rougemont, *Love in the Western World,* trans.
Montgomery Belgion [New York: Pantheon Books, 1956], pp. 42, 59, 60,
283–287). Freud had the same trouble with Dora ("Fragment of an Analysis
of a Case of Hysteria," *Collected Papers,* III)—or, perhaps, Dora had the
same trouble with Freud—and he relied heavily on the notion of transference
to guide him through the analysis, although even that did not seem to be
enough. Through the phenomenon of transference Freud attempted to answer the same question that de Rougemont asks about the final moral
validity of romantic love. De Rougemont asks, "Marry Iseult?" in order to
embarrass passion and draw it into the higher organization of faith—that
is, to "transcend" passion. Freud spoke of passion through the notion of
"transference-love" and attempted to bring it under the higher control of
total insight.

pearance of a theological movement such as the death-of-God theology, in which the traditional Protestant view of transcendence is said to have collapsed into immanence, means, if only psychologically, that those of our culture for whom this movement is meaningful are undergoing changes in their normative understanding of human fulfillment. The collapse of transcendence into immanence reflects an inner psychic movement in which the criterion of self-limitation is being replaced by one of self-completion. In this sense, theological existentialism can be understood as a cultural vista response and the death-of-God theology a therapeutic doubting of the normative claims that underlie the Protestant Christian's crisis of conscience.

At this point the psychology of distance, implicit in the theology of transcendence, articulates directly with Freud's psychoanalytic thought. Freud's psychology is really a psychology of distance—of the collapse and recovery of distance. It is a clinical commonplace that vista responses are direct expressions of superego processes. The superego, then, is a structure of distance. All that has been said of the superego can now be said of distance. Thinking dynamically and not metapsychologically, the key construct is transference, which refers to an appearance of the forces that create repression and the superego. The therapeutic thrust of this psychology is therefore against the superego, against distance. From the dynamic point of view, Freud's psychology "collapses" distance. The third or iconic reading of Freud's thought follows from this: the religious image of the Devil, so intimately associated with the problematic of the superego, is an image of distance. Understanding and interpretation, when directed to such religious images, move against distance and therefore create another problem: the recovery or winning of distance.

Theological recommendations of transcendence have psychological form: they are recommendations that the superego be transcended. Consider once again Roland Bainton's description of Luther's tremors, this time with regard to their bearing on what he calls "the man of our secularized generation." His description is quite consistent with this interpretation of distance in Luther's experiences. Bainton writes:

> The man of our secularized generation may have difficulty in understanding the tremors of his medieval forebear. There are indeed elements in the religion of Luther of a very primitive character, which hark back to the childhood of the race. He suffered from the savage's fear of a malevolent deity, the enemy of men, capricious, easily and unwittingly offended if sacred places be violated or magical formulas mispronounced. His was the fear of ancient Israel before the ark of the Lord's presence. Luther felt similarly toward the sacred hosts of the Saviour's body; and when it was carried in procession, panic took hold of him. His God was the God who inhabited the storm clouds brooding on the brow of Sinai, into whose presence Moses could not enter with unveiled face and live. Luther's experience, however, far exceeds the primitive and should not be so unintelligible to the modern man who, gazing upon the uncharted nebulae through instruments of his own devising, recoils with a sense of abject littleness.[9]

It is the tension between God the high and the sense of abject littleness that we now characterize as the sense of distance.

Through an iconic reading of Freud, we can see the means by which the superego can, by way of its correlate religious image, be penetrated, and understanding can emerge. At this point, the force of Freud's psychology is not so much against the doctrine of transcendence as it is against the psychological infrastructure undergirding that doctrine. The Protestant Christian's experience of his transcendent God presupposes the anguished conscience. What is the fate of this paradigm if its infrastructure undergoes alteration? Psychoanalytic psychology moves against distance, against the high reaches of the Protestant's spiritual perception. It asks whether such distance is "false distance." Must this distance be collapsed? And, if distance is to be won, is it to be recovered "on the other side" of the collapse of distance?

Before pursuing this question further, we note the im-

[9] Bainton, *Here I Stand*, p. 31.

portance of the problem of distance in post-Protestant interpretations and in the death-of-God theology. If the imagery of distance is in fact implicit or latent in the theological view of transcendence, we should expect that the post-Protestant group would not only find it necessary to discuss the meaning of distance, but also that they should do so far more explicitly and directly than do such theological figures as Niebuhr and Tillich. This turns out to be very much the case. Norman Brown finds distance central to no less than the following considerations: genital organization, subject-object relation, repression, and the work of the Devil. For Brown, distance must be collapsed if symbolical consciousness is to be achieved.

> In vicarious experience there is both identification and distance. . . . Representative institutions depend upon the distance separating the spectators from the actor on the stage; the distance which permits both identification and detachment; which makes for a participation without action; which establishes the detached observer, whose participation consists in seeing and is restricted to seeing. . . .
>
> The detached observer: subject and object distantiated; the subject-object dualism. The dualism which distantiates subject and object, allows the subject only pictures. . . . Pictures: spectral images on the inside, which represent external reality to the subject. Cognition then, as well as politics, is mediated through representative institutions. Correspondence is then a relation of likeness, or copying, or imitation, between internal images and external reality; instead of correspondence as sympathy, or action at a distance, or active participation. . . .[10]

Bakan makes similar although far more therapeutically recognizable use of the notion of distance. He believes that not only psychotherapy but also all human development require a critical phase in which agentic attitudes dominate the psychological life of the person. As these attitudes increase, the need to project them through images becomes more and more necessary. These attitudes are finally given dynamic and projective ex-

[10] Brown, *Love's Body*, pp. 119–120.

pression in the figure of the Devil. So it is that the Devil, agency, the superego—indeed the very possibility of projection itself—all reflect psychic distancing. Bakan, however, uses distance to refer to insight, what Brown means by "action at a distance."

> In the religious allegory, God holds the content unconscious, and the Devil is the counterforce which renders the material conscious. The task involved in Freud's self-analysis was that of bringing the unconscious into consciousness. Continuing the allegory, an alliance of the ego with the Devil was necessary to make it possible to achieve the requisite "distance." Thus by permitting successful intervention of the Devil the person wins "distance." Hence, paradoxically, the Devil must cause his own destruction. By bringing the demonic into the light, the demonic is stripped of its demonic character. More prosaically this can be stated as follows: the disease of the neurotic is his guilt. This guilt is, in itself, an evil and its removal is good. However, within the neurosis the guilt is a punishment for evil. Within the neurosis a counterforce to the punishing imago is required. Hence there is an alliance with such a counter-imago as will allow all to become open, accessible to consciousness. If God is a guilt-producing imago, then the Devil is the counterforce. But the Devil's very permissiveness is the cause of his own destruction. Having permitted all to become open, the infantile character of both imagos is revealed and "distance" with respect to each is won.[11]

Also notably different from Brown's discussion is Bakan's clear association of female sexuality with the processes by which agency is mitigated—that is, with the processes by which distance is collapsed.

Bakan echoes Brown's conviction that psychoanalysis is a stage of consciousness higher than Protestantism but that without Protestantism there could not have been psychoanalysis. However that may be, it does seem clear that the kind of therapeutic consciousness that both conceive is rooted in the psychological interpretation of the problem of distance and its relation to

[11] Bakan, *Freud,* pp. 232–233.

immanence and immediacy. This integration requires an expansion of our understanding of self-transcendence, an expansion that has not been made explicit by the theological existentialists, although, as we have argued, such explication is probably consistent with their deepest, albeit unacknowledged, intentions. Accordingly, a constructive argument—were we to indulge in one—should begin by noting that the centrality of distance constitutes the permanent psychological contribution of Protestantism to religious self-understanding. The permanent psychological contribution of psychoanalysis is the precise way in which distance, apparently so hostile to immanence at the inception of the crisis of conscience, subsequently opens up into immanence in the resolution of the crisis. If the collapse of distance is the contribution of depth psychology to Protestant theology, then the recovery of distance becomes the next and crucial question.

Philip Rieff does not speak explicitly of the psychology of distance, probably because, as noted, his point of view so closely resembles that of the theological existentialists, in whose thought a psychology of distance remains unexplicated. Still there is a presupposition of a psychology of distance in his work. Distance is a superego phenomenon, and in the collapse of distance we find reflected the collapse of the superego. That collapse is also a release of transference, for transference is an internal as well as an interpersonal, cultural, and existential-theological problem. The collapse of the superego is identical with what Rieff calls deconversion and the rise of the analytic attitude.

> The sacralist cures, therefore, by recalling the individual to some principle of legitimacy, by reinforcing, through sacramental action, the cultural super-ego, and by re-enacting its internalization. He speaks for some corporate identity within which the individual can feel secure in his personal identity. The analyst, on the other hand, must deal with individuals beyond salvation, that is, beyond salvation through communal purposiveness. Therefore, the understanding of the individual's own authority is the final step in resolving a corporate identity that no longer serves to integrate the self.

Earlier therapists, being sacralists, guarded the cultural super-ego, communicating to the individual the particular signs and symbols in which the super-ego was embodied or personified. In this sense, earlier therapists assumed priestly powers. The modern therapist, however, is without priestly powers, precisely because he guards against the cultural super-ego and, unlike the sacralist, is free to criticize the moral demand system. Rather, he speaks for the individual buried alive, as it were, in the culture. To be thus freed from a tyrannical cultural super-ego is to be properly bedded in the present world. Analysis is not an initiation but a counter-initiation, to end the need for initiations. The modern therapeutic idea is to empty those meanings that link the individual to dying worlds by assents of faith for which his analytic reason tells him he is not truly responsible. In this way, by acts of interpretation, the sacred becomes symptom. Sacred images are, then, the visible forms not of grace but of sickness. The sacralist yields to the analyst as the therapeutic functionary of modern culture.[12]

The triumph of the therapeutic is most recognizable as the collapse of social distance. As Rieff wryly remarks, "I fear we are getting to know one another."

The death-of-God theology shares Freud's dynamic intuitions, and the psychology of distance is the clue to the psychological meaning of this movement. Altizer's proposed coincidence of opposites and eternal recurrence, in addition to their religious and philosophical meanings, are also referable to dynamic events in the life of the self. They are the result of his "theological interpretation of the Oedipus complex."[13] Altizer summarizes his interpretation as follows: "This fantastic myth, to which Freud clung as the literal truth, can only truly be meaningful if it is interpreted theologically: the Oedipus complex is the primordial project of murdering God, only the death of God can provide an adequate explanation for the origin of repression."[14] Yet his is

[12] Rieff, *Triumph,* pp. 76–77.
[13] Thomas J. J. Altizer, *Mircea Eliade and the Dialectic of the Sacred* (Philadelphia: Westminster Press, 1963), chaps. vii and viii.
[14] *Ibid.* p. 161.

not a theological interpretation in the sense in which Tillich, for example, "interprets" Freud. It is true that Tillich's God of theological theism and the transcendent God that Altizer rejects are the same God whom Nietzsche said "had to be killed." I have called these images of God the transference-God, the distantiated God who produces and then resolves the crisis of conscience. Tillich, however, attempts to move beyond this formulation by linking the superego to his theological analysis of human estrangement, only to reintroduce distance by way of the concept of the God above God, although the more overt intent of his theologizing is always in the direction of immanence. In so doing, he inadvertently ontologizes the vista motif into the structure of his Christian anthropology.

But Altizer's theological interpretation of the Oedipus complex presupposes the permanent collapse of the superego, of just that distance; it is this that distinguishes him from theological existentialism and allies him with the post-Protestant group. For Altizer, the superego is that psychic structure that underlies the repressive history so long established by God the high spiritually and conceptually in the Christian doctrine of transcendence. Through his theological interpretation this structure dissolves, because Altizer identifies Freud's unconscious with Eliade's understanding of the sacred, and by implication, therefore, he also identifies the superego (Freud) with the meaning of the profane in Eliade's thought. His interpretation, the introduction of a coincidentia in place of the dualism of immanence and transcendence, therefore collapses the barrier between conscious and unconscious. As we have seen, the dynamic function of the harsh superego is to maintain repression and its corollary, the distinction between conscious and unconscious. Like Brown, whom he admires, Altizer speaks of a release of energies subsequent to this dissolution, energies that were formerly bound by the transcendent but are now accessible to the experienced inwardness of the self. And he associates this release with a disclosure into human awareness of the image of the mother: "the Oedipus complex is at bottom a desire for the primal paradise, and the sexual desire for the mother is fundamentally a desire for union with unfallen being."[15] The superego collapses, creating in the ego a mystical sense of cosmic inwardness.

There is, however, no attempt to effect a recovery of distance in Altizer's concluding proposal of a creative willing of the self. His work, therefore, prompts a "constructive" question: Is a recovery of distance possible, which will not abrogate the "sheer immediacy of being"?[16]

---

*Transcendence and
social distance*

THE writings of William Hamilton and Paul Van Buren also propose in effect what I have called the collapse of distance, although their discussions give more emphasis to social distance. Psychological distance and social distance are, of course, inseparable. The collapse of transcendence issues in new capacities for social intimacy and involvement and, as such, presupposes internal changes as well. Implicit here is the risk of loss of centeredness and the distance that this requires. Hamilton's recommendations are far more conventionally therapeutic than are those of Altizer. Following the route of ego psychology and its amend-

---

[15] *Ibid.,* p. 153.

[16] Altizer's discussion bears on the question of a recovery of distance only at the point of regression or transference, which is a retrograde movement against the superego. But the connection between this and Eliade's thought does not concern us. The logic of our discussion does suggest that one can move beyond Freud to a number of different, more dynamic, understandings of religion, including that represented by Eliade; but this discussion also suggests that further distinctions must be made regarding the thought of Freud and Eliade. One line of thought lies in Jung's notion of transference as "conjunctio" and coincidentia. One cannot simply identify the sacred with Freud's unconscious. Without working out the psychological roots of Eliade's theory of religion and its very intimate relation to the Freud-Jung problem, it is not possible for this discussion, in Altizer's words, to "move beyond Freud and Eliade" (*ibid.,* p. 175).

ments of classical psychoanalysis, Hamilton bypasses the possibility that the death of God is accompanied by a release of fantasy. Hamilton says:

> Oedipus shows us the individual's psychological bondage, Orestes
> shows us his freedom and struggle for harmony. . . .
>
> Psychologically we are in a new world beyond the oedipal
> state, and religiously we are in a new world as well. . . .
>
> To be freed from the parents is to be freed from religion,
> the religious a priori, religion as necessary, God as meeter of
> needs and solver of problems. Orestean theology means the end
> of faith's preoccupation with inner conflict, of the struggle of
> faith, of the escape from the enemy God, of the careful confession
> of sin.[17]

Instead, Hamilton prefers the rational categories of ego psychology, placing developmentally lower value on infantile sexuality in favor of regression in the service of the ego, or what is
sometimes called "independent ego energies." The sense of immediacy that the experience of primary dependency creates,
which Christian theology has dealt with classically through its
doctrine of Creation and existentially through the concept of
estrangement and which psychoanalysis has dealt with through
transference and all that it implies, Hamilton ignores by means
of the principles of ego psychology. In a fashion somewhat reminiscent of behaviorism, Hamilton uses ego psychology as a methodological solution to a psychological problem, in this case the
problem of distance. He achieves or recovers distance without,
however, attending to the retrograde emphasis of Freud's thought
and the imaginative—as well as the moral—possibilities that this
emphasis contains. Having "mastered" the problem of infantile

---

[17] William Hamilton, "The Death of God Theology," *The Christian Scholar,*
LXIII, No. 1 (Spring 1965), 42–43. This discussion polarizes and separates
"psychological bondage" and "personal freedom" much as the theological
existentialists do. For this reason the solution is psychologically and perhaps even religiously dangerous; although it frees us from the terror and
oppression of the past, it also denies the therapeutic power of a confrontation with the past. It implies that psychological bondage is not theological
and that personal freedom is not psychological.

sexuality by assuming ego energies independent of it, Hamilton
is in a position to propose for the modern self a domesticated
Kierkegaardian leap from the oedipal phase into Orestean, urban
responsibility, leaving behind the nuclear problematic of superego, repression, and transference. He bypasses the possibility of
a release of fantasy, particularly the reality of the image of the
mother that underlies Altizer's interest in the history of religion.
Hamilton's proposals, therefore, lead to a "theology of the secular" rather than to a theological analysis of religious images.

Unlike Altizer, both Hamilton and Van Buren envisage the
collapse of the transcendent as releasing energies primarily for
social involvement. Hamilton's God, who is the "meeter of needs
and solver of problems," is what I have called the transference-
God; release from the bondage of oedipal psychological organization frees the modern self to relate more fully to his neighbor
and to meet the responsibilities of urban life generally.

In effect, Van Buren shares with Hamilton and Altizer the
same dynamic critique of theological existentialism, although
his method is language analysis and he does not employ psychological categories regularly and consistently. The theological
notion of transcendence is approached in Van Buren's discussions
through the use of R. M. Hare's now familiar notion of the "blik."
His attempt to analyze the blik is an attempt to render the opacity
of Biblical narrative and its central images transparent to understanding by submitting it to the verification principle. However,
the application of the verification principle, when applied to the
blik, has consequences that are not simply cognitive and intellectual. Energies formerly given over to an intellectual preoccupation with belief and the nature of its object are released. These
energies are freed for moral action, for participation in the life of
"the others." Following Bonhoeffer, Van Buren says: "The experience of transcendence is Jesus' being-for-others."[18] But, is
not being "remarkably free" tantamount to being released from
the introverting, repressive effects of the transference-God?

[18] Paul Van Buren, *The Secular Meaning of the Gospel* (New York: Macmillan, 1963), p. 132.

The problematic situation that is created for the believer by his blik is really not very different from Adler's discussion of the psychological problem of distance, for the very presence of the blik creates a kind of distance that, when seen through or interpreted—Van Buren speaks of disclosure or discernment[19]—makes a higher degree of moral participation psychologically possible. The dynamics of this new freedom are, in Van Buren's own words, the dynamics of interpersonal relationships. He says:

> We have already suggested some of the dynamics of interpersonal relations which may result from an encounter with a free man. If our reaction is positive, we may feel attracted to him and we may be encouraged to be more free ourselves, or at least challenged to be more free. Our fears may be calmed simply by the presence of one who is unafraid and free from the fears and anxieties which bind us. On the other hand, our reaction may be negative: we may be threatened by a free person; we may feel judged in our insecurity and bondage. This is an odd experience and if we speak of it at all, we will do so with odd words. We might say there is a certain mystery about it, a mystery of the depths of human personality and relationships.[20]

Language analysis, then, according to Van Buren, seems to have a therapeutic function, in the expanded sense in which we have discussed transference, for this discussion is highly reminiscent of Freud's psychological discussions of "the great man."[21] By invoking the rhetoric of therapeutic psychology, Van Buren declares the connections between his use of language analysis and the intuitions of depth psychology. His use of language analysis is therefore a therapeutic for religious method. It is an attempt to recover distance on the other side of transference without, however, exploring its deeper dynamics.

From time to time we have noted briefly the way in which problems in theological response to Freud do touch on considerations in the writings of psychology itself. Although psychology as

[19] *Ibid.*, p. 143.
[20] *Ibid.*, pp. 137–138.
[21] See Freud, "The Moses of Michelangelo," *Collected Papers,* IV.

a discipline does not find any advantage in a discussion of theology, nevertheless the psychology of personality, at least at this specifiable point, does seem to be struggling with the same dilemma that besets both theology and the death-of-God group, at least in terms of our higher psychological reading. This is true at least for those writings that are sometimes referred to as "humanistic psychology" and more colloquially as the "third force."[22] Does the problem of distance pertain to humanistic psychology's theoretical meanderings?

In its broadest outlines the methodological strategy of these writers is to define their concern in triangular relation to behaviorism and psychoanalysis, the two stereotypical options in American psychology, in order to work out a third position that combines the objective bias of empirical work and the subjective bias of the more dynamic clinical work. In so doing, they attempt, like theological existentialism and like the third reading of Freud, to transcend the subject-object dichotomy.

More important, however, is their attention to what is in effect a moral psychology of socialization, where the dynamic of distance is at work. This can be seen if we note the position of psychoanalytic psychology generally in these theories of socialization, especially the significance given to the superego. The norms for optimal development in the third force are usually mounted on a criticism of psychoanalytic theory, especially the reductiveness of the theory of infantile sexuality. In each case, the theoretical point of departure for the proposed reformulation of health and maturity is a developmental critique of the superego.[23]

---

[22] This reference is primarily to the work of Allport, Maslow, and Carl Rogers, although by implication it includes such earlier neo-Freudians as Sullivan, Horney, and Fromm and, in ego psychology, the work of Erikson as well.

[23] For example, Gordon Allport defines functional autonomy and propriate striving in relation to lower and earlier organizations and has described the latter through the notion of the superego. (See *Pattern and Growth in Personality* [New York: Holt, Rinehart and Winston, 1961], chap. x, and *Becoming*, pp. 68–74.) Maslow builds his psychology of being on the transcendence of deficiency motivation and, in terms of sociality, a transcending of the environment. (See Abraham H. Maslow, "Health as Tran-

The third force advances this particular kind of argument concerning the nature of socialization with a good deal of regularity. Development is construed to be in one way or another a double movement; it is first a movement in the direction of socialization, which, when completed, makes possible a subsequent disengagement of psychic energies from social form, energies that can then return to the self. Although by means of very different categories, the development of the individual is projected as one of initial socialization, in which the self is formed in the image of others, and subsequent disengagement, in which it "transcends" environmental formations and becomes unique.

We sense here the same debate with psychoanalysis that theological existentialism has engaged in. For theological existentialism is also under the impression that superego forms of socialization involve adjustment and simple internalization and that these must, once they have been acquired, be transcended. Like theological existentialism, these theories of personality claim that transcendence can be negotiated theoretically and can be achieved developmentally without reference to the dynamics of repression and the subsequent release of fantasy and religious images.[24]

---

scendence of Environment," *Toward a Psychology of Being* [Princeton, N.J.: D. Van Nostrand, 1962].) Carl Rogers's notions of acceptance, congruence, full-functioning person, and the like, presuppose a "feeling through" (not a "working through" as Freud said) of "conditions of worth." These conditions of worth are early introjects and as such are identical with Freud's superego. (See *Client-Centered Therapy,* pp. 498–503.) Fromm's productive orientation is a transcending of nonproductive (i.e., oedipal) orientations. (See Erich Fromm, *Man for Himself* [New York: Rinehart, 1947], pp. 62–107.) Sullivan sought a "process" view of self and society to break out of the mechanism of Freudian theory—"parataxic distortion" is his rewriting of the notion of transference, and it presupposes his reading of Whitehead. (See Harry Stack Sullivan, *The Inter-Personal Theory of Psychiatry* [New York: W. W. Norton, 1953], pp. 28, 102.) Erik Erikson's "revisions" are far more subtle, although they are regularly addressed to such Freudian notions as superego, identification, and libido theory. (See Erikson, *Identity.*) Because all of these theories seek to move an understanding of development beyond superego organization, and because that organization is also problematic for theology, they could in this sense be called death-of-god psychologies.

24 Of these writers, Erikson, Maslow, and, to a lesser extent, Fromm attempt to expand Freud's analysis of fantasy and dream into wider social (Fromm),

For the most part, however, this dichotomy between personal inwardness and social commitment remains unresolved in personality theory, despite the strenuousness of methodological discussions. The dichotomy has its origins in the subject-object dichotomy and infects the understanding of structural and dynamic dimensions of selfhood as well. Such personality theories as Allport's, Fromm's, Rogers's, and Sullivan's, like theological existentialism, in their own way make a fatal distinction between the developmental and whatever lies beyond mere socialization. In so doing, they lack the necessary presuppositional equipment for a generic intersubjectivity, which would undergird such distinctions as these between earlier and later, regression and development, and childhood and selfhood. Such a theory would protect both personal inwardness and creative sociality. That personality theory shares with theological existentialism the same sort of dilemmas no doubt in part accounts for the fact that the psychological writings of the third force have been extremely attractive to pastoral and systematic theologians.[25]

The collapse of distance: final consequence of Freud's psychology

THE implications of the notion of distance for the collapse of the transcendent must now be carried one step further. None of the death-of-God theologians is *directly* concerned with the

sociohistorical (Erikson), and socioreligious (Maslow) contexts. In this attempt to retain dynamically active images in a theory of the self, they share affinity with Altizer, Bakan, and Brown. (See, for example, Erich Fromm, *The Forgotten Language* [New York: Grove Press, 1951]; Erikson's analysis of the dream of a young man studying to be a missionary, in "The Nature of Clinical Evidence," *Insight and Responsibility*, pp. 57–70; and Maslow's discussion of what is in effect a psychology of religious conciousness in *Religions, Values, and Peak-Experiences* [Columbus, Ohio: Ohio State University Press, 1964].)

[25] Thomas C. Oden, *Kerygma and Counseling* (Philadelphia: Westminster Press, 1966), and Don S. Browning, *Atonement and Psychotherapy* (Philadelphia: Westminster Press, 1966), are typical of such efforts.

meaning of mass culture for the meaning of transcendence. And those who concern themselves at all seem interested in the moral rather than the imaginative features of mass culture. Theological existentialism creates a gap at this point through its notion of the self that transcends social adjustment. But this conclusion presupposes a mechanistic reading of socialization such that neither the theological nor the psychosocial dimensions of self-hood articulate at any point. Given this model as I have argued, transcendence becomes as mechanistic as the modes of adjustment it seeks to correct.

It becomes simply amusing to trace this dichotomy through post-Protestant writings and death-of-God theology. In the work of Brown and Rieff, inwardness and sociality are polarized in ways even more extreme than in theological existentialism—mysticism and therapeutic adjustment. In the death-of-God debate, where it reappears in the work of Altizer and Hamilton, extreme inwardness (sheer immediacy of being) bears little resemblance to the moral participation that urban responsibility requires. Inward, psychic depth and authentic sociality are split further and further apart. If there is a psychological dimension to theological and psychological theory, then perhaps these different "theories" themselves in a sense testify to the fragmenting effects of the collapse of the transcendant on conceptions of socialization. In each case, however, the question of mass culture is not broached, in spite of the fact that the collapse of the reality of transcendence, a sense of distance, the removal of the obstacle, all point to a radical immanentism.[26] A recovery of distance, I now argue, can occur only "on the other side" of such a collapse. We therefore return to the notion of transference, one way of speaking psychologically of what theology has meant by immanence, this time in its cultural and social rather than in its individual and psychotherapeutic manifestations. In this context, we may speak of the collapse of social distance and the problem of identity. In doing so, we carry Freud's analysis of religion—and the task of this study as well—to its conclusion.

[26] See Gabriel Vahanian, *The Death of God: The Culture of Our Post-Christian Era* (New York: George Braziller, 1957), chaps. viii and ix.

The problem of transference in mass society is helpfully put forward by Allen Wheelis in his discussions of the place of identity, or rather the absence of identity, in the context of mass society, particularly in his discussion of the "sociology of transference."[27] The last fifty years of American life, Wheelis argues, have been characterized by a steady decline of the effectiveness of the superego as the primary source of identity formation and as the structure organizing internal psychic depth and its social forms of expression. Like Erik Erikson, Rollo May, and others, Wheelis notes that the central therapeutic problem that confronted psychoanalysis at its inception—which in fact occasioned its appearance and to which its implicit moral psychology was addressed—was neurosis and not identity. The classic psychoanalytic techniques for the investigation of unconscious childhood conflicts presupposed a firm sense of personal identity on the part of the patient. It was assumed that clarification of conflicts in infantile sexuality would release the patient for nonneurotic living. According to this argument, psychoanalysis articulates with the prevailing social climate and its particular normative understanding of the relation between self and society.

The touchstone of Wheelis's argument is the assumption that personal identity and social and technological change are always in tension. A sense of personal continuity and sameness can support only limited participation in changing social and economic forms. One must either deny change and live in a psychically constricted relation to the social and economic environment or undergo a deepening sense of personal ambiguity with regard to one's own inner self-consistency.

Wheelis carefully describes this dilemma:

> Neurotic suffering in the present is coming more and more to derive from a quite different process. Society does not embody such generally accepted patterns of value, and the individual is caught in a dilemma: if out of the multitudinous choices of modern life he commits himself to certain values and with them builds a

[27] Allen Wheelis, *The Quest for Identity* (New York: W. W. Norton, 1958), pp. 159–173.

durable identity, he is apt to lose contact with a rapidly changing world; if he does not commit himself, but maintains an alert readiness to move with the current, he suffers a loss of the sense of self. Not knowing what he stands for, he does not know who he is. This occasions the anxiety which is coming to be the name of our age. Any development that threatens further to liquify this already fluid sense of identity may increase anxiety to an unendurable pitch and hence prompt the ego to exclude the threatening wish or perception from awareness.[28]

The crisis in identity is understood psychodynamically as the decline of the superego. The point of contact between discussions of the superego, identity, and Rorschach psychology would be the M response, the experience of movement. Beck says that "the more original and deviating movement associations are representatives of very deep wishes, innermost psychologic activity. . . . The psychologic activities that M projects to the surface are therefore of a kind that can only materialize in the image of a human being. . . . The nuclear M or movement association is thus one in which a whole human being is engaged."[29] M responses are the psychological side of Tillich's formulation of centeredness. Through M we glimpse the psychological infrastructure of that movement of the self which Tillich for example characterizes as "going-out from a center of action." Tillich formulates this movement as the principle of growth and the function of self-creation.[30]

The strong superego is an "internal transference" of the ego to the superego. The declining power of the superego to bind impulses appears now at the cultural level as cultural transference.

[28] *Ibid.,* p. 129. Any doubt regarding Wheelis's debt to Freud is dispelled by comparing his description with Freud's: "The dwindling of the conscious individual personality, the focusing of thoughts and feelings into a common direction, the predominance of the affective side of the mind and of unconscious psychical life, the tendency to the immediate carrying out of intentions as they emerge—all this corresponds to a state of regression to a primitive mental activity, of just such a sort as we should be inclined to ascribe to the primal horde" (Freud, *Group Psychology and the Analysis of the Ego,* trans. James Strachey [New York: Bantam Books, 1960], p. 70).

[29] Beck *et al., Rorschach's Test,* I, 72.

[30] See Tillich, *Systematic Theology,* III, 30–32.

Cultural transference, however, is not mass hysteria either in the colloquial or in the clinical-diagnostic sense, for hysteria as a clinical problem requires a reduction in the harshness of the superego. In such cases, the psychoanalytic "lifting of superego repressions" does not dissolve the superego as a psychic structure; instead, it simply makes its dictates more transparent and more accessible to the deeper intentionality of the self. Social and technological change, however, have performed that therapeutic function on the cultural superego and, through that, on the individual superego. Defenses, against which patient and psychoanalyst formerly labored long and hard, now dissolve before their eyes; but the deeper currents of intentionality formerly held in abeyance by infantile conflict do not so readily appear. Their absence has escaped much clinical theory.

> No one is altogether free of unconscious conflict, and to the extent that it is present and can be analyzed, transference can be resolved or diminished. In these days, however, more and more often the aspirations directed toward the analyst are the product, not of unconscious conflict, but of the loss of the eternal verities which formerly bound these aspirations. This culturally determined loss of institutional absolutes creates the same potential for transference as exists when security is lost by unconscious conflict. There is the same propensity to direct toward the analyst the yearning, the fear, and the hate. In these circumstances transference cannot be analytically resolved. For psychoanalysis does not surmount culture, but is part of it. It provides no escape from culturally determined problems.[31]

Two points require special emphasis in this description of cultural transference. First, in both its individual and social forms, cultural transference is experienced inwardly as an "intense, preoccupying yearning" for a sense of stable centeredness. In this yearning we find the experiential conclusion of Freud's argument against religion. Here Freud's analytic of religion, of the superego, of transference, comes to an end. For once

[31] Wheelis, *Quest,* p. 171.

the patterns of repression are disclosed, the superego is no longer the agent either of repression or of control. Yet, repression has been the occasion of theology's argument for transcendence. Even the unconscious portions of the ego are closer to awareness, and the ego must therefore be the source of control. It can no longer depend on society for control but only for release. Given an experience of this kind, paradigmatic synthesis between transcendent God and anguished conscience is not simply fragmented—that has been happening for some time—but is permanently dissolved. The structure of self-understanding as a structure of guilt to which the experience of justification has therapeutically ministered, that very structure dissolves. This is the psychodynamic meaning of the collapse of the transcendent— a meaning that has fundamental ontological and theological consequences and that cannot be separated from these consequences. All distance is lost, be its referent God the high, denied elements within the self, or social relation. Transcendence, we may say, dissolves into "intense, preoccupying yearning." It is a yearning without, apparently, form or object.

In the presence of this particular type of experience, existential theology is helpless. Having lost touch with its psychic roots, it loses touch with its divine object. Its strategies of reparation have been based on a particular understanding of the structure of self-limitation as a structure of guilt. When that structure itself changes radically, then theology (one can hear the theologian say) should change radically. Theology must become "relevant" to cultural change. Such a radical adaptation has been the intent of the death-of-God theology as well as of recent theologies of the secular. But even these theologies have been unable to incorporate the intense, restless, preoccupying yearnings of modernity. Theology, now dissociated from the vagrant yearnings to which it formerly gave transcendent referent, psychic structure, moral direction, and social control, that theology now itself becomes a yearning. Theology becomes a passion all its own, an enthusiasm without an object, a yearning with only apparent form. Theology has become the illusion of structure.

In the following chapter, I will argue that this state of affairs is not so terminal as it appears, that there are, so to speak, resources for this state of affairs, but that these resources lie in the conclusion of the analytic point itself. And the analytic point, I will argue, is not so analytic as it seems. It is a function of particular readings of Freud. There are resources in the very collapse of distance itself for the recovery of distance.

Seven: Transition: nostalgia, hope, and the recovery of distance

Distance and fantasy

THERE is a second point of importance in Allen Wheelis's description of cultural transference, and in its implications there is, I think, an unexpected possibility for what can be called the "recovery of distance." In both its individual and social forms, the yearning of which Wheelis speaks cannot be analytically resolved. It cannot be so resolved because the type of psychological conflict that in the past has been accessible to analytical resolution consisted in a form of repression that was associated with a firm, even harsh, superego. However, as Wheelis argues, the social process itself now performs what classic psychoanalysis considered to be the essence of therapy; analytic intervention of the classic sort, therefore, creates an effect quite the opposite of its original intent. Intervention only augments these psychological processes and can only provide the patient—the "patient" being, to use one of Rieff's terms, our hospital culture—with an even greater sensitivity to feeling and to whatever remains of what Freud called the dictates of conscience. The use of the word "intervention" is itself mistaken. The old cure becomes a new disease—or, as this transition implies, a much older disease—and both physician and patient fall ill to that disease.

Perhaps the theologians are right after all. It is not out of place to note that much of Wheelis's criticism of his own profession has a distinctly Niebuhrian ring to it. For Wheelis objects to psychoanalysts who insist that "insight" continues to be therapeutic in spite of accelerating social change and its psychodynamic consequences and who do so to avoid a deepening sense of ambiguity regarding the efficacy of their own calling.

There are important similarities between Wheelis's moral psychology of cultural transference and Rieff's description of a new social character, the therapeutic. But there is a more important and far more fundamental difference, and in that difference lies the possibility that what has been almost entirely an *analytic* of religion could become something more. Rieff's therapeutic type is quite ready to conduct his experimental life with enthusiasm and with a sense of permanent gratitude for his liberation from the authority of the past. But Wheelis's intimations regarding an identityless social type suggest that the collapse of transcendence and the subsequent release of transference affect into social form really has the opposite effect: restless, intense, preoccupying yearning. This yearning is accompanied by but not reducible to the simply dynamic remission of energies formerly cared for by faith and its institutional guardians. It is not simply accountable to interdictory neutrality, to adjustment psychology, or, for that matter, to moral neutrality. It betrays, to use Wheelis's own term, a "quest" for something a good deal more primary.

Wheelis's analysis of intense, preoccupying yearning and longing is related structurally to the loss or collapse of transcendence, to the collapse of distance. It implies, incidentally, that the death-of-God theology is a social as well as an intellectual phenomenon. Dynamically, it is related to the decline of the superego and the release of yearning and fantasy that the superego organized and maintained, individually and socially. We can also speak of the collapse of *social* distance, the loss of a firm sense of identity which can provide the basis for relating the individual to the more affective forms of social life—the result can be seen with special clarity in the imagery of mass culture.

The phenomenon of a collapse of distance makes it possible at least to raise the question of a recovery of distance. Prior to recognizing the collapse of distance, it was not possible to speak of winning distance in an authentic sense. Transcendence and fantasy were opposed to each other, according to theological existentialism. There, fantasy moves "against" distance and the presence of fantasy threatens to collapse distance. Therefore, the way to a recovery of distance lies in the way in which we think psychologically about fantasy. The iconic reading of Freud helps at this point, especially as it has been presented by Brown and Bakan and in Marcuse's reinterpretation of the Freudian distinction between fantasy and reality. According to this distinction, reality is "unpleasant, useful and correct," and fantasy is "pleasant, but becomes useless, untrue." In this framework, fantasy is accessible, in Wheelis's terms, to analytic resolution. That is, it can be reduced interpretively to feelings and attitudes about the ordinary, workaday world. This view is assumed by theological existentialism in its use of the subject-object dichotomy. Fantasy is held in check psychologically by the reality principle and theologically by the principle of transcendence.

In this sense the fantasy so central to Freud's thought, the oedipal fantasy, can be understood only as one fantasy alongside others. Or else it is a master fantasy, the one fantasy of which all others are reflections. In either sense fantasy is understood as simply the projection of a subjective wish, even of the oedipal wish. And in either sense fantasy exists in tension with transcendence, for it is evaluated as being merely subjective, that is, as unobjectified subjectivity requiring reduction to the reality of the reality principle or to the reality of the subject-object dichotomy. I have referred to this view as a lower reading of Freud and of the problem of fantasy, so central to his work.

An iconic approach to the problem of distance and fantasy is necessary. Let us approach fantasy from a perspective not entirely affected either by the reality principle or the principle of transcendence, and in so doing think of fantasy as evincing phenomenal significance in its own right. As such it cannot be accounted for by either the reality principle or the pleasure principle, entirely. From this perspective fantasy signifies neither the absence of the real, nor the presence of pleasure, but rather the inception of imagination. Such an approach dignifies fantasy, and in this very act we are able, in Marcuse's words, to begin "to restore imagination to its rights." Under these conditions the meaning of the Oedipus fantasy can no longer be restricted to "mere fantasy." It is a structure of limitation through which human possibility must go. The Oedipus story is a story about the origins of the capacity for imagination. Or, to couch our third reading entirely in the language of lower readings: it is a fantasy about the act of fantasy itself. For this reason Freud's psychology must be viewed not primarily as a theory of personality nor as a clinical theory, but as a dynamic theory of imagination.

Therefore, the presence of fantasy means, not the collapse of transcendence, as theologians fear, but the beginning of imagination. In the light of our third reading the disposition of fantasy is now a problem in interpretation, rather than an object of theological-doctrinal statement or clinical application. What was merely subjective has become objective, and this movement opens the way for a higher objectivity. The transition to this higher objectivity we call the recovery of distance. Now the problem of fantasy and distance, which we inherit from a higher critique of theology, confronts us directly.

Religious existentialism is more explicitly concerned with the problem of distance than is usually recognized. Rollo May, for example, has been interested in what he calls the phenomenological bases of psychotherapy. He calls for a phenomenological approach to Freud and does so through the phenomenon of distance.[1] May believes it was Freud's ever present "mythology" that saved him from the full mechanistic implications of his determinism. More than any other existential psychotherapist, May is indebted to both the psychological work of Freud and the ontological thought of Paul Tillich, and the problem of distance serves to draw these two perspectives together.

[1] May, "On the Phenomenological Bases of Psychotherapy."

May presents three principles that unite Tillich's ontology and Freud's image of man, the last of which attempts to resolve the problem of distance. These three principles are addressed to the nature and meaning of neurosis, transference, and the uncon-scious. They constitute what is in effect May's "reading" of Freud, in the light of his commitment to existentialist thought. His view of transcendence emerges from his critical commentary on Freud.

There is first the principle of centeredness. Centeredness con-sists in an active, self-determining relation to the social world, accompanied by a sense of inner continuity and sameness. Neu-rosis is viewed as a distortion of centeredness, a shrinking of possibilities in order to maintain centeredness. May likens cen-teredness to Husserl's understanding of integration. The second principle is encounter and relation, the personal possibility of going out from centeredness to participate in the life of other beings. May sees transference as a distortion of encounter, a distortion forcing the person to "go out too far." This distortion is not only a clinical problem, he believes, but is also the "psycho-cultural phenomenon of the organization man," the threat of overparticipation by which one's own intrinsic powers are sacri-ficed in the interest of approval by others.

The third principle, most important for our concerns, alludes to the ontological meaning of Freud's concept of the unconscious. May distinguishes between awareness and consciousness. The former is a capacity persons share with animals, but the latter is the distinctively *human* form of awareness, the capacity not just to know something, but also to know that one knows it. This distinction is also formulated as "awareness at a distance" and as "being aware of distance." The first describes unconscious experience, the latter the actualization of unconscious experience, the goal of psychotherapy.

> The animal who walks on all fours . . . has infinitely greater awareness in many ways than I. . . . [A] dog's alertness at a great distance by senses of smell and hearing is a source of endless amazement. . . . But when man rises on two legs, stands upright

and sees, he does not sense at a distance but is aware *of* a distance between himself and the world. This distance . . . is correlated with consciousness.[2]

In this fashion May is able to speak of the distinction between being aware of repressed experience and knowing that one is aware. When insight occurs in therapy, the patient may say that he has known it all the time. What May calls sensing at a distance is therefore directly referable to repression and superego processes. Sensing at a distance, we now conclude, characterizes our vista responses and the externalized and distantiated God-image that produces the anguished conscience of Protestant spirituality.

A discussion of distance very similar to May's, this time at the point of societal rather than psychological concerns, occurs in a recent study by Gibson Winter. Although he does not discuss the problem of distance directly, it is important for his study as a whole, both methodologically and anthropologically. The basis of Winter's view of distance, however, is his view of the function of symbols, wherein:

> . . . a symbol is the mode of the self's openness toward the world; it is also the mode of its distance from the world—distance through which it surpasses the immediacy of its environment and transforms what surrounds it from an environment into a situation. The subject-object relation implies a standing-over-against the other or the situation. Thus, being "situated" rather than being "conditioned by an environment" implies a self which can set itself apart from its world while at the same time being open toward that world.[3]

The process of symbolization is fundamental to understanding societal identity or societal centeredness. Starting with the work of the personality sciences, especially that of Erik Erikson, Winter describes self-awareness as "a power of self-transcending distance, which depends upon consistency in internal awareness

[2] *Ibid.*, p. 182. May draws on the work of Erwin W. Strauss, *Phenomenological Psychology*, trans. in part by Erling Eng (New York: Basic Books, 1966).
[3] Winter, *Elements*, p. 104.

and social responses." On the social level self-awareness means:

> . . . a grasp of the forces at play in the shaping of social rela-
> tionships; it includes awareness of the values and institutions
> which condition the decisions and activities of the everyday
> world. Awareness of the conditioning forces of the past, sensi-
> tivity to tradition, and understanding of the regularities which in-
> form our day-to-day activities furnish the reflective distance
> which makes policy a work of freedom.
>
> The conception of social policy as that which is shaped by
> human reflection presupposes social consciousness—a distance
> from the conditioning structures of the pregiven social world.
> To this extent, the conscious development of social policy presup-
> poses a science of man's social world or its equivalent. When the
> past ceases to be taken for granted as a sacred past of tradition,
> man has gained sufficient distance from, and consciousness of,
> that past in order to make it his own and to reshape it to his
> needs and interests. This is essentially the work of objective re-
> flection; it is theoretical reflection on the conditioned character of
> practice; we have identified this task with the human sciences.[4]

Neither of these writers gives attention to the retrograde
thrust of the self as it is embodied in fantasy and myth. They do,
however, presuppose the therapeutic process—May in the work of
Freud, Winter through the work of Erikson—and in this sense
they have already incorporated the psychological collapse of
distance into their phenomenological point of view. In fact, they
both imply that phenomenological approaches require or presuppose the psychological collapse of distance, of which we have
spoken, and they embody the recovery of distance methodo-

---

[4] *Ibid.,* pp. 264–265. Daniel Bell provides further support to our argument in
his sociological analysis of modernity and mass society by means of what
he calls "the eclipse of distance." He writes: "Not only is physical distance
compressed by the newer modes of modern transportation . . . but the very
techniques of the new arts . . . act to eclipse the psychic and aesthetic
distance between the viewer and the visual experience. . . . My thesis would
be that the 'eclipse of distance' between oneself and experience as the defining feature of modernity is the consequence of changes in the social
environment (notably the increased amount of interaction between persons
in the mass society) and that both mass culture and high culture are re-
sponsive to these underlying impulses" ("Modernity and Mass Society: On
the Varieties of Cultural Experience," *Studies in Public Communication,*
No. 4 [Autumn 1962], pp. 3–34. See esp. pp. 26–27 and n. 34.).

logically. We have already suggested that there is a correlation between the harshness of the superego and the bifurcation of subject and object in theological epistemology. The emergence of a phenomenological emphasis in theological studies may have some higher psychological significance. A phenomenological approach may be a therapeutic for theological method and its epistemological assumptions.

A structural discussion of distance is found in Martin Buber's recent attempt to clarify further the two fundamental attitudes of I-Thou and I-It, this time somewhat more accessible to developmental implications but in no sense entirely so. Buber speaks of a twofold movement which constitutes the principle of human life. First is "the primal setting at a distance" and, second, "entering into relation." The first is presupposed in the second, for "one can enter into relation only with being which has been set at a distance, which has become an independent opposite."

The event of distancing, therefore, occurs developmentally first and is ontologically prior.

> An animal's "image of the world," or rather, its image of a realm, is nothing more than the dynamic of the presences bound up with one another by bodily memory to the extent required by the functions of life which are to be carried out. This image depends upon, it clings to, the animal's activities.
>
> It is only man who replaces this unsteady conglomeration . . . by a unity which can be imagined or thought by him as existing for itself. . . . Man is like this because he is the creature (*Wesen*) through whose being (*Sein*) "what is" (*das Seiende*) becomes detached from him, and recognized for itself. It is only the realm which is removed, lifted out from sheer presence, withdrawn from the operation of needs and wants, set at a distance . . . which is more and other than a realm. Only when a structure of being is independently over against a living being (*Seinde*), an independent opposite, does a world exist.[5]

[5] Martin Buber, *The Knowledge of Man,* trans. Maurice Friedman and Ronald Gregor Smith; ed. Maurice Friedman (New York: Harper & Row, 1965), p. 61.

Here Buber relates the structure of being, the capacity of the self to be an independent opposite, and the existence of a world, all by means of the phenomenon of distance. To know being is itself, for Buber, to recover distance.

Relation proceeds from this event of distancing and is dependent on it; the second movement is added to the first: "Man turns to the withdrawn structure of being *(Seiende)* and enters into relation with it." This is the act and work of entering into relation with the world as such, which Buber refers to as the synthesizing apperception, the apperception of a being as a whole and as a unity.

> But a man does not obtain this view simply from the "setting at a distance" and "making independent." These would offer him the world only as an object, as which it is only an aggregate of qualities that can be added to at will, not a genuine wholeness and unity. Only the view of what is over against me in the world in its full presence, with which I have set myself, present in my whole person, in relation . . . only in such an opposition are the realm of man and what completes it in spirit, finally one.[6]

Distance, Buber concludes, provides the human situation; relation provides man's becoming in that situation. Only man gives distance to things that he comes upon in his realm; only man is capable of the acceptance of otherness.

These three approaches link the structure of being (ontological), actualization of the unconscious (psychological), and social consciousness (sociological) to what we have called the problem of recovering or winning distance. Although Buber, like the other two, does not discuss the problem of fantasy as such, he prompts us to reformulate our own question: Is there any sense in which fantasy can achieve the status of independent being, of otherness? Perhaps the reduction or interpretation of fantasy can be carried out at the ontological level as well as the psychological and social dimensions of the self. We turn to this question of the otherness of the religious image through the phe-

[6] *Ibid.,* p. 63.

nomenon of nostalgia in the context of the work of Erik Erikson
and Mircea Eliade.

Distance and nostalgia

WHEELIS's sociology of transference is conducted, for the most
part, under the auspices of the second or dynamic reading of
Freud, with some overtones of the first or metapsychological reading. According to the mechanistic view, transference is the loca-
tion of energies and attitudes in the wrong object; according to
the dynamic view, it is regression. If we draw on a higher reading
of this phenomenon, on a psychology of mythic structures, then
the intense, preoccupying yearning of which Wheelis speaks
might also be designated as nostalgia. Transference is a form of
nostalgia. Nostalgia is also the dynamic meaning of immanence,
which is accentuated as the result of the collapse of transcendence.

Did not Freud speak of nostalgia, although he preferred the
word "longing," choosing to cast the "ultimate" cause of neurosis
in terms of separation and desire for reunion? "As if the still
very undeveloped creature did not know what else to do with his
longing." Longing, Freud seems to be saying, is the "cause" of
neurosis. As we have noted, David Bakan finds in the separations
accompanying the oedipal conflict a more profound separation,
a separation of the self from the mystery of its own being, a
mystery that cannot in turn be "separated" from the mystery of
its origins.

Is the yearning of which we now speak so different from
a fundamental metaphor rooted deep in the matrix of Reinhold
Niebuhr's highly dynamic Christian anthropology, the metaphor
of the homelessness of the self? That metaphor has an undeniably
important place in the fabric of his thought. It is most likely
to be recognized in his discussions of the self's longing for for-

giveness and for its subsequent completion in the transcendent life of God. But it can be said without overstatement that the metaphor of homelessness also underlies the conceptual structure of Niebuhr's thought, providing it with its dynamic base. For, as he is so fond of saying, the self "lives" at the "juncture" of nature and spirit—between self-limitation and self-completion, between transference and transcendence, or, as we now prefer to say, between nostalgia and hope.

The religious image of the Devil can also be reconstrued as a nostalgia for the demonic. These structures may not be accessible to analytic resolution, as Wheelis argues; but they might, perhaps even for that reason, be all the more appropriate to hermeneutical resolution, especially if the rules for interpretation allow a dynamic discussion without being dominated by it. Must the mythic and the psychological be dissociated, in order that their differences be respected?

We have already alluded to Bachelard's proposal for a higher or secondary psychoanalysis of science and objective knowledge, in which he seeks "the reverie beneath the experiment." So we have been seeking, through a higher or third reading of Freud, the psychological infrastructure of theology, the reverie beneath the doctrine, now conceived as nostalgia for the demonic.

Yet, this is not reductionism, as theologians might fear, for as Bachelard says: "Psychically, we are created by our reverie— created and limited by our reverie—for it is the reverie which delineates the furthest limits of our mind."[7] Thus Bachelard emphasizes the *sui generis* nature of fantasy by speaking of it as reverie and metaphor. In the act of interpretation one passes from metaphor to reality. Reverie is not "merely" psychological. It has structural status and deserves to be dignified as that which lies "over against" the self, in relation to which the possibility of becoming, and of becoming an independent opposite, occurs.

There is a methodological shift in our argument, in this attempt to reformulate the classic Protestant meaning of imma-

---

[7] Bachelard, *Psychoanalysis of Fire*, p. 110.

nence through a comparison with psychological materials, that is, in terms of nostalgia. The movement is twofold, first from structure to dynamics, and then a return to structure on the basis of dynamics: from doctrinal thinking to its dynamic substrata and then a return to structure, reformulating in this return the meaning of structure as the religious image. Or, again, from object, to subject, and then a return, with an iconic definition of the objective. Or again, from doctrine to psychoanalysis, and from there to hermeneutics.

If we accord such dignity to fantasy—or, rather, if we recognize the dignity that it has always possessed—then the dilemma that Wheelis has posed can be viewed from a different perspective. The yearning of which he speaks is accessible to hermeneutical inspection and possible resolution. In this regard, the work of Brown and Bakan is an attempt to locate a religious image and submit it to a nonreductive interpretation, showing at the same time the function of the religious image in the dynamics of the self. With this interpretation, distance is recovered. The winning of distance consists in the interpretation of the deepest nostalgias of which a society is capable.

In this context the writings of Erik Erikson are especially valuable and relevant. For, like Bakan and Brown, his psychoanalytic tools also link together the image of the Devil, the superego, and Protestant spirituality. He has attempted to show how the self moves beyond or transcends these in the formation of identity. Erikson has clarified much that lies between the early developmental and the later existential, through the use of historical images of identity. His writings are important for Protestantism not simply because he wrote a book about its leading historical figure, but because his efforts, like the efforts of that theology itself, seek to clarify the dynamics of development as the self moves beyond superego organizations.

Erikson's work is transitional, a link between the psychological meanings of classic Protestantism and the contemporary problem of the fluidity of fantasy and mass society. In this sense it is fair to say that he has psychologized and decentralized the

Protestant ethic (Weber) by transforming the externalized sense of work and vocation into the internal developmental task. David Riesman has proposed the phrase the "hardness of the material" to characterize the objects of work to which the inner-directed social character addresses itself.[8] In the Eriksonian schema, one now works on himself rather than on the external, material world, but there is just as much work to do, for there are eight tasks—enough for a lifetime or, in Erikson's words, for the entire life cycle.

But in a broader and more important sense, Erikson's work is also a psychological hermeneutic of the Protestant sense of spiritual vocation, and no doubt this in part accounts for its attractiveness among contemporary religious leaders. In addition to writing his psychology of Luther's identity formation, Erikson has also chosen to write about the problem of identity in mass society. In fact, his writings are essays on the art of self-preservation in mass society, and crucial to this self-preservation is a psychological understanding of the Protestant past.

Erikson synthesizes much of the diversity found in post-Protestant interpretations of Freud. Like Brown and Bakan, he links the superego, anality and repression, and the religious image of the Devil, and, like Rieff, he is concerned with the dilemmas of identity in mass society. Identity is the phenomenon that joins the religious images of the past to the problem of the erosion of the self in mass society. Because of the intimate connection between ego and society in Erikson's work, he is saying, in effect, that all fantasy is identity-fantasy.[9] If, as Bachelard indicates, it is reverie that creates the self, then we could also say that social reverie creates the social self. Perhaps the intense, preoccupying yearnings of which Wheelis speaks have more form than he himself implies; perhaps these yearnings take on form as social reverie, as nostalgia for religious images of identity. The clarification of the relation between these historical images and

[8] David Riesman and Nathan Glazer, *The Lonely Crowd* (Garden City, N.Y.: Doubleday Anchor Books, 1954), p. 136.

[9] See chap. vi, pp. 190–91 above.

contemporary forms of experience and yearning is the function of a higher psychological interpretation.

Erikson's efforts to interpret the latent images of Protestantism are, therefore, attempts to gain distance on the past. The result of such higher psychological interpretation is the recovery of distance through the interpretation of nostalgia. Erikson's work moves the debate between theology and psychology forward, raising other questions: What are religious structures? What bearing do they have on contemporary forms of experience in mass culture? For this reason, in addition to being considered an ego psychologist, Erikson should also be considered a moralist, concerned with the capacity of the past to facilitate new paradigms of identity that, however, do not simply repeat preceding ones.

It is not difficult to see how the work of Mircea Eliade helps explore this very question. Unlike Erikson, Eliade's work is unhelpful at the point of the psychological interpretation of contemporary forms of experience, despite his not entirely occasional forays into the realm of mass culture through the analysis of ideologies,[10] in a manner reminiscent of Tillich's habit of searching out secular forms of ultimate concern. But Eliade does much to clarify the new "object" that emerges from Protestantism as a result of a third reading of Freud.

Eliade always has been thoroughly impatient with Freud and more concerned with the way in which psychoanalysis reflects the underlying spiritual malaise of modernity, in its emphasis on functionalism, historicism, and empiricism. This is, however, a rejection of mechanistic and dynamic-clinical views of Freud's thought that is reminiscent of the theological criticism already discussed at length. For this reason Eliade has refused to close entirely the study of the history of religion to Freud, and he has even tentatively defined his own work as "metapsychoanalysis," the study of man not only as an historical being

[10] Mircea Eliade, *Myth and Reality* (New York: Harper, 1963), chap. ix, and *Myths, Dreams and Mysteries* (New York: Harper, 1960), chap. i.

but also as a living symbol, through the use of "a more spiritual technique, applicable mainly to elucidating the theoretical content of the symbols and archetypes."[11] This approach is very similar to what we have called a third or iconic reading of Freud.

For Eliade the problem of reductionism turns on the status assigned to the religious symbol. It is the image alone that reveals; the symbol is an autonomous mode of knowledge that possesses and evinces intrinsic cognitive value. Most important, it is the symbol, as it is woven into mythic narrative, that transcends the plane of "immediate experience," the immediate experience of yearning, which cannot be adequately described by empirical and rational modes of analysis. Symbols, then, are metaempirical realities, transcending the immediate experience of modernity without being dissociated from it.

The point at issue for our own argument is Eliade's methodological distinction between history and structure. Structure refers to images that embody a unity and wholeness that man in his historical life and thought lacks. Because he lacks unity and wholeness, he knows the difference between what is possible and his own actual, historical condition; and he yearns for being through the medium of its mythic forms. Religious structures are, therefore, autonomous; they exist "out there," neither as projections nor as the hypostasized reality of dogmatic theological statement.

The dynamic component of Eliade's phenomenology is nostalgia, the desire to participate in mythic structures and, through them, in unfallen being: "The desire to be always, effortlessly, at the heart of the world."[12] Eliade's work may also be important for resolving the methodological dilemma of theology and psychology, the dilemma of projection and introjection, the dilemma of having separated developmental processes and their projec-

[11] Mircea Eliade, *Images and Symbols,* trans. Philip Mairet (New York: Sheed and Ward, 1961), p. 35.
[12] Mircea Eliade, *Patterns in Comparative Religion,* trans. Rosemary Sheed (Cleveland: World, 1963), p. 383.

tions of religion from doctrinal statements asserting that faith must be internalized by the believer.

A higher reading of Freud permits a metapsychoanalysis of objective religious structures and of subjective desires through which the self relates itself to such structures. There is therefore some connection between Wheelis's analysis of social yearning, Erikson's work linking the problem of identity to a particular religious image, and Eliade's general approach to the problem of understanding religious structures.

Ralph Harper has defined nostalgia in a similar manner:

> Homesickness or nostalgia is an involuntary conscience, a moral conscience, positive rather than prohibitory. It reminds a person, by way of giving him the experience, of the good he has known and lost. Nostalgia is neither illusion nor repetition; it is a return to something we have never had. And yet the very force of it is just that in it the lost is recognized, is familiar. Through nostalgia we know not only what we hold most dear, but the quality of experiencing that we deny ourselves habitually. This is why nostalgia is a moral sentiment.[13]

For Harper the phenomenon of nostalgia is inseparable from that of distance.

> Heidegger has spoken of man as a "Wesen der Ferne," a creature of distance, a being who can transcend or surpass himself. Whatever meaning one gives to transcendence, whether it be "vertical" or "horizontal," whether it be epistemological or religious, there is also the fact of man's being distanced as well as distancing. When he feels himself distant from home . . . distance comes to mean alienation. . . .[14]

Through the interpretation of nostalgia, one gains distance. If nostalgia is our own "new" word, our religious word, for immanence, is there a "new" word, a religious word, for transcendence?

[13] Ralph Harper, *Nostalgia: An Existential Exploration of Longing and Fulfillment in the Modern Age* (Cleveland: Western Reserve University Press, 1966), pp. 26–27.
[14] *Ibid.*, pp. 141–142.

Distance and hope

WE have suggested that the classic Protestant dialectic of immanence and transcendence, insofar as it is accurately portrayed in our neo-Reformation theologians, must be reformulated under the auspices of a higher reading of Freud's thought, that immanence is not really so different from the phenomenon of nostalgia, that interpretation of religious structures can be seen as a winning of distance, and that the winning of distance requires its own particular object. Now we consider the second part of the reformulation, again in a cursory and unsystematic way to be sure, simply attempting to annotate some of the consequences of our juxtaposition of theological and psychological materials.

Transcendence and immanence are dialectical, by theology's own definition. If nostalgia is the iconic meaning of immanence, then the corresponding meaning of transcendence is hope. Hope, like nostalgia, therefore becomes in this context a religious category. It is implied in the meaning of nostalgia. Hope is the result of gaining distance on the past, on one's age, on the social other, and on oneself.

Again, the grounds for this conclusion lie entirely in the particular reading given to the psychological materials. According to the more mechanistic readings of Freud's thought, the opposite of transference is control and delay, the capacity to suspend impulse gratification in the interest of reality-testing. We can call this view a "lower" reading of the psychology of hope. A more dynamic rendition of this aspect of Freud's thought is the process of insight, of understanding. However, the third reading suggests that these are dimensions of a broader, more total understanding of the self and that hope in this sense is the truly inclusive phenomenon.

Theological existentialism has given us a doctrine of transcendence that is rather inattentive to nostalgia; consequently, nostalgia has asserted itself into the very center of that experience of transcendence. The result has been a strange inversion: the faith that transcends history is in danger of becoming itself a nostalgia, of becoming merely historical. By means of the psychology of distance, we are led to explicate theological doctrine in the context of its more dynamic and iconic substrata.

William Lynch has discussed the psychology and metaphysics of hope in a way compatible with much of this discussion. According to him, a psychology of hope is a psychology of the immediate. He defines hope as a "sense of the possible," and the activity of hoping as a kind of wishing for or wanting reality, "a single human energizing and wishing faculty that comes close to being man himself."[15]

Lynch distinguishes hope from its self-destructive opposite, "the absolutizing instinct," and the key to the distinction is fantasy. The absolutizing instinct refers to the human tendency to pour floods of confusing fantasy on the object, and hoping therefore overcomes this absolutizing tendency. It is imagination that conquers fantasy, that makes the bold passage through fantasy to discover reality.[16] At the religious level, Lynch's absolutizing instinct resembles what we have called the transference-God and the harsh superego.

The passage from fantasy to reality, from nostalgia to hope, suggests that interpretation is a fundamental activity of religious thought, and the work of Paul Ricoeur is extremely helpful at this point. For Ricoeur, hermeneutics and therapeutics are closely related. But his use of psychological materials has already been anticipated in the writings of Philip Rieff. As noted, Rieff finds Freud's psychology not only to be therapy, but also to be a "religious hermeneutic." He speaks of Freud's "tactics of interpretation" directed to the opacity between emotion and mind, between experience and expression, and in particular to the

[15] William F. Lynch, S. J., *Images of Hope* (Baltimore: Helicon Press, 1965), p. 141.
[16] *Ibid.*, Epilogue, pp. 243–247.

relation between language, the unconscious, and the body. Further, Rieff believes that "Freud does not imply base meanings at all," that he "does not merely lower what was elevated, but elevates what was once lowered."

This view of Freud is developed by Paul Ricoeur in conjunction with the problem of interpretation; he speaks of distance at two points, and by implication at a third point as well. First, Ricoeur speaks of distance in terms of pure description and mystery and in terms of the paradox of being both master of one's body while at the same time being given over to it. On the one hand, there is Descartes's understanding of thought wherein the mind holds "clear and distinct ideas *at a distance from itself*"; this is to be distinguished from the attempt "to *identify* with the definite experience of existence which is myself in a corporeal situation." This, Ricoeur says, resembles Marcel's "conversion from 'objectivity' to 'existence,' . . . a reorientation from 'problem' to 'mystery.' "[17] The passage from objectivity to existence is, therefore, a collapse of distance, and the reflection on it bears some similarity to a recovery of distance. The subject-object dichotomy receives, if only at the level of thought, its first therapeutic gesture.

There is a second specific reference to distance. In his discussions of hermeneutics, Ricoeur distinguishes three types of relation between consciousness and symbols. These relations must be considered whenever one wishes to develop rules and ways for thinking about religious symbols.[18] There is first of all the original condition of primitive naïveté, of the immediacy of the symbol, a direct connection between the religious consciousness and symbols. This state of mind or religious attitude, of course, is not available to modern man, who continually prefers to seek out the causes, function, and origins of myth, ritual, and belief. Modern

[17] Paul Ricoeur, *Freedom and Nature: The Voluntary and the Involuntary,* trans. Erazim V. Kohák (Evanston, Ill.: Northwestern University Press, 1966), p. 15.

[18] Paul Ricoeur, *The Symbolism of Evil,* trans. Emerson Buchanan (New York: Harper & Row, 1967), pp. 347–357.

man prefers awareness of myth as myth, of the logos of the mythos. He dissolves myth into explanation, preferring truth without belief. This second relation or frame of mind Ricoeur calls "truth at a distance." It raises questions about myth and symbol at the level of comparison, not commitment; it runs from one symbol to another without regard for the existence and subjectivity of the interpreter.

The third stance or attitude of mind Ricoeur calls a second immediacy, a second naïveté, a postcritical equivalent of a precritical hierophany, a return to the immediacy of belief and therefore to the powerful immediacy of religious symbols—but all this on the basis of distance, on the basis of the premises required by "demythologization." Ricoeur says: "But if we can no longer live the great symbolisms of the sacred in accordance with the original belief in them, we can, we modern men, aim at a second naïveté in and through criticism. In short, it is by *interpreting* that we can *hear* again."[19]

The movement from thought at a distance to existence and the movement from truth at a distance to hermeneutics are, however, special moments in a wider, more general movement that can be characterized as a general shift from phenomenology to hermeneutics. It is a highly dynamic one and would have been impossible for Ricoeur to make without Freud's thought.[20] Freud's psychology makes this transition possible. Ricoeur is fascinated by Freud's hermeneutical style, which he incorporates —only up to a point, of course—into his own work. And it is the hermeneutical style that Freud makes possible that interests us most of all here.

Ricoeur argues first that phenomenology and psychoanalysis do in fact share important similarities. For example, both have an epoche. Phenomenology displaces immediacy of conscious-

---

[19] *Ibid.,* p. 351.
[20] Ricoeur, *De l'Interpretation,* esp. pp. 368–383, 408–424, 476–478, 504–506, and 521–529. I have relied heavily on the discussion of Ricoeur's study of Freud by Don Ihde, "From Phenomenology to Hermeneutic," *Journal of Existentialism,* VIII, No. 30 (Winter 1967–1968), 111–132.

ness through a deliberate bracketing, in order to show the naïveté of the natural attitude. Psychoanalysis also displaces immediacy through its distinction between surface ego and depth factors that lie behind or beneath the surface sense of reality. Both seek the origins of meaning first encountered in the experience of the world of perception: psychoanalysis through its search for the roots of regression, phenomenology in the problem of the lived body. And both focus their work on language rather than perception, recognizing that language always exceeds any simple immediacy of knowing.

However, the fundamental significance of Freud's thought lies not in its likeness to phenomenological description, but in its independent contribution: Psychoanalysis is the necessary discipline of an antiphenomenology, for it demands that the Cogito pass through a particular kind of experience for reflection on symbols to become possible.[21] This requires the abandonment of immediate consciousness, of the pretension of consciousness to rule the senses. There is a "false cogito" which must be given up. One must abandon the concept of the object so that the object can become once again a "transcendental guide."

The Cogito must pass through the experience of narcissism. The movement from phenomenology to hermeneutics is therefore a movement from object to subject, the Cogito must participate in the desire of the ego for immortality. Hence Ricoeur calls psychoanalysis a "semantics of desire,"[22] and he insists that "interpretation must pass through human desire"[23] in order to make possible an "archaeology of the subject." It is the subject that must be purified so that hermeneutics can once again be undertaken.

Although narcissism is the "thorny" psychological point, the point at which the methodological movement from phenomenology to hermeneutics undergoes a complete inversion, Ricoeur also speaks of the fantasm, the mythic exemplification of nar-

[21] See esp. Ricoeur, *De l'Interpretation,* pp. 410–416.
[22] *Ibid.,* p. 15.
[23] Paul Ricoeur, "The Atheism of Freudian Psychoanalysis," *Concilium,* XVI (1966), 59–72, esp. p. 61.

cissism. In so speaking he moves from what we have called metapsychological and dynamic to iconic considerations. Narcissism is the narrow passage by which the fantasm comes into view. What Ricoeur means by "fantasm" is by no means new to our discussion, however. He means the Oedipus myth, thereby invoking, it is correct to say, all the additional psychological processes that, as we have seen, can be attached to it. Antiphenomenology becomes a passageway to hermeneutics.

Consequently Ricoeur is prepared to ask several questions, all turning on the nature of the fantasm, all very similar to our discussion of nostalgia and religious structures: "Is there, in the affective dynamism of religious belief, the wherewithal to rise above its own archaism?" Is the fantasm "only the vestige of a traumatic memory," or is it "a symbol, capable of providing the first stratum of meaning to an imaginative presentation of origins, more and more detached from its function of infantile and quasi-neurotic repetition, and more and more suited to an investigation of the fundamental meanings of human destiny?"[24]

These are questions that Freud's thought—and only Freud's thought—makes possible. Ricoeur draws into relation the activity of interpretation and the deepest developmental processes that Freud's own interpretive powers were capable of elucidating. Conversely, they are also questions that theology makes impossible. We have attempted to untangle and interpret these theological objections. As long as one remains in the theological circle —at least in the circle of Niebuhr and Tillich and their equivalents—such questions are "irrelevant." Doctrinal modes of thought and statement insist that psychology deals only with "a vestige of a traumatic memory." We therefore conclude that theological objections to psychoanalysis are, at their deepest level, objections to the existence of religious images and to hermeneutics.

Ricoeur's answers to these questions lie in the formulation of a double movement, of regression and progression, which he calls

[24] *Ibid.*, p. 69.

archeology and teleology. By means of the fantasm and through
its interpretation, the past is disowned and surpassed. The force
of interpretation converts the fantasm, understood now as a religious symbol, into an instrument of discovery. In such fashion,
religion, in the hands first of psychology and then of interpretation, overcomes its own archaism and makes possible a new
relation to reality. Ricoeur's final step consists in bringing the
fantasm under the power of the Biblical dimension of sin. Hermeneutics has as its task the destruction of all that remains of
the archaic. Freud's antiphenomenology is a hermeneutics that
juxtaposes an infantile, idolatrous consolation and a "higher"
consolation, the consolation of spirit. The deprivation of the first
consolation generates the second. By insisting that interpretation
must pass through human desire, Ricoeur returns, hermeneu-
tically, to the full range of symbols, images, and myths described
"at a distance" by the phenomenology of religion; and he returns
to thought that is no longer conceived of as "thought at a distance." Concrete reflection on symbols is possible once the archaism of the subject has been opened to interpretation.

In the work of Ricoeur, then, we find a thoroughgoing and
extensive incorporation of Freud's psychoanalytic thought into
a methodological progression. In fact, Ricoeur is so impressed
by Freud's thought that one wonders whether pure description,
in his hands, has a defensive function. It is a third or iconic reading that makes incorporation possible, and that third reading is
inseparable from the phenomenological approach, a point we saw
already anticipated in the work of May and Winter. What we
have called the gap between family and history (Niebuhr) and
the subject-object dichotomy (Tillich) are healed in Ricoeur's
movement through Freud to hermeneutics.

Ricoeur's use of distance suggests a double movement somewhat similar to our own. His dialectic between archeology and
teleology seems to be formally identical with that between nostalgia and hope. We need not explore here the central difference,
namely Ricoeur's sense of continuity between his use of Freud's
antiphenomenology, on the one hand, and the dogmatics of Barth

and Bultmann, on the other hand. From our own point of view, it is extremely difficult to return to theologies that, by definition, require the absence of dynamic and iconic considerations in their anthropology and methodology. By shifting psychological processes to the level of thought, Ricoeur provides methodological support for the structural considerations of Eliade and the societal analyses of Erikson.

Unfortunately—or, perhaps, fortunately—there seems to be no one figure whose work embodies concretely and extensively the kind of clarification at specific points that our discussion requires. However, Jung's work embodies a constructive carrying forward of the consequences of a higher psychological criticism of theology, and with these remarks our discussion concludes. The energies of Jung's thought, person, and work were given over primarily to the psychological meaning of the doctrinal-theological notions of sin and faith and the systematic-theological notion of transcendence, on the one hand, and, on the other hand, to rethinking the significance of Freud's psychological "discoveries." This is the force of analytical, rather than psychoanalytic, psychology.

Although Jung's thought does not provide solutions to our problems, what is important and attractive is the style of his investigation. His work gives focal attention to the several dilemmas that we have inherited from theological existentialism. At this point, the fact that a theory can move from, say, structural to dynamic and from dynamic to societal considerations is as important as the specific content of the theory. For we are in search of a style that coordinates different dimensions. There have been, in other words, enough Jungian "solutions" for some time to come; but there can never be enough—at least at this point in theology's decline or ascent—Jungian questions.

Jung's thought is incredibly elusive, provocative, and rich. He is a "bridge" figure, one who sees and relates many things, leaving to others the task of finding a clearly recognizable focus or center, sacrificing organization to richness. But Jung's concerns are fundamentally dynamic rather than structural, societal, or methodological. He explores the Protestant experience and the limits of Freud's thought at this point. In its most general meaning, Jung's formula, the union of opposites, refers to an attempt to bridge the gap between the developmental and the existential, between becoming and self-understanding, between anthropology and methodology, the fundamental divisions of theological existentialism.

The link between these opposites—and there are, in Jung's thought, many, many more of them—is the image or symbol, the preferred general term being archetype, which is always religious by virtue of its historical and universal givenness. Yet there is a strictly psychological side to the archetype, a more immediate side, and this is the phenomenon of fantasy. With Jung we return to the grounds of our initial objection to theology, its ignorance of and even opposition to the psychological process of fantasy. In Jung the relation between immanence and transcendence is reformulated as the relation between fantasy and archetype, or, rather, as the transition from fantasy to archetype. This dynamic touches on all other aspects of the nature of the self and the process of individuation.

The characteristic Jungian event or moment in the process of individuation is the breakdown of the persona.[25] "Persona" is Jung's term for those aspects of the self that resemble societal expectations. It is, therefore, equivalent to Freud's superego, and changes in the relation between the persona and the ego are not so different from what Wheelis and others have called the decline of the superego. The breakdown of the persona introduces a new possibility, that of fantasy or reverie, and this psychological event in turn opens up social and religious aspects of the self. The wider, more universal reveries, the archetypes, become experientially accessible when individual factors in personality are transcended.

Jung named the technique for bringing about this process "active imagination," and he referred to its psychological consequences as the "transcendent function."[26] Together, these in effect provide a double movement, of collapse and recovery of

[25] C. G. Jung, *Two Essays on Analytical Psychology,* trans. R. F. C. Hull (New York: Meridian Books, 1956), pp. 166–172.
[26] *Ibid.,* pp. 224–238.

distance. In the interpretive movement away from individual fantasy to collective archetype, distance is won. "Archetype" is Jung's word for transcendence. Yet the appearance of the archetype presupposes a transformation of all those lower functions that Freud called superego, repression, regression, and transference. The sense of connectedness between these and archetypes led Jung into his explorations of the psychology of doctrine. Far more than Freud, Jung was concerned with the psychology of doctrine in addition to religious experience. For him, theology was inseparable from religious experience, although, as we have seen, Freud was far closer to this position than lower readings suggest. Unfortunately Jung tended, like the theologians, to render a lower reading of Freud in order to develop his own psychology.

The double movement of collapse and recovery of distance is not only developmental, but also societal. The creative chaos that results from alterations in the relation between ego and persona Jung called the teleological significance of regression, recalling Erikson's emphasis on the developmental task as a crisis with positive as well as negative outcomes. If the preceding arguments have been correct, we would expect the notion of transference to be central to both regression and progression (in Ricoeur's terms, archeology and teleology) in this style of thinking, and this is exactly the case.[27] Jung spoke of the transference as a conjunctio, a compositum in which opposed feelings first flare up and then open themselves to a higher resolution or coincidentia. It is the retrograde crucible out of which individuation appears. Yet transference is a life process in both its regressive and progressive aspects. Without it the ego is cut off from the whole of mankind and from spirit. Jung generalized: "What our world lacks is the *psychic connection*,"[28] and that connection he called transference. This double movement of regression and progression,

---

[27] C. G. Jung, "Psychology of the Transference," *The Practice of Psychotherapy,* trans. R. F. C. Hull ("Bollingen Series XX," Vol. 16; New York: Pantheon Books, 1954), esp. 167–201.

[28] *Ibid.,* p. 321.

although it is conceived of developmentally, engages the collective dimensions of life. For the archetypes are social reverie, social transference, and as such they are referable to what we have called mass or popular culture. Here Jung parts company with Eliade and Ricoeur and joins company with Erikson: Contemporary yearning does have form, the form of images. The archetypes have social and historical as well as developmental-personal meanings.

The elucidation and interpretation of such images requires a particular method. Jung spoke of his own approach as the phenomenological standpoint, the methodological dimension of active imagination and the transcendent function; sometimes he used alternative terms such as "the phenomenology of religious experience."[29] It is a dynamic phenomenology of fantasy: "By means of 'active imagination' we . . . make the discovery of the archetype";[30] fantasy is the first beginning of spiritualization.[31] In this approach Jung really presupposes an ontology of projection, a search for what we will call ontic fantasy, the fantasy of being and the beingness of fantasy. Once again, the image mediates and resolves the circular debate between introjection and projection, between subject and object. Jung says that: ". . . it is not the conscious subject but the unconscious which does the projecting. Hence one meets with projections, one does not make them."[32] But the withdrawal of projections is not a return to subject-object reality, but to a creative relation to other life—and to other archetypes.

So Jung unites many concerns—structural, dynamic, societal, and methodological. It is his style, one that closes gaps and

[29] C. G. Jung, *The Archetypes and the Collective Unconscious,* trans. R. F. C. Hull ("Bollingen Series XX," Vol. 9, Pt. I; New York: Pantheon Books, 1959), 54–72.

[30] C. G. Jung, *The Structure and Dynamics of the Psyche,* trans. R. F. C. Hull ("Bollingen Series XX," Vol. 8; New York: Pantheon Books, 1960), 211.

[31] C. G. Jung, *Freud and Psychoanalysis,* trans. R. F. C. Hull ("Bollingen Series XX," Vol. 4; New York: Pantheon Books, 1961), 180.

[32] C. G. Jung, *Aion: Researches into the Phenomenology of the Self,* trans. R. F. C. Hull ("Bollingen Series XX," Vol. 9, Pt. II; New York: Pantheon Books, 1959), 9.

seeks continuity, rather than his specific solutions that is important. In this sense his psychology is another post-Protestant interpretation of Freud, for in his thought the implicit psychological concerns of Protestant thought and spirituality become explicit. Threading its way through these concerns, and through his work as a whole, is the final coincidentia, a general principle of both individual and historical self-understanding—in his own words, "backward-looking images" and "forward-looking anticipations."[33] What we have called nostalgia and hope.

Conclusion

If our arguments have been correct, if there is implicit psychological meaning in the formulations of theological existentialism, if there is far more continuity than seems apparent between these and the post-Protestant uses of Freud and the final considerations of distance, then we have reached a point of closure and summation. We could formulate our final conclusion in one of two ways, both consistent with the fundamental question that has vexed our study from beginning to end, the question of continuity or discontinuity.

On the one hand, we must say that in the collapse of the transcendent referent of Protestant spirituality and its subsequent release into structureless social yearning, we have followed out to its end-point the grim and comfortless conclusion of Freud's "analytic" of religion, his "antitheology." The depths of nostalgia embodied in and contained by the structure of Protestant spirituality are released into awareness and expressed in social behavior. Freud's psychology is the end of the Protestant era; it moves at all points against that understanding of transcendence. One must, it seems, choose, and in choosing one, reject the other.

[33] *Ibid.*, Vol. 9, Pt. I, 279.

On the other hand, this very conclusion, as we have also suggested, appears to contain a second possibility unanticipated by this first conclusion, restricted as it is to the theological and psychological materials. The yearning that is inaccessible to analytical resolution, and that previously was accessible only to dogmatic and ecclesiastical resolution, may once again be accessible to resolution, this time to hermeneutical resolution. The yearning that appears in the form of cultural transference, and that is the dynamic form of what theology has meant by immanence, contains the possibility of transcendence. Freud moves against theology; but theology points the way for a higher psychology.

If this is so, then we must conclude that the analytic point, so much anathema to theological orthodoxy and so necessary to psychological orthodoxy, appears to have contained all along a double possibility—not only for the collapse of distance, but for the recovery of distance as well. Has theological orthodoxy all the while *secretly embodied* both the possibility of the collapse and recovery of distance, of the dialectic of nostalgia and hope?[34] Theological orthodoxy seems to have opposed not only the unveiling of that secret, but also the very notion of its presence in its midst. But that depends on how you look at it—that is, on whether you stand inside or outside the theological circle, or, now that the distinctiveness of a third or iconic reading of the Freud materials is visible, inside or outside the neurosis. From this second perspective, it would seem that theological existentialism has, quite to the contrary of the first, carefully nurtured and jealously guarded that alternative, attempting to protect the possibility of a higher psychology from the reductionisms of mechanistic, adjustment psychology and romantic psychologies of individuality and internality.

Our pursuit of this psychological core in theology has led

---

[34] In suggesting that theology has "secretly" embodied this double possibility, I have adopted and transposed to a different context Medard Boss's argument to the effect that Freud's psychology "secretly" states the Heideggerian understanding of *Dasein,* despite its more superficial, apparently mechanistic and objectifying approach. See Boss, *Psychoanalysis and Daseinsanalysis,* pp. 97, 284.

in particular to the implicit or latent images that provide the raw material for doctrine. We have stumbled upon the reverie beneath the doctrine. We could then also conclude that theological orthodoxy has secretly embodied images. In the Protestant imagination, at any rate, it would seem that the form of nostalgia is the religious image. It is this, the image, that theology at once rejects and yet at the same time, in a more subtle way and for that reason perhaps in a more significant way, "secretly" nurtures, protects, and carries forward. It is the religious image that, in the hands of Freud's hermeneutical style, can be seen to mediate between objects of faith and psychic depth.

In the case of the Protestant experience at any rate, it seems clear that the image of the Devil is by and large the most dynamically active religious image. This image and its underlying dynamics have been extremely problematic for our theological materials. So much so that at times it seems that the image of the Devil has itself inadvertently become an image of transcendence, wherein transcendence is conceived of as extreme and alien distance, the object of an ambivalent nostalgia. We have found the image of the Devil archetypal in this particular theological imagination, standing for and giving expression to the psychically dark side of human life. In our analysis, the theological image of the Devil is referable to repression and the superego. This image, when unclarified, makes it necessary to think of faith rather as an abrogating than as a therapeutic-interpretive transcendence of repression. It is therefore the barrier between the analytic point and its deeper, reparative possibilities. But it is also, in the hands of the proper form of interpretation, the link between these. The image of the Devil is, to use that by now overworked phrase, the connecting term, the iconic link between immanence and transcendence, between the collapse of distance and the recovery of distance—and, for that matter, between male and female, mother and father, self and society, subject and object, anguished conscience and transcendent God.

At least in the spiritual dynamics of Protestantism, the image of the Devil is apparently an interposition whose presence

and subsequent overcoming is necessary for the self's final integration. Like the subject-object relation in theological epistemology,
one cannot know the world without it, and yet one cannot know
God with it. The genre of theology that we have discussed has
tended to be distinctly uninterested in nostalgias for the demonic,
except as these are brought under the sure and certain control of
the doctrine of God's transcendence. But that is where the trouble
begins. For in that case, nostalgia itself comes under suspicion.
What theology means by dialectic, when submitted to what metapsychology calls the "economic factor," does suggest, however,
that redress is possible. A higher psychology, one oriented toward
the interpretation of religious images, makes possible a "letting
be" of such nostalgias. The reverie beneath the doctrine becomes
visible, and one is free to think anew of different doctrinal
meanings.

These dynamic considerations take on societal meaning
through the notion of identity. We can ask the question again, at
another point: Does theological orthodoxy secretly embody new
possibilities for identity? Identity is the very wide and inclusive
sense of personal being, the roots of which lie midway between
those transcendent images of self that religion provides and those
images put forward through the "first mythology" of all growth,
the mythology of the family, so arduously documented by Freud.
We have found evidence of much unresolved tension between
these two mythologies in the thought of Reinhold Niebuhr and
Paul Tillich. And we have found impulses deep within the fabric
of psychoanalytic thought that press the self forward to transcend the first mythological world and to enter the second. In its
haste to transcend the first mythology of development, theological
existentialism has unwittingly elevated and ontologized a good
deal of that mythology into the substance of faith. And in its perception of this, psychoanalysis has continued to find religion,
especially theology, at best ambiguous.

Insofar as these mythologies remain entirely distinct from
one another, there will always be two identities for the self—
superego images and images that transcend to the point of dis-

sociation the vicissitudes of that first mythology. The yearnings, the longings, the nostalgias of post-Protestant man, our conclusions suggest, are for religious images of identity, the moral consequences of good interpretation. More precisely, his is nostalgia for superego images, in order to discover images of hope. It may be helpful for purposes of analysis to speak of two mythologies, but the task of religious thought strives for a unitary interpretation in which the two coalesce in the unity of man. For that reason, it seems psychodynamically unwise to speak of "post-Protestant" or "post-Christian" man at all—or, for that matter, of "Christian" man or of the "Christian" point of view, insofar as it is rigorously juxtaposed to a secular one.

Yet these images of identity, our conclusion also suggests, will have as their context the imaginations of mass society. If mass society is, in our cumbersome phrase, heir to the superego, then the modern self, caught in the yearning of cultural transference, is forced to fashion images of its own and to draw its materials from the immediacies of its own experience. By and large, approaches to mass society—or, more properly speaking, to popular culture—follow the same divisions that have beset our study of Freud and theology. Those divisions appear most generally in the distinction between "high culture" and "low culture." Thus theological existentialism seeks to protect the (high) transcendent dimensions of the self and the moral integrity of the family from the (lower) effects of mass society. In the death-of-God theology, we find this dissociation of what is high from what is considered low carried forward in even more extreme fashion. The writings of Gabriel Vahanian and Harvey Cox focus this extremity, the one finding in the immanentism of mass culture the end of transcendence, the other proposing that theology must begin precisely at this point. Cox's proposals are, of course, under the control of his theology of secularization.

Social science seems to be concerned these days with attitudes, opinions, influence, and diffusion—that is, with the way in which individuals, groups, and institutions manipulate one another,[35] or, with broad functional analyses of media.[36] They carry forward in their own way the behavioristic and dynamic sides of our discussion, respectively. Literary critics—who might be expected to exercise an iconic approach—have for the most part named mass culture the "lower" portion of culture and have accordingly assigned it to the social scientists, much as a physician makes a referral. And the social scientists have obligingly taken the case. However, their methods and interests preclude an approach to mass culture based on a theory of the imagination, be that theory literary, theological, or even psychological. On the other hand, the custodians of such a potential theory quickly point out that they cannot include fads and popular things in their discipline.[37]

Yet our investigation concludes that what is usually called popular culture is at once the result of the collapse of a theological dimension in human life and also an attempt to recover some sense of religious form. If the yearnings of cultural transference are nostalgias and if these nostalgias are, so to speak, seeking form, then perhaps popular culture is better understood as a diffuse mythopoetic apparatus thrown into motion by the collapse of the transcendent, one that serves—adequately or not, that is not the point—to "minister" to the nostalgias of many.[38] We may, for example, approach the portrayal of violence on television through such notions as "aggressive fantasies"[39]—but we might also speak of nostalgia for the demonic. Or we may note in the detective story obsessive-compulsive behavior. But one might

[35] See, for example, Carl I. Hoveland and Irving L. Janis, eds., *Personality and Persuasibility* (New Haven: Yale University Press, 1959).

[36] See, for example, Charles R. Wright, *Mass Communication: A Sociological Perspective* (New York: Random House, 1966).

[37] See, for example, Richard Hoggart, *The Uses of Literacy* (Boston: Beacon Press, 1961).

[38] An approach that moves in this direction is William Stephenson, *The Play Theory of Mass Communication* (Chicago: University of Chicago Press, 1967).

[39] See, for example, Joseph T. Klapper, *The Effects of Mass Communication* (New York: The Free Press, 1960).

also speak of a nostalgia for innocence, which underlies the more apparent preoccupation with guilt.

Are the imaginative wanderings of mass culture "mere fantasy," are they "merely psychological"? Or do we have in the vulgar notion of "psychological escape" a methodological barrier that prevents a fresh and far more penetrating look at the popular imagination? For that barrier is clearly reminiscent of the separations that have vexed theological approaches to immanence, speaking as they do of the theological and then placing this in opposition to the "merely psychological." Is it possible, then, for a theological analysis of self-understanding to follow the immanental imagination, the nostalgia, of mass society? Is mass society a hermeneutical situation?

Just as images are dynamically active in the formation of doctrine and faith, opening up for thoroughgoing reformulation the meaning of transcendence, so our argument also calls for a methodology that will close some of the gaps manifest in the theological formula of the subject-object relation and its transcendence—a formula that, as noted, appears in much of psychology's like-minded attempt to formulate a third approach beyond behaviorism and psychoanalysis. Our discussion suggests that the power of images does affect methodology.

Both theology and psychology attest to the fact that methodologies are finally rooted not just in "experience," but that there is an ultimate circularity between a master image and a particular methodology. This may well be one way of summarizing Freud's contribution not only to psychology, but to religion and theology as well. We should recall that Freud wrote *The Interpretation of Dreams* early in his career and that the "speculations" came later. In the tangles of clinical technique, theory, metapsychology, and the "applications" of psychoanalysis, strands of myth can be recognized from time to time. What we have spoken of as thought, person, and work are themselves comprehended by a mythic structure. Yet Freud did not simply create the Oedipus myth, nor did he simply apply it. That myth emerges, so to speak, as a result of a particular kind of interpretive readiness to be accessible to, and distant from, psychic depth.

Theology, too, seeks to ground its method in a mythic structure, the form of revelation. But theology in practice proceeds for the most part in a manner opposite to that of depth psychology. Depth psychology begins with surface appearances—with everyday life—moves to depth, and then returns to surface on the basis of depth. Theology begins with an image of depth, one, however, that has come to acquire many of the characteristics that we ordinarily assign to everyday life. Theology then proceeds, unaware of these characteristics, to correlate or to apply its mythic structures to the forms of everyday life. In theology, the mythic is a given, it is taken for granted. In depth psychology, however, the mythic must be won anew in each investigation.

This difference of approach can be quickly illustrated by placing Tillich's definition of revelation in a psychological context. "A revelation," Tillich says, "is final if it has the power of negating itself without losing itself."[40] This theological principle is rooted mythologically in the historical witness to the Crucifixion and Resurrection. The essence of psychoanalysis, as we have argued, lies in the establishment of a transference relation and in its subsequent resolution. Because transference is far more than a clinical process, and because it is the medium for both disease and cure, it is also a medium about which it can be said that it negates itself without losing itself. It is therefore, in an important sense, Christological in form. Yet the theologian cannot understand this, for his applications begin with an image that is for the most part detached from its original depth and that does not allow him to carry that image into the psychic depths of contemporary life. He can only apply it; he cannot behold it. Psychoanalysis often has the reverse difficulty, for it cannot "ascend" to the mythic without incurring for itself a sense of methodological impropriety. Demythologization neutralizes the possibility of a higher psychology of religious images.

[40] Tillich, *Systematic Theology,* I, 133.

Our conclusion therefore inquires whether or not it is possible to have a method that does not confuse nostalgia with hope, a method that provides both psychic closeness to and distance from the alleged objective priority of myth in all cultural analysis and in all formulations of self-understanding, thereby permitting a plurality of master images to emerge in any investigation. Its "correlation" would not be from a master myth (kerygma) to a cultural situation; it would require the elucidation of situational myths, the historical gathering of many master myths, and the creation of interplay between the two in the context of levels of meaning. Such a methodological style would permit what Erikson has called a "disciplined subjectivity" to enter into one's hermeneutical formulations. Such a method will obviously be, as we have already seen, phenomenological, addressed both to "modernity" as well as to the classic images.

What our discussions call for, therefore, is a phenomenology of fantasy, a dynamic phenomenology of images by means of which objective and subjective, faith and psychic depth, myth and dream are rendered in a manner accessible to the nostalgias of the modern self. These nostalgias can, perhaps, give form to social identity and, when properly interpreted, release the substance of hope.

These remarks are no more than suggestions or proposals, although they are derived directly from the conclusion of this study. They are, I believe, the consequences of its initial task, to pursue as exhaustively as possible an engagement between the thought of Freud and that particular form of theology most accessible to his thought. The conclusion is simple. There is a psychological side to this theology and the psychology thus evoked is clearly Freud's. He has given us a glimpse of the psychic roots of that theology in a way heretofore unattempted; and once this glimpse has been acknowledged, there is no simple return to theology. But, contrary to the expectations of that theology, once its psychological side has been acknowledged, a new series of considerations appear; transcendence is neither simply lost, nor can it be found again in any simple way.

In this conclusion, characterized as it is by anticipated and unanticipated features, lies the deepest paradox—the deepest "dialectic"—of a style of theology that has sought by its own admission to be and to remain essentially dialectical. The impact of Freud's thought on this theology lies therefore least of all in a particular decision—for faith, or for psychoanalysis. The impact of Freud can best be stated in this regard as "making possible." The permanent contribution of psychoanalysis lies in its impulse to complicate, to expand, to enrich, to double back and look again and again—not to deny closure or commitment, but to make possible the suspension of closure in the interests of something more. So Freud's thought makes possible a transition to a different style not of theological analysis but of interpretation and religious understanding. Although his thought does not suggest the content of such work, it does necessitate complexity and dynamic movement in defining problems, in selecting resources, and in projecting solutions. Therefore, his work marks the end of the Protestant era, and his psychology is a psychology of secularization. And for this reason his work separates us, insofar as we will let it, from our own immediate theological heritage.

Under the impact of such a separation, what are we to do? Are we, as theology would have it, to "wait without idols,"[41] a counsel that in effect asks us to hope without yearning? Or are we, as lower readings of psychoanalysis would have it, to yearn without hope? That is the dilemma with which we began. "Everything new must have its roots in what was before,"[42] Freud wrote. Everything new is rooted dynamically in the past; nothing new is entirely so; the meaning of what is new lies in knowing exactly its relation to what is old. Let that be our epitaph for a theology that, although it from time to time confused the child and the man, the old and the new, must nevertheless remain the active past for whatever is to come. Theology repeats the past; interpretation authorizes the future. Only under such conditions can religious thought—and that amorphous entity, the modern self—enter the second half of life without repeating the first.

[41] Gabriel Vahanian, *Wait Without Idols* (New York: George Braziller, 1964), chap. v.
[42] Freud, *Moses and Monotheism,* p. 22.

Annotated bibliography

One: The problem

For further elaboration of the validity and meaning of what Gordon W. Allport means by the Leibnitzian emphasis, consult any of the final chapters in Parts II, III, IV, or V, *Pattern and Growth in Personality* (New York: Holt, Rinehart and Winston, 1961).

For a thoroughgoing review of the Lockean and Leibnitzian trends, see Edwin G. Boring, *A History of Experimental Psychology* (New York: Appleton-Century-Crofts, 1950), chaps. xxiv and xxv.

For three major surveys of experiments testing psychoanalytic theories, see David Rapaport, *Emotions and Memory* (Baltimore: Williams and Wilkins, 1942); R. R. Sears, *Survey of Objective Studies of Psychoanalytic Concepts* (New York: Social Science Research Council, 1943); and E. R. Hilgard, "Experimental Approaches to Psychoanalysis," *Psychoanalysis as Science*, ed. E. Pumpian-Mindlin (Stanford, Calif.: Stanford University Press, 1952), pp. 3–45. These surveys are discussed by David Shakow and David Rapaport, *The Influence of Freud on American Psychology* ("Psychological Issues," No. 13; New York: International Universities Press, 1964).

For a general discussion of the reception of Freud's ideas, see Shakow and Rapaport, *The Influence of Freud*, chap. iv. For an excellent review of neo-Freudian thought as a response to Freud, see Ruth L. Munroe, *Schools of Psychoanalytic Thought* (New York: Holt, Rinehart and Winston, 1955). For a discussion of Freud from the point of view of existential psychology, see Rollo May, ed., *Existence: A New Dimension in Psychology and Psychiatry* (New York: Basic Books, 1958). For a review that discusses both, see Dieter Wyss, *Depth Psychology: A Critical History*, trans. Gerald Onn (New York: W. W. Norton, 1966). For a critical discussion of Freud and psychoanalysis from a phenomenological point of view, see Adrian Van Kaam, *Existential Foundations of Psychology* (Pittsburgh: Duquesne University Press, 1966).

For illustration of the polarity in Protestant theological response to Freud, see Albert C. Outler, *Psychotherapy and the Christian Message* (New York: Harper, 1954), and David E. Roberts, *Psychotherapy and a Christian View of Man* (New York: Scribner's, 1953). See also Seward Hiltner, *Pastoral Counseling* (New York: Abingdon-Cokesbury Press, 1949), pp. 26–33.

For a helpful general discussion of the theological figures and issues that form the background of this study, see John B. Cobb, Jr., *Living Options in Protestant Theology: A Survey of Methods* (Philadelphia: Westminster Press, 1962), and Edward Farley, *The Transcendence of God* (Philadelphia: Westminster Press, 1960).

For two careful Roman Catholic responses to Freud, see Roland Dalbiez, *Psychoanalytical Method and the Doctrine of Freud*, trans. T. F. Lindsay (London: Longmans, Green, 1941), and Albert Plé, *Chastity and the Affective Life*, trans. Marie-Claude Thompson (New York: Herder and Herder, 1966).

For examples of pastoral psychology, see Henry Balmforth, *An Introduction to Pastoral Theology* (New York: Macmillan, 1937); John Sutherland Bonnell, *Pastoral Psychiatry* (New York: Harper, 1938); and Rollo May, *The Art of Counseling* (Nashville, Tenn.: Cokesbury Press, 1939). The work of the pastoral psychology movement is best represented by two journals, *The Journal of Pastoral Care* and *Pastoral Psychology*.

Two: Anthropological response to Freud: Reinhold Niebuhr

FOR an early discussion of the concept of self in Niebuhr's work, see *Does Civilization Need Religion? A Study in the Social Resources and Limitations of Religion in Modern Life* (New York: Macmillan, 1927). For representative statements, see *Moral Man and Immoral Society: A Study in Ethics and Politics* (New York: Scribner's, 1932); *The Nature and Destiny of Man* (2 vols.; New York: Scribner's, 1953); and *Self and the Dramas of History* (New York: Scribner's, 1955). For Niebuhr's use of the word "structure" with reference to the self, see *Nature and Destiny of Man*, I, 269–276. For a more detailed discussion of Niebuhr's thought with regard to the self, see Gordon Harland, *The Thought of Reinhold Niebuhr* (New York: Oxford University Press, 1960), and Nathan A. Scott, Jr., *Reinhold Niebuhr* ("Pamphlets on American Writers," No. 31; Minneapolis: University of Minnesota Press, 1963).

For illustration of Freud's structural approach, which permits a distinction between psychic apparatus and the "energies or forces" active in it, see *An Outline of Psychoanalysis,* trans. James Strachey (New York: W. W. Norton, 1949), chap. iv. See also "The Anatomy of the Mental Personality," *New Introductory Lectures on Psychoanalysis,* trans. W. J. H. Sprott (New York: W. W. Norton, 1933), and *The Ego and the Id,* ed. and trans. James Strachey (New York: W. W. Norton, 1961). For a detailed discussion of structure in psychoanalytic theory, see Merton M. Gill, *Topography and Systems in Psychoanalytic Theory* ("Psychological Issues," No. 10; New York: International Universities Press, 1963); for a simpler discussion, see

K. M. Colby, *Energy and Structure in Psychoanalysis* (New York: Ronald Press, 1955).

The four categories used in this review are familiar to general psychological discussion. Hall and Lindzey, for example, organize their comprehensive analysis of personality theory around structure, dynamics, development, and research methods (see Calvin S. Hall and Gardner Lindzey, *Theories of Personality* [New York: John Wiley, 1957]). For an approach similar in style, see Munroe, *Schools of Psychoanalytic Thought.*

For philosophical discussions of Freud's mechanistic thinking, see Martin Buber, "Guilt and Guilt Feelings," *The Knowledge of Man,* ed. Maurice Friedman; trans. Maurice Friedman and Ronald Gregor Smith (New York: Harper & Row, 1965); Jean-Paul Sartre, *Being and Nothingness: An Essay on Phenomenological Ontology,* trans. Hazel E. Barnes (New York: Philosophical Library, 1956), pp. 557–575; Medard Boss, *Psychoanalysis and Daseinsanalysis,* trans. Ludwig B. Lefebre (New York: Basic Books, 1963), pp. 28–34, 70–74, and 85–89; Maurice Merleau-Ponty, *The Structure of Behavior,* trans. Alden L. Fisher (Boston: Beacon Press, 1963), pp. 177–181; Gordon W. Allport, "Scientific Models and Human Morals," *Personality and Social Encounter* (Boston: Beacon Press, 1960). For a general review of this concept, see Floyd W. Matson, *The Broken Image: Man, Science and Society* (New York: George Braziller, 1964).

Discussions of Freud's theory of the instincts often distinguish between the first and second instinct theory. For reference to the first instinct theory, see "Types of Neurotic Nosogenesis," *Collected Papers* (5 vols.; "The International Psycho-Analytic Library," ed. Ernest Jones; New York: Basic Books, 1959), II. For references to the second instinct theory, see *Beyond the Pleasure Principle* and "Two Encyclopedia Articles," *Collected Papers,* V.

For Freud's discussion of the ego and the superego understood metapsychologically, see "The Anatomy of the Mental Personality," *New Introductory Lectures; The Ego and the Id;* and, for a summary, see *Outline of Psychoanalysis.*

For a discussion of the theory of identification, see Anna Freud, *The Ego and the Mechanisms of Defence,* trans. Cecil Baines (New York: International Universities Press, 1946).

Representative discussions of anxiety by Freud can be found in "Anxiety and Instinctual Life," *New Introductory Lectures,* esp. pp. 122–130; *The Problem of Anxiety,* trans. Henry Alden Bunker (New York: The Psychoanalytic Quarterly Press and W. W. Norton, 1936); *A General Introduction to Psychoanalysis,* trans. Joan Riviere (New York: Washington Square Press, 1952), chap. xxv; and *Civilization and Its Discontents,* trans. Joan Riviere (Garden City, N.Y.: Doubleday, 1958). For a review of Freud's theory of anxiety, see Rollo May, *The Meaning of Anxiety* (New York: Ronald Press, 1950), pp. 112–127.

For a theological discussion of Freud's theory of anxiety, see Fred Berthold, Jr., *The Fear of God: The Role of Anxiety in Contemporary Thought* (New York: Harper, 1959). For a discussion of the centrality of infantile anxiety to the neo-Reformation theological conception of sin, see Fred Berthold, Jr., "Theology and Self-Understanding: The Christian Model of Man as Sinner," *The Dialogue Between Theology and Psychology,* ed. Peter Homans (Chicago: University of Chicago Press, 1968).

For Freud's social thought, see his *Civilization and Its Discontents,* esp. pp. 44–53, 90–105; *Totem and Taboo,* trans. James Strachey (New York: W. W. Norton, 1952), esp. pp. 140–146, 156–161; *Moses and Monotheism,* trans. Katherine Jones (New York: Vintage Books, 1955), pp. 101–105, 169–176; *Group Psychology and the Analysis of the Ego,* trans. James Strachey (New York: Bantam Books, 1960), esp. pp. 69–84.

For Freud's discussion of "the great man," see *Moses and Monotheism,* pp. 136–142, and "The Moses of Michelangelo," *Collected Papers,* IV, esp. 282–283. For a discussion of Freud's concept of himself in relation to the figure of Moses, see David Bakan, *Sigmund Freud and the Jewish Mystical Tradition* (Princeton, N.J.: D. Van Nostrand, 1958), chap. xvii.

For specific discussions by Freud of scientific method, see "Instincts and their Vicissitudes," *Collected Papers,* IV; *An*

Autobiographical Study, trans. James Strachey (New York: W. W. Norton, 1952), pp. 110–112; and "A Philosophy of Life," *New Introductory Lectures.*

For references to Freud's methodological remarks, understood in a more general sense to include his work and even his teaching, see *Collected Papers,* IV, 60 (the distinction between conventions and phenomena); *ibid.,* V, 358–371 (the distinction between interpretations and constructions); and *ibid.,* V, 376–377 (the distinction between dogmatic and genetic modes of teaching).

For a summary discussion of the period of self-analysis in the development of Freud's thought, and for bibliographic materials, see Shakow and Rapaport, *The Influence of Freud,* pp. 41–50. For examples of the interpretation of the Freud-Fliess relationship as emotional, see Ernest Jones, *The Life and Work of Sigmund Freud* (New York: Basic Books, 1953), I, chaps. xi–xiv; Bakan, *Freud,* chap. viii; and Erik H. Erikson, "The First Psychoanalyst," *Freud and the Twentieth Century,* ed. Benjamin Nelson (New York: Meridian Press, 1957). For examples of the interpretation of the relationship as a means of carrying out intellectual-scientific discussion, see Ernst Kris, "Introduction," in *The Origins of Psychoanalysis: Letters to Wilhelm Fliess, Drafts and Notes: 1887–1902,* ed. Marie Bonaparte *et al.* (New York: Basic Books, 1954), and Wyss, *Depth Psychology,* pp. 71–97. Shakow and Rapaport themselves take an intermediate position.

Three: Methodological response to Freud: Paul Tillich

FOR a discussion of transference as an internal phenomenon, see Heinz Kohut and Philip F. D. Seitz, "Psychoanalytic Theory of Personality," *Concepts of Personality,* ed. Joseph M. Wepman and Ralph W. Heine (Chicago: Aldine, 1963), esp. pp. 120–121. Kohut and Seitz point out that, although Freud for the most part spoke of transference as an interpersonal phenomenon, his original definition was an endopsychic and metapsychological one. For a discussion of transference in its social form, see Allen Wheelis, *The Quest for Identity* (New York: W. W. Norton, 1958), chap. v. Almost every discussion of psychoanalysis includes a discussion of transference. For an extremely good general discussion of the meaning of transference in psychoanalytic theory and technique and for bibliographical materials, see Karl Menninger, *Theory of Psychoanalytic Technique* (New York: Basic Books, 1958). For a discussion of transference in the context of pastoral care, see E. Mansell Pattison, "Transference and Countertransference in Pastoral Care," *The Journal of Pastoral Care,* XIX, No. 4 (Winter 1965), 193–202. For a discussion of transference in Freud's psychology that likens it to the "personal existence" motif in existentialism, see Wyss, *Depth Psychology,* pp. 404–413. For example, Wyss discusses the work of Buber and Scheler under the title "Partnership and Transference." For an extended discussion of transference in existential psychiatry, see Boss, *Psychoanalysis and Daseinsanalysis,* chap. xiv.

For a general discussion of the subject-object relation in Protestant theology, see James Brown, *Subject and Object in Modern Theology* (New York: Macmillan, 1955).

For a review of Buber's thought in relation to psychotherapy, see Maurice S. Friedman, *Martin Buber: The Life of Dialogue* (Chicago: University of Chicago Press, 1955), chap. xxi. A concise discussion by Buber of Freud's psychology can be found in "Guilt and Guilt Feelings," *The Knowledge of Man.* For a review of Buber's thought in relation to George Herbert Mead and, by implication, to certain aspects of social science, see Paul E. Pfuetze, *Self, Society, and Existence* (New York: Harper, 1954).

For further discussion of the subject-object relation in Barth's thought, see Brown, *Subject and Object in Modern Theology.* For a concise posing of this problem, see Joseph C. Weber, "Feuerbach, Barth, and Theological Methodology," *Journal of*

Religion, XLVI, No. 1, Pt. I (January 1966), 24–36. For an especially concise statement of the subject-object dichotomy as the basic focus for a theological criticism of psychology, see Emil Brunner, "Biblical Psychology," in *God and Man: Four Essays on the Nature of Personality,* trans. David Cairns (London: SCM Press, 1936). For a critical discussion of this aspect of Brunner's thought, see Fred Berthold, Jr., "Objectivity and Personal Encounter," *Journal of Religion,* XLV, No. 1 (January 1965), 39–45.

For an illustrative statement of Bultmann's understanding of the limits of what is properly psychological in self-understanding, and for the relation between this and "the subjective" and "fantasy," see "Paul," in *Existence and Faith,* trans. Schubert M. Ogden (New York: Meridian Books, 1960). An especially concise statement regarding the subject-object relation in Bultmann's thought is found in his "What Sense Is There To Speak of God?" trans. Franklin H. Littell, *Christian Scholar,* XLIII, No. 3 (Fall 1960), 213–222. For a helpful discussion of this problem, see Schubert M. Ogden, *Christ Without Myth* (New York: Harper, 1961), pp. 22–44. See also Ogden's "Myth and Truth," *McCormick Quarterly,* XVIII (January 1965), Special Supplement, 57–76.

Four: A retrospective
interlude

For important studies in the psychology of religion, see William James, *The Varieties of Religious Experience* (New York: Modern Liberary, 1902); E. D. Starbuck, *Psychology of Religion* (New York: Scribner's, 1903); G. A. Coe, *The Psychology of Religion* (Chicago: University of Chicago Press, 1916); J. H. Leuba, *A Psychological Study of Religion* (New York: Macmillan, 1912); and G. S. Hall, *Adolescence* (2 vols.; New York: D. Appleton, 1904). See also *The Journal of Religious Psychology, Including its Anthropological and Sociological Aspects,* published from 1904 to 1916. For a collection of readings, see Orlo Strunk, ed., *Readings in the Psychology of Religion* (Nashville, Tenn.: Abingdon Press, 1959). For a review discussion of this group and their approach, see Seward Hiltner, "The Psychological Understanding of Religion," in Strunk, ed., *Readings,* and Paul Pruyser, "Some Trends in the Psychology of Religion," *Journal of Religion,* XL, No. 2 (April 1960), 113–129.

For a discussion of the biographical context of the psychologies of James and Hall, see Boring, *History,* pp. 505–524.

For a review of the changes undergone in American psychology during the first decades of this century, see Boring, *History,* pp. 505–524, 641–653; Gardner Murphy, *An Historical Introduction to Modern Psychology* (London: Routledge & Kegan Paul, 1949), chaps xv and xviii; and Shakow and Rapaport, *The Influence of Freud,* pp. 36–41, 65–78.

For a good discussion of a phenomenological approach to behaviorism and the problem of objectivity, see T. W. Wann, ed., *Behaviorism and Phenomenology: Contrasting Bases for Modern Psychology* (Chicago: University of Chicago Press, 1964).

For examples of the American school of pastoral psychology, see Carroll A. Wise, *Pastoral Counseling: Its Theory and Practice* (New York: Harper, 1951); Wayne Oates, *The Christian Pastor* (Philadelphia: Westminster Press, 1951); Hiltner, *Pastoral Counseling;* and Paul Johnson, *The Psychology of Pastoral Care* (Nashville, Tenn.: Abingdon Press, 1953). The single most informative text is Hiltner's. Also see his "Freud for the Pastor," *Pastoral Psychology,* V, No. 50 (January 1955), 41–57. For a discussion of Freud in relation to theology, see Hiltner's "Freud, Psychoanalysis, and Religion," *Pastoral Psychology,* VII, No. 68 (November 1956), 9–21. For a heavily psychoanalytic interpretation of the Christian pastoral ministry in the Protestant tradition, see Oates, *The Christian Pastor.*

For a highly illustrative discussion of the process of pastoral counseling, which includes both case material and theological interpretation, see Knox Kreutzer, "Some Observations on Approaches to the Theology of Psychotherapeutic Experience," *Journal of Pastoral Care,* XIII, No. 4 (Winter 1959), 197–208.

---

*Five: Three post-Protestant
interpretations of Freud*

FOR a discussion in which sexuality is taken as an interpretive basis for criticizing theological existentialism, see Valerie Saiving Goldstein, "The Human Situation: A Feminine Viewpoint," *The Nature of Man,* ed. Simon Doniger (New York: Harper, 1962), pp. 151–170.

For a general discussion of the implications of Freud's psychology for existential psychology, see May, ed., *Existence,* chaps. i and ii.

For a discussion of Freud's thought in relation to both Judaism and secularization, and in the style of radical theology, see Richard L. Rubenstein, *After Auschwitz: Radical Theology and Contemporary Judaism* (New York: Bobbs-Merrill, 1966). Rubenstein's approach is put into more explicit and formal theological context in *The Religious Imagination: A Study in Psychoanalysis and Jewish Theology* (New York: Bobbs-Merrill, 1968).

---

*Six: Transcendence, mass culture,
and the psychology of distance:
an interpretation*

BASIC sources in the death-of-God theology discussed in this book consist of the following: Thomas J. J. Altizer, *Mircea*

Eliade and the Dialectic of the Sacred (Philadelphia: West-
minster Press, 1963); William Hamilton, *The New Essence of
Christianity* (New York: Association Press, 1961), and "The
Death of God Theology," *The Christian Scholar,* LXIII, No.1
(Spring 1965), 27–48; Paul Van Buren, *The Secular Meaning
of the Gospel* (New York: Macmillan, 1963); and Gabriel
Vahanian, *The Death of God: The Culture of our Post-Christian
Era* (New York: George Braziller, 1957).

The school of Rorschach interpretation used in these discussions is that of Samuel J. Beck, Anne G. Beck. Eugene E. Levitt,
and Herman B. Molish, *Rorschach's Test, Vol. I: Basic Processes*
(New York: Grune and Stratton, 1961). A briefer and less technical review of its materials may be found in Beck, "The Rorschach Test: A Multi-Dimensional Test of Personality," *An
Introduction to Projective Techniques,* ed. Harold H. Anderson
and Gladys L. Anderson (Englewood Cliffs, N. J.: Prentice-Hall,
1951). For the Klopfer discussion of vista responses and distan-
tiation, see Bruno Klopfer, Mary D. Ainsworth, Walter G.
Klopfer, Robert R. Holt, *Developments in the Rorschach Technique, Vol. I: Technique and Theory* (New York: Harcourt,
Brace & World, 1954), I, 145–166, 376–388. For a brief discussion of the Rorschach test in relation to existentialism, see
Henri F. Ellenberger, "A Clinical Introduction to Psychiatric
Phenomenology and Existential Analysis," May, ed., *Existence.*
For a thorough discussion of this, see Roland Kuhn, *Phénoméno-
logie du Masque: À Travers le Test de Rorschach,* trans. from
the German by Jacqueline Verdeaux (Bruges: Desclée de Brou-
wer, 1957).

For discussions of the death of God that also employ psycho-
logical categories but in a somewhat different way, see Richard
A. Underwood, "Hermes and Hermeneutics: A Viewing from the
Perspectives of the Death of God and Depth Psychology," *Hart-
ford Quarterly,* VI, No. 1 (Fall 1965), 34–53, and Daniel C.
Noel, "Still Reading His Will? Problems and Resources for the
Death-of-God Theology," *Journal of Religion,* XLVI, No. 4
(October 1966), 463–476.

For sociological discussion of the problem of identity and

mass society, see David Riesman, Nathan Glazer, and Ruell Denney, *The Lonely Crowd* (Garden City, N.Y.: Doubleday Anchor Books, 1954); Helen Merrell Lynd, *On Shame and the Search for Identity* (New York: Science Editions, 1961); and Erich Fromm, *The Sane Society* (New York: Holt, Rinehart and Winston, 1955). For a brief review of this problem and some of the better-known bibliographic references, see Hendrik Ruitenbeek, *The Individual and the Crowd* (New York: New American Library, 1965). For theological discussions of contextual ethics that attempt to resolve this problem, see Paul L. Lehmann, "The Decline and Fall of Conscience," *Ethics in a Christian Context* (New York: Harper & Row, 1963). For a dissenting opinion informed by psychological understanding and convinced that certain Protestant views of conscience are foreign to Hebraic and Pauline teaching, see Krister Stendal, "The Apostle Paul and the Introspective Conscience of the West," *Harvard Theological Review*, LVI, No. 3 (July 1963), 199–215.

Seven: Transition: nostalgia, hope,
and the recovery of distance

FOR Eliade's view of psychoanalysis and the history of religions, see Mircea Eliade, *Images and Symbols*, trans. Philip Mairet (New York: Sheed and Ward, 1961), pp. 9–32. There is no careful and thorough study of the implicit psychology of Eliade's theory of religion. For a discussion of the problem of structural and historical approaches in Eliade's thought, see Robert Luyster, "The Study of Myth: Two Approaches," *Journal of Bible and Religion*, XXXIV, No. 3 (July 1966), 235–243.

There are a number of helpful discussions in philosophical phenomenology of the problem of distance. Heidegger discusses distance in conjunction with "de-severance" and "distantiality," in *Being and Time*, trans. John Macquarrie and Edward Robinson (New York: Harper & Row, 1962), pp. 138–148, 163–168; his later thought deals with "the nearness of distance" in *Discourse on Thinking,* trans. John M. Anderson and E. Hans Freund (New York: Harper & Row, 1966), pp. 86–90. John Wild uses the phenomenon of distance to develop a philosophical ethic in *Existence and the World of Freedom* (Englewood Cliffs, N.J.: Prentice-Hall, 1963), pp. 108–113, 140–149.

Maurice Merleau-Ponty briefly discusses the problem of distance in *The Phenomenology of Perception,* trans. Colin Smith (London: Routledge & Kegan Paul, 1962), pp. 265–267. For a discussion of the problem of distance in Jung's psychology, see Victor White, O.P., *God and the Unconscious* (Cleveland: World, 1961), chap. vii. White uses the problem of distance to develop a psychological theory of Aquinas's understanding of revelation.

For a discussion of the superego in relation to religious structures and for helpful bibliographic reference, see Wolfgang Lederer, *Dragons, Delinquents and Destiny: An Essay on Positive Superego Functions* ("Psychological Issues," No. 15; New York: International Universities Press, 1964).

For theological reviews of Jung's work, see Raymond Hostie, S.J., *Religion and the Psychology of Jung,* trans. G. R. Lamb (London: Sheed and Ward, 1957); Hans Schaer, *Religion and the Cure of Souls in Jung's Psychology,* trans. R. F. C. Hull (New York: Pantheon Books, 1950); and David Cox, *Jung and St. Paul* (London: Longmans, Green, 1959). For psychological discussions see Jolandi Jacobi, *The Psychology of C. G. Jung* (New Haven: Yale University Press, 1962), and Gerhard Adler, *Studies in Analytical Psychology* (New York: Putnam's, 1967). The approach of this study is better represented by Julius Heuscher, *A Psychiatric Study of Fairy Tales* (Springfield, Ill.: Thomas, 1963); Herbert Fingarette, *The Self in Transformation* (New York: Basic Books, 1963); and Erich Neumann, *The Origins and History of Consciousness,* trans. R. F. C. Hull (2 vols.; New York: Harper Torchbooks, 1962).

For a discussion of Jung's approach to the problem of mass culture, see Neumann, *Origins,* II, Appendix II.

Index